MW00625873

The Month of Their Ripening

10-11-2019

To Tod—
Ripen well, friend!

The Month of Their Ripening

North Carolina Heritage Foods through the Year

GEORGANN EUBANKS

Photographs by Donna Campbell

Paintings by Carol Misner

THE UNIVERSITY OF NORTH CAROLINA PRESS

Chapel Hill

This book was published with the assistance of the Blythe Family Fund of the University of North Carolina Press.

Designed by Jamison Cockerham
Set in Arno, Chaparral, and Malina types
by Tseng Information Systems, Inc.

All photographs, except those otherwise noted, by Donna Campbell.
All interior and jacket paintings by Carol Misner.

Manufactured in the United States of America

The University of North Carolina Press has been a member
of the Green Press Initiative since 2003.

LIBRARY OF CONGRESS CATALOGING-IN-PUBLICATION DATA
Names: Eubanks, Georgann, author. | Campbell, Donna, 1951– | Misner, Carol.
Title: The month of their ripening : North Carolina heritage foods through the year /
Georgann Eubanks ; photographs by Donna Campbell ; paintings by Carol Misner.
Description: Chapel Hill : The University of North Carolina Press, [2018] |
Includes bibliographical references and index.
Identifiers: LCCN 2018001366 | ISBN 9781469640822 (cloth : alk. paper) |
ISBN 9781469640839 (ebook)
Subjects: LCSH: Food habits—North Carolina—History. | Diet—North Carolina. |
Cooking—North Carolina. | Cooking, American—Southern style.
Classification: LCC TX360.U62 N67 2018 | DDC 641.59756—dc23
LC record available at https://lccn.loc.gov/2018001366

For

STELLA BAILEY

and

BOMER HENRY EUBANKS

master gardeners and grandparents

Contents

Remind yourself that the one you love is mortal,

that what you love does not belong to you,

it is given you for the present time, not irrevocably or for ever,

but just like a fig or a bunch of grapes at the season of ripeness.

EPICTETUS from *The Golden Sayings*

Figures

Preface

I CAME TO KNOW IT WAS SEPTEMBER WHEN MY GRANDFATHER PULLED out the dented buckets from his toolshed and nodded for me to follow him. We'd trek across the dam beside his hand-dug pond, watching the bass pop up after the long-legged insects that skated on the water's surface. We did not dawdle. We went straight for the sturdy trellis on the far bank, a jackleg assembly of galvanized pipe that he'd put up long before I was born. I tagged along without a word between us. This was the man who'd let me plant my first row of butter beans the year before, at age five.

The frame was barely visible now that the pipes had become the bones of a thick, green, undulating tunnel of climbing vines. They hung heavy with fat bronze scuppernongs under the first half of the leafy canopy. Smaller purple-hulled muscadines waited at the far end of the trellis. A firmament of bees droned above the tunnel, swooping in and out of the greenery. The scent of sun-warmed fruit oozed over us as we stepped into the shaded cave and began to pick. When I encounter that fragrance now, I am back in his world, that world under the trellis.

I could reach the clusters of grapes along the sides of the light-dappled tunnel. Granddaddy would pull down the higher ones. He had already taught me how to squeeze the hard hulls between my teeth to release sweet juice and chewy innards where the seeds were stored. We ate and picked and ate some more.

In North Carolina, scuppernongs are our official state fruit, and they are at their best only in early fall. We are forced to wait — the whole passage of a year between tastes — which makes them so much sweeter.

* ● ◐ ◖ ◕ ◔ ◆ ◄ ■ ◕ ◗ ◆

This book explores a dozen such North Carolina foods that are exemplary of our state's culture and history. The seasonal fruits, vegetables, dairy, and seafood to be considered—some wild and others cultivated—offer more than physical nourishment. They help to elaborate our collective story—past and present—as people of many tastes and habits. They are part of the vernacular of North Carolina kitchens and our varied landscape. Some also serve as bellwethers of North Carolina's environmental future.

Organized by the month of their arrival, these heritage foods are quite perishable and therefore most precious in their fresh form. They epitomize the kinds of flavors that make us long for the harvest, yearning for their bright tastes on our tongues, even as we pull out preserves and frozen facsimiles from the fridge in bleakest winter. Writers of fiction, poetry, and essay have extolled their virtues. Discerning restaurants and drive-by diners incorporate them into their seasonal menus. But most important, these are foods that are not available year-round. We have to long for them, and in that longing is their special character.

It is easy to become complacent, thanks to the profusion at the grocery—fruits and vegetables shipped green from afar, ultimately turning up near-ripe in the produce section. This staged array lasts all year long, but at what cost? For instance, how many modes of transportation did it take to ship those blackberries in February from Chile? Or how true to their real ripened character are the figs that have traveled 3,000 miles from a tree in California? How much fuel did these products consume before we consumed them? And who has not despaired at the taste of a bright red but cardboard-flavored winter tomato that began life in a greenhouse under hot artificial light, its roots shot through with synthetic nutrition?

As novelist and naturalist Barbara Kingsolver explains in *Animal, Vegetable, Miracle*, "For modern kids who intuitively believe in the spontaneous generation of fruits and vegetables in the produce section, trying to get their minds around the slow speciation of the plant kingdom may be a stretch."

Thus, for our own sake and the benefit of our children, we need to recapture the practice of anticipation. Then later we can savor the rewards of those authentic, local, seasonal foods whose arrival is driven by nature, not commerce.

Food, memory, and season are inextricably linked, most directly by the gift of smell. As Diane Ackerman, in *A Natural History of the Senses*, puts it, "Hit a tripwire of smell and memories explode all at once. A complex vision leaps out of the undergrowth."

It's not a stretch, then, to consider how, beyond fond family memories, once-a-year foods also help us to build community, containing for us the sweet and savory traditions particular to place, climate, soil, and season. Chef Peter Hoffman, writing in the magazine *Edible Manhattan*, pretty much sums it up: "Food unique to a certain time and place still calls out to us with a power and urgency that ubiquitous dishes found on menus in all 50 states never can."

Terroir, a concept most commonly discussed in relation to wines, is the combination of unique environmental factors that affect a crop beyond the variety of the plant itself—external factors, such as soil, water, sunshine, and the slope of the land. Few states have the biodiversity of North Carolina, with its range of climate, soil, and altitude. Some plants flourish all across the state; others are more discretely regional. Either way, our state's food-ways are born of a special bounty and regional interpretations across many kitchens.

North Carolina oyster lovers have been known to invoke the term "mer-roir" when considering the relative salinity associated with the location of oyster beds in the state's many inlets. In December, when little else is being harvested, oysters are a most delicious prize and the subject of great debate among aficionados about whether the bivalves of Stump Sound on the back-side of Topsail Island in Pender County or the oysters from Stumpy Point in Dare County have the finest taste. Of course, there are many other con-tenders, too, but most oyster lovers would agree that there's hardly anything better on a crisp, starlit night than an oyster roast where the hardwood fire is smoldering beneath the metal altar on which the oysters are laid, bathing all comers in a savory scent that clings to our clothes until bedtime. Such a sweet communion of salt, smoke, and friends: elbow to elbow, each with one hand gloved and the other bare, twisting an oyster knife; then, at intervals, raising up our half shells for the sacred slurp.

It can be misleading when you google the phrase "unique foods in North Carolina" only to land on a list of brand names: Pepsi, Cheerwine, Texas Pete, Krispy Kreme, Hardee's, Bojangles, K&W, Lance, and Mt. Olive Pickles—all interesting products with daring stories of bootstrap entrepreneurship behind them. But in this project, I aimed to meet the growers and fisherfolk, the professional and home cooks who are carrying on culinary traditions more deeply rooted in North Carolina terroir than these commercial products are.

Among the twelve foods considered here, some have been better known in the past, such as the intensely sweet Ridgeway cantaloupes of Warren County, cultivated as early as the 1880s by German farmers who worked their magic on the local soil and then shipped their harvest by train up the East Coast to such restaurants as the one in New York's Waldorf-Astoria Hotel. Today there is only one farmer left, a descendent of those early German settlers, who grows the original Ridgeway.

Likewise, shad, the focus for March, is the largest member of the herring family but not as well known or plentiful in North Carolina as it was during the Civil War. Back then, one commercial shad fishery was reportedly shut down and the proprietor imprisoned by Union forces in an effort to cut off a key food source for hungry Confederate troops come spring. Even as herring have been dreadfully overfished in the commercial waters off the coast, shad still swim inland and upstream in our eastern North Carolina rivers each year, and they are prized both for sport and sustenance.

Other foods considered here are much more commonly known and appreciated. The month of May presents the story of two purveyors of soft-shell crabs: Murray Bridges of Colington Island, who has mentored many younger fishermen, including his good friend Willy Phillips, who sells thousands of dozens of the creatures each year, working out of a roadside seafood market on Highway 64 in Columbia, North Carolina.

The February essay moves among goat dairies — one developed by Lilian Steichen Sandburg, the poet Carl Sandburg's wife, in 1945 near Flat Rock, in the western mountains. Her goat breeding expertise led to the relocation of the national headquarters of the American Dairy Goat Association to Spindale, North Carolina. Sampling the first goat's milk of the year may not be to everyone's taste, but its nutritional value and the creative dishes into which "the other white milk" is now being applied could yet change some minds and palates.

Along the way, each essay also provides suggested destinations where you might sample these foods, take in a local celebration, or learn more about the agricultural and historical resources of the region. And when there's a recipe that you won't find elsewhere, that's included, too.

So let us begin. Herein we joyfully celebrate a dozen North Carolina native foods ready to taste in the month of their ripening and then to pine for as another year goes by. They provide us with both nourishment and the rare chance to practice the art of anticipation.

The Month of Their Ripening

January

Snow

IN NORTH CAROLINA, SNOW BLOOMS IN THE AIR AS SUDDENLY AS A bank of dogwoods in spring, and—like the dogwood—we can never precisely predict its coming and going. It rarely piles up high enough or lingers long enough in most areas of the state to grow gray and sooty.

In January, there is little else in nature that presents itself to us that we can eat. Snow, however, is a dessert that literally falls from the sky, and when it does, North Carolinians—particularly in the Piedmont and points east— declare it a party. For us, snow never fails to quicken the pulse and slow the pace. Snow gives us license to loosen up. It brightens the view and blankets the landscape with a flag of truce. And once the snow piles high enough, we make snow cream, a very simple treat like ice cream, which normally accompanies the most universal celebration across cultures—a birthday party.

Even for mountain folk who get the most of it, snow requires an adjustment from business as usual to an almost gleeful awareness of possible hazards and the promise of certain culinary and other pleasures. One winter, teaching writing to middle schoolers in western North Carolina, I learned about the passionate stirrings that come even among those who get the most snow.

With nearly 1,700 residents, Burnsville is the Yancey County seat. The town was established in 1834, a year after the celebrated Nu-Wray Inn opened. From the Nu-Wray, where both Elvis Presley and Mark Twain allegedly dined and spent the night, you can step beyond the porch into the town square and see mountaintops in every direction. The subtle gradations of color in the peaks surrounding the village produce a visual Doppler effect: the shades of blue grow lighter the farther away the mountain. Yancey County has seventeen peaks that are higher than 6,000 feet, the highest being Mount Mitchell (the tallest east of the Dakotas), where twenty-one inches of snow fell in twenty-four hours in January 2016.

Thus, despite the warm name, Burnsville is North Carolina snow country, a place where a visitor might assume that children and adults would be quite accustomed to the more-than-occasional presence of the white stuff, as abundant as the biscuit flour that was once stowed in the Nu-Wray pantry. But even here, snow is still a cause for celebration.

It was January when the local arts council hired me to teach five classes on creative writing to every student at East Yancey Middle School, about a mile from the Burnsville town square. Right after lunch period on a gray and biting afternoon, I was about to give my third lesson in the series to a rambunctious group of seventh graders — mostly boys — who had been relegated to ISS, or "In-School Suspension," for troublemaking. The principal had warned me at the beginning of the week that this group had burned out three teachers before Christmas break. He was grateful that I was at least holding down one class period for the first week of the new year while he cobbled together substitutes to fill the rest of these students' day. More than once, I'd caught a glimpse of him in the hall outside the room, making sure I was still there.

On this particular day, my lesson was about writing vivid description. With the fourth-period bell the students rushed to their seats, and I entered the ring. "So who can tell me," I said, "what is a simile?"

A hand shot up. "Is that like when the whole school goes to the gym on Fridays for a program?"

It took me a minute. "No. That is an *assembly*," I said.

Travis, the boy who had offered his best guess, grinned. Though he might not have known what a simile was, he knew how to get my goat. Travis was a handsome kid and a strong junior-varsity football player, I had been told. His cheeks had a perpetual flush, as if he'd just dashed in from the field. Travis also had leadership ability, but this trait was usually directed toward guiding others into his mischief.

I explained how a simile is a figure of speech that compares two unlikely things using the words "like" or "as." Puzzled faces. I gave some examples: "Her face looked like a baloney sandwich. The wind blew like a freight train." There was a glimmer of recognition among those who were listening.

"Okay," I said, "so that's a simile." I wrote the word on the board with my back turned. Someone called out that the word looked like "smile."

"Uh-huh," I said, turning around to face them once more. "Now, what's a metaphor?"

Utter silence, and then a big-wristed boy in the back row, whose arms seemed to be outgrowing his sleeves before our very eyes, threw his arm up and blurted, "Cows!"

The class laughed. I didn't get it.

"What's a meadow fooooor?" Travis hollered like a cheerleader and jumped up, shaking his hands loose in the air like pom-poms.

"Cows!" the class roared back. Travis then sat, crossed his arms, and stared at me.

I felt like I was pulling helplessly on the end of a long rope attached to a large, unmoving cow. This was not a new feeling in my role as guest artist in the schools.

And then, out of nowhere, chaos erupted. The students jumped out of their seats. Some desks fell over. Books hit the floor like claps of thunder. They ran for the bank of windows on the south side of the classroom. It had begun to snow outside — small but discernible flakes, flying by fast. The students examined the heavens and the earth and then, just as suddenly as they had risen, moaned and went back to their seats.

"It's just a'blowing," Travis declared. He explained to me that snow in Burnsville comes two ways — either "a'blowing," meaning flurries were flying sideways but not accumulating, or "a'laying," which meant school might get out early because it was already sticking.

I told them we'd listen for any important announcements about early dismissal over the intercom, which I half hoped for myself. They hushed, and I started ad-libbing. "The native people in Alaska . . ."

"Eskimos!" the big boy in the back shouted.

"Yes," I said. "The Eskimos or Inuit people have lots of different words for snow, because snow can take so many forms and shapes up there near the North Pole. So let's come up with some similes for snow. You all know already about wet snow and dry snow, right? Snow that sticks and snow that flies. Sometimes it's big flakes; sometimes they're small."

Nods around the room.

A sullen girl raised a limp hand. "Are we going to have to *write* again today?" she whined.

"Let's just talk this out." I smiled. "I'll write whatever you all say on the board."

I asked them to complete the sentence "The snow fell like _____."

They called out their answers as fast as I could chalk them up: "Popcorn!" "Chicken feathers." "Salt." "Sugar." "Grits." "Ice cream!"

Then their ideas began to come more slowly and grow more fanciful: "Moths." "Q-tips." "Ashes." "Chalk dust." "Stuffed animal guts," Travis said. "My grandaddy's beard at the barbershop!" said another boy in the back.

All excellent similes, I told them, and I hoped they might remember the concept. Their expertise with snow, because of its frequency in Yancey County, made their images and associations all the more fanciful. I noticed, too, how so many of the first similes had naturally referenced something edible.

The term "edible memory" comes from the University of Wisconsin sociologist Jennifer A. Jordan. In her 2015 study, *Edible Memory: The Lure of Heirloom Tomatoes and Other Forgotten Foods,* Jordan explains that she came to the concept as she considered the power of food as ritual in her own childhood. Even though her grandmother was an excellent scratch baker, she would always have a certain store-bought mix for spice cake whenever her granddaughter visited. The boxed mix even came with its own baking pan.

"We'd open the package, add water, and mix it up directly in that aluminum pan," Jordan writes. "Later we'd ice it with the foil packet of bright white frosting that also came in the package. An important part of the whole experience was the time spent in the kitchen together, mixing up the cake, and then eating it washed down with glasses of milk, catching up on the important events in the lives of a nine-year-old and an eighty-year-old."

Jordan was struck by how such food memories sit deep within us, how particular meals and the preparation of certain foods — even something as banal as a boxed cake mix — can shape someone's identity and sense of place in the world. As she put it, "Something happens when we eat: the transformation, even transubstantiation, of these molecules into energy and strength. . . . But it can also transform into social bonds and memories, connections within families and communities and larger social groups — as well as stark divisions and distinctions, ways of resisting or oppressing, controlling and rebelling. Food — its production, consumption, and distribution — shapes and transforms a range of places as well: kitchens and dining tables, fields and forests." She goes on: "Edible memory encompasses ways of talking about the world, but also ways of acting on and moving through the world. I found edible memory propelling people into action — to save seeds, to plant gardens, to eat meals, and tell stories."

For North Carolinians, the ritual of making snow cream from the simplest ingredients — sugar, snow, vanilla, and cream — evokes a particular place and time for many of us. Memories of this dish, like Jordan's spice cake, often involve grandparents, impromptu preparation, enormous anticipation, and a strong sense of belonging.

In his memoir *I Was There When It Happened*, the musician Marshall Grant tells a story of longing for snow cream. Grant played bass for Johnny Cash, and in January 1957, Grant, Cash, and the guitarist Luther Perkins were driving back to Tennessee from New York City after an appearance on *The Jackie Gleason Show*. "We were coming into North Carolina," Grant writes, "when John said, 'Boy, I wish we would run up on some snow somewhere. I sure would like to have some snow cream.'"

Born in Bryson City, in the North Carolina mountains, and raised in Bessemer City, near Charlotte, Grant had often traveled the elevated stretch of highway that would eventually carry the trio up and over the Smoky Mountains into Tennessee and on to Nashville. He was pretty sure that they were not likely to find any snow until they reached North Carolina's Soco Gap. Grant told Cash to be patient. (At an altitude of 4,340 feet, Soco Gap is a mountain pass on U.S. 19 in the Balsam Range that runs between Maggie Valley and Cherokee and marks the beginning of the Qualla Boundary of the Eastern Band of Cherokee Indians.)

The musicians made a stop in the village of Black Mountain to prepare. They bought a dishpan, plastic bowls, spoons, sugar, milk, and vanilla and then kept rolling. In another fifty miles, at the top of Soco Gap, Grant's forecast came true: they found the ground covered in snow. The men pulled over and walked some distance off the road into the woods to gather a clean patch, because the snow had clearly been there a while.

> We filled the dishpan, went back to the car, and whipped up a fine batch of snow cream. There was a park bench nearby, and the three of us were sitting there enjoying our treat when all of the sudden we heard a strange noise coming up the bluff toward us. "What *is* that?" John asked, and Luther and I replied at the same time, "I don't know!"
>
> We found out real quick when a big Smoky Mountain black bear poked his head over the rise. I guess he'd smelled our snow cream and wanted some for himself.

The trio grabbed their gear and raced toward Grant's '54 Plymouth. They watched the bear in the rearview mirror as it sniffed around the bench while they descended out of sight, their tongues still numb from the snow cream.

In North Carolina, the western mountains actually help to protect the rest of the state from chilling winds, temperatures, and precipitation blowing in from the west. According to the State Climate Office, altitude is the most important factor in the temperatures and hence the amount of snow we experience across the state. As you head east from the Appalachian Mountains, the landscape slopes downward into the rolling Piedmont and then flattens out as it descends toward the ocean. As the Climate Office describes the extremes, "The average annual temperature at Southport on the lower coast is nearly as high as that of interior northern Florida, while the average on the summit of Mount Mitchell is lower than that of Buffalo, New York."

The "fall line" in North Carolina is the geological marker that defines the boundary where the hard igneous rocks of the Piedmont transition into the softer sedimentary rocks of the Coastal Plain. As the landscape lowers farther across the eastern side of the fall line, the probability of a good snowfall also declines. Historic Highway 1, running northeast and southwest up the Eastern Seaboard, was built along this fall line, more or less. Today's Interstate 95, a bit farther east, forms the boundary that weather forecasters often use to point out where a winter storm is likely to transition from snow (on the western side) to frozen rain, sleet, or just plain rain to the east.

A snow deep enough to supply the ingredients for snow cream is therefore less and less likely the father east you go in the state, and arguably the memories of snow cream are thus more dear (or at least rare) in the eastern direction. I set out to test this hypothesis by inviting some of North Carolina's most distinguished storytellers on both sides of the fall line to share their snow cream memories.

Writer and editor Dawn Shamp was raised in Roxboro, the seat of Person County, on the Virginia border. Her part of the Piedmont tends to get more snow than the better-known Research Triangle area, just to the south. During snow events the county becomes a favored destination for roving television reporters who are dispatched to the media market fringes to describe, on the quarter hour, the changing nature of every flake that falls. (Just in case you are not from here, snow is always news in the Piedmont, sometimes worthy of canceling regular programming.)

Shamp, who now lives in Durham, confirmed the slightly greater accumulations of snow she experienced as a girl in Roxboro, the memory of which seemed to magnify her enthusiasm: "Oh my gosh, I loved snow cream when I was a kid. I can taste it right now. Nothing compares. The most vivid memory I have is being in Grandma's kitchen, watching Aunt Susie mix up a batch of snow cream in a giant (I mean, *giant*) opaque Tupperware bowl for my cousins and me, then her dishing it up into these smaller, pastel-colored Tupperware bowls."

Types of bowls, you will soon notice, are key to many snow cream memories. Tupperware, of course, is an important generational marker for those raised in the 1960s. I, too, have this memory of the sound of sugar and snow scraping against the bottom of a giant plastic bowl that was brought down only for special occasions and that had to be stowed out of the way on a high kitchen shelf because it took up so much space. I asked Shamp if the enormous bowl happened to be the same one that her grandmother used to mix her corn bread dressing and then store it in the fridge before holiday baking commenced. Affirmative.

According to eBay, this would be the "Two-Piece Vintage Tupperware Large Fix N Mix Bowl," which held twenty-six cups and came with a white sealing top. The bowl would have been either Pastel Yellow or Jadeite Green. Shamp's grandmother's was Jadeite, as was my mother's. Thus, the accoutrements of cooking or serving edible memories take on a nostalgic luster themselves, just like those dented buckets my grandfather and I used to gather scuppernongs.

* * * * * * * * * * * *

Novelist and short-story master Jill McCorkle grew up in Lumberton, where I-95 runs near the heart of town on one side and the Lumber River snakes by on the other. Lumberton is therefore east of the fall line in North Carolina, and a good snowfall was very rare there. "My mother would put out a big yellow Pyrex bowl on a high post that was in the yard," McCorkle said. "It had been a stand for the bird feeder. She warned us that we could only eat what fell directly into that bowl up high. No fair scooping anything up anywhere else. No yellow snow."

When the bowl finally filled up, the children brought it inside. Jill's mother, Melba, would inspect the snow suspiciously and then stir in a mixture of sugar, milk, and vanilla. "We'd eat some and then keep the rest in the freezer for months and taste of it from time to time," Jill said.

I asked what kind of milk her mother used — evaporated, sweetened condensed, whole milk, or half and half? McCorkle said quickly that Eagle Brand Sweetened Condensed Milk was the essential ingredient in her mother's lemon pie but never her snow cream. They used regular milk. However, during the big snow of 1973, when she was a high school freshman, Jill recalled how she and three friends bundled up in coats and hiked through deep snow to a Lumberton convenience mart. There they bought chocolate chip cookie dough and a can of Eagle Brand Sweetened Condensed milk, which is thick as syrup and just as sweet. Rather than going home to bake cookies and make another batch of snow cream, the group ducked down an alleyway and took turns eating the raw dough and passing the can of Eagle Brand as if it were Mad Dog 20/20. "Then we waddled back home," McCorkle said. Such is the permission to indulge during a good snow.

Fiction writer and James Baldwin scholar Randall Kenan was raised in the 1960s in the farming community of Chinquapin, in Duplin County near the Northeast Cape Fear River, around sixty miles east of the fall line. Describing the family recipe in the hands of his great-aunt, whom he called Mama, Kenan makes her snow cream sound both delicate and elegant: "Mama would brush a significant quantity of fresh snow into a pan. She would sprinkle it with a little sugar; pour in maybe a third of a can of evaporated milk, depending on the amount of snow. She would add a few drops of vanilla extract, and stir lightly. Ain't that how everybody does it?"

Evaporated milk, in which 60 percent of the liquid has been removed or evaporated, is a thrifty alternative to fresh milk. This concentrate in a can takes up less space than whole milk, does not require refrigeration, and has a shelf life of many months. Because it is heated in the evaporation process, it takes on a slightly darker color and a caramelized natural sweetness, though no sugar is usually added in the processing. Evaporation also concentrates the nutrients and calories. The low price made it highly popular during the Depression era, with which Kenan's great-aunt Mary would have been very familiar.

I also asked the current North Carolina poet laureate, Shelby Stephenson, about his snow cream experience. Raised on a farm in Johnston County, right along the fall line, he was quick to suggest that the closer to the cow, the better the snow cream. His mother used fresh cream from the family cow, he

Novelists Jill McCorkle (from Lumberton) and Randall Kenan
(from Chinquapin) say they rarely saw snow while growing up in eastern North
Carolina. They are pictured here at a literary event at a public library in Hillsborough.

said with nostalgia, and as poets laureate tend to do, he soon wrote and sent me this remembrance of Johnston County snow:

Bring Back the Snow Cream

My mother could make it
off the bat, beating the vanilla
and milk from our cow, some sugar
and there it was, the snow

still falling outside
bumping
the big oak limbs at
the kitchen window

and she hummed
when she'd make it

what a longing
memory throws over
the smell I could feel
in that kitchen

For more historical data on snow cream, I then turned to *The State* — once a weekly magazine in North Carolina, now a monthly called *Our State*. With its long practice of holding up a mirror to the state, revealing the habits, quirks, and passions of Tar Heels, the magazine often turned its attention to the subject of snow cream, which in turn stirred up memories from many readers. The snow cream recipes offered over the years also reveal variations in the types of milk and other ingredients used in family recipes. Some *State* readers called for the addition of an egg or two, which would be mixed in with the other kitchen ingredients. The brave ate the eggs raw in their snow cream (not necessarily aware of the risk of salmonella poisoning); others simmered the ingredients on the stove and let the mixture cool before pouring it into the snow.

The egg formula mimics the recipe for custard-based homemade ice cream that is nowadays simmered and then poured into the canister of an ice cream freezer wherein a dasher — cranked by hand or electricity — is

Shelby Stephenson, poet laureate of North Carolina, stands at a window watching the weather in the Johnston County plank house where he was born. (Used by permission of the photographer, Jan G. Hensley)

surrounded by rock salt and ice and will eventually produce ice cream. The eggs provide added fat and emulsifiers that help make the ice cream soft and creamy.

In a 1981 story in *The State* called "The Snow Eaters," the writer Maxine Carey Harker interviewed families in the eastern town of Grifton about their snow cream practices. A member of the Noble family was adamant about her preference for a raw egg in the recipe, having tried both cooked and raw egg mixtures. She also shared her resistance to canned milk. "I use dairy milk. I don't like the condensed taste." Despite her insistence upon adding a raw egg, Ms. Noble also made known her abhorrence of any "eggy" taste in the snow cream, which she countered with nutmeg—a durable spice that goes back to the first century. According to Hindu writings from India's Vedic period, nutmeg can also cure headaches: handy, since snow cream eaten quickly and in great quantity can cause throbbing temples.

By contrast, Dorothy Hall Ruth, of High Point, wrote a dismissive letter to the editor of *The State* in January 1983 regarding the use of eggs in snow cream: "I was so amused at the recipes calling for eggs, milk, sugar; they were making custard and pouring it raw over the snow! . . . Real snowcream is made with thick cream from fresh cow's milk, sugar, and vanilla. Mama would skim a sheet of thick cream from a crock of milk—cold and heavy—sweeten it and add vanilla."

An entirely different school of Tar Heel snow creamers extolled the virtues of sweetened condensed milk, which, one would presume, would eliminate the need for any additional sugar. This canned formula, called Eagle Brand, was developed by a Texas inventor named Gail Borden in 1856 to combat food poisoning and other illnesses that were common before the era of mechanized refrigeration. Just as Mr. Duke's Bull Durham Tobacco found favor on the battlefields of the Civil War, Mr. Borden's Eagle Brand milk gained wide acclaim among the Blue and the Gray, because the canned product traveled well in soldiers' ration bags.

The Gladsen family, of Grifton, told Maxine Carey Harker that not only did they prefer Eagle Brand milk for their snow cream, but they also topped it with Cool Whip, for good measure.

When a craving for snow cream hit the Barfield household, the patriarch would get in the family car and drive north until he found snow, Harker reports. Mr. Barfield then loaded up several coolers with the found snow and brought them home. To his main ingredient he added two eggs, one can of evaporated milk, one and a half cups of sugar, and one tablespoon of vanilla. Then he would cover the mix with a velvety blanket of chocolate syrup and promptly consume his frozen trophy before making any more for the rest of the family.

Another father described in Harker's narrative won the favor of the neighborhood kids by making snowballs for the children to chomp on. He would punch a hole with his finger into the middle of each ball and fill the cavity with molasses.

The addition of alcohol to snow cream has also apparently been a long tradition with some North Carolinians. T. H. Pearce, of Franklin County, responded to the story about the Grifton citizens' snow cream habits with something of a rant. In his letter to the *State* editor, Pearce explained that his neighbors had always avoided any potential harm — from pollution in the snow or from uncooked eggs — by simply adding a sufficient amount of homemade Franklin County apple brandy to their snow cream. "That stuff would neutralize anything," he wrote.

● ● ● ● ● ● ● ● ● ● ● ●

Vanilla and sugar — the other two essential ingredients in snow cream — also bear brief consideration. Photographer and seasoned southern cook Donna Campbell, who accompanied me in the field research for most of this book, makes a simple syrup of sugar and water, which she chills in the fridge while the snow is collecting outside in a metal bowl, which also conducts the cold particularly well. The chilled syrup, then mixed with cream and vanilla, is whisked frugally into the snow until the texture is like ice cream. Having the sugar already dissolved means it disperses more evenly and does not compete with the potentially grainy quality of the snow. (Where I live in the Piedmont, snow rarely comes without some crunchy sleet in advance of the fluffier product.)

Good vanilla is also critical, and Donna always keeps a bottle of genuine Mexican vanilla on hand for the occasion. According to the former Chez Panise pastry chef and food writer David Leibovitz, you can also use dried vanilla beans to make your own vanilla sugar in advance. The beans, he says, can be stored in a jar of sugar, which will take on the vanilla flavor after a couple of weeks. Or you can make a vanilla infusion by adding vanilla beans to whiskey, vodka, or rum to create an adult version of snow cream.

The temptations of eating snow have a long history. The Chinese were probably the first to make fruit and wine slushes and iced desserts from mountain snow that they harvested and transported over great distances, but dairy
products were not used in these concoctions.

Alexander the Great demanded that snow be brought to him from the
Alps to cool his drinks in summer, and Nero reportedly poured honey on
snow for his culinary pleasure (not unlike the molasses application). Other
stories credit Nero with the invention of "Italian ice," because he also compelled his servants to run up the Apennine Mountains to bring home snow
sufficient to mix with fruit. By the sixteenth century, Italians were dropping
snow into their wines to chill them.

But it wasn't until the discovery that salt lowers the freezing point of ice
that the making of ice cream, as we now know it, began. As early as 200 BC,
the Chinese were packing canisters containing a syrupy mixture of rice and
buffalo milk in ice and saltpeter to freeze the mixture. But it was a Philadelphia inventor named Nancy Johnson who created and patented the
first hand-cranked ice cream freezer in 1843. Arguably, the making of snow
cream—so much simpler and quicker—takes us back to something purer.
Or is it?

Warnings against eating snow began to gain traction in the late 1800s
as industrialization swept over the United States and the country's increasingly crowded cities were seen as especially dangerous. In 1892 the journal
Annals of Hygiene warned that "in a large, crowded city like New York there
are always myriads of disease germs or seeds floating in the air; snow-storms
always purify the atmosphere by catching hold of the seeds in the air and
carrying them down to the ground; hence, after a fall of snow, the air is puri-
fied, but the snow itself is defiled." The writer, a physician, strongly urged
parents to prevent children from eating snow to avoid the germs that produced measles, diphtheria, and scarlet fever.

A later round of warnings about the hazards of eating snow began in
the era of nuclear testing, in the late 1950s and early 1960s. Nuclear fallout
had tainted the snow, some warned, and eating snow cream had become
suspect. In one story a 1960s mother made snow cream for her son and was
then roundly scolded by her sister for allowing the boy to eat all he wanted.

Shamed, the mother promptly forced the child to eat—of all things—a raw egg as a cure.

Other parents of the era were more reasonable or lackadaisical, depending on your point of view. Durham resident Debbie McGill remembers how her mother, Bobbie, read a warning about radioactive snow in the *Durham Morning Herald*, but when her daughters asked if they could make snow cream, she joined them in the festivities. How much could it hurt? she reasoned. Eating snow was, at best, a once-a-year event.

Tar Heels in their sixties and seventies have told me that the general rule passed down to them was to avoid the very first snow and allow it to accumulate before partaking. "Six inches is a good minimum," one man from Fayetteville told me. In answer to my email on the subject, Dr. Michael Burchell, in the Department of Biological and Agricultural Engineering at North Carolina State University, wrote, "The only thing I can tell you is that we used to eat it all of the time in rural North Carolina, and there were only two rules: don't eat the first snow of the year, and never eat yellow snow!"

John Pomeroy, a Canadian scientist at the University of Saskatchewan, told National Public Radio's Anne Bramley that snow can have a "scrubbing brush" effect on the atmosphere so that the air (or the snow) gets cleaner as the storm proceeds, and eager snow eaters should wait a few hours for this effect.

As recently as the twenty-one-inch snowfall on Mount Mitchell in 2016, which expanded into a blizzard of record proportions as it rolled up the East Coast, newspapers began a new round of warnings against snow consumption, citing a 2015 study published in the journal *Environmental Science: Processes & Impacts*. The study showed that snowflakes absorb particulate pollutants, and further, exhaust fumes from vehicles may interact with snow and freezing temperatures in a way that compounds the concentration of chemicals such as benzene, toluene, and xylenes—all carcinogens—in snow. The study implied that big cities with large and lingering annual snowfall amounts are at the highest risk from this phenomenon. It concluded that as climate change research continues, researchers must take account of how snow and ice carry and concentrate pollutants and how this phenomenon may amplify the health impacts of carbon emissions around the globe.

In 2015, cultural anthropologist Sarah Baird suggested that snow-eating is less likely to be a cultural practice in urban areas anyway. Writing in *Mod-*

ern Farmer magazine, she said, "The popularity of snow cream is unique in that it's not a regionally specific dish — it's a rural-specific one. Growing up in a non-urban area or small town has more impact on whether or not one knows the joys of snow cream than growing up in the plains of the Midwest or the slushy Mid-Atlantic. 'Both my dad (southern) and mom (northern) made snow cream growing up,' says Ellie Lawrence, a graduate assistant at Appalachian State University. 'My 22-year-old little brother keeps a can of sweetened condensed milk in his college dorm room for snow!'"

Given all this information, should we now consider ourselves to be living in the post-snow-cream era? Is this heritage food already done for? It is an individual decision, of course. However, it is possible, I learned, to buy your own personal snowmaker for home use. The SNOPRO Snowmaker is a small unit that operates on the same principle as the larger machines that are used on ski slopes. The smallest home model starts at less than $400, and you can input your zip code on the company website to see if the purchase makes sense where you live. (The machine still requires sufficiently consistent freezing temperatures outdoors to make the snow.)

Frankly, I'm surprised that some small-appliance manufacturer hasn't already devised a countertop snow cream machine — a miniature kitchen appliance that would operate on the same principle as commercial snow guns but would have its own indoor snow chamber to generate freezing temperatures and capture the snow in a handy removable canister. Then again, what kind of machine-made edible memory would that be?

Rural or urban, if you are chary of snow-eating the old-fashioned way, I found some consolation. According to Appalachian lore, there is another, healthful practice to undertake with snow when it first arrives.

In 1967, the *Asheville Citizen-Times* columnist John Parris wrote about a mountain woman named Nancy Rathbone who lived in Haywood County and swore that the first snow of the season was the key to her health, but not because she *ate* the snow.

"You know," she said, "when the first good snow comes, a snow that's about shoe-mouth deep, I get out in it and wade about in it barefooted. Been doin' it since I was big enough to toddle about. And I'm nigh on to 73." Rathbone went on to tell Parris, "Reckon you think I'm a mite tetched in the head.

Well it could be that I am. But I'll tell you one thing. And it's a fact as true as Scripture. I am one that never has a cold in the winter. Never have had one and don't expect to get one as long as I'm able to walk." Rathbone prescribed a barefoot walk in the first ground-covering snow. Ten minutes or so is all it takes.

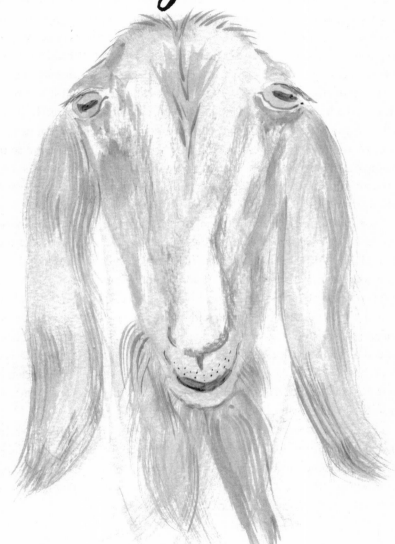

February

Goat's Milk

IN SIGHT OF THE BLUE RIDGE MOUNTAINS ONE FEBRUARY MORNING, a chill wind jittered the limbs of a leafless oak as photographer Donna Campbell and I let ourselves into the fenced area of a historic goat farm. We headed toward a second gate that opened into the bigger pasture, where a mixed herd of white Saanen, darker Nubian, and brown and white Toggenburg goats were grazing. At once a group of them looked up and began trotting toward us. A black and white Nubian with long, floppy gray ears led the pack and poked me in the side with her nose as I closed the gate behind me. It was a bit intimidating, with so many curious goats beginning to clot around us.

The eyes of a goat are glassy and large as shooter marbles. The pupil, however, is a horizontal bar of jet black. When a goat stares directly at you, it's like an inquisition: the intensity can be unnerving. After a sniff or two, the Nubian turned and walked a few steps away, giving her full attention to the grass again. The other goats satisfied their curiosity by sniffing and staring at us, and then they, too, backed off. I noticed all of them wore collars with identification tags.

Two yearling Toggenburgs trotted down the worn path some distance and turned to each other. They both reared up on their hind legs and then dropped slowly, butting heads in slow motion — the goat version of tai chi.

In another direction, a mature Nubian stood swaying her head nonchalantly, as if unaware of the dark, round-bellied barn cat sitting in front of her, staring off into the distance. Then, with great precision, the goat lifted one hoof and stepped directly onto the cat's tail. The cat, without looking back, pranced away to reposition herself for another indifferent pose. The goat soon followed, stepping even closer to the cat's tail, which slowly curled up and down, seeming to dare the goat to do it again. This was clearly the routine of their relationship, a barnyard pas de deux.

I could have observed the herd for hours except for the knife of a wind blowing down from Big Glassy, the granite outcropping above us, so called because of the tendency for precipitation to freeze on the rock face that rises above the Carl Sandburg Home, a National Historic Site that figures prominently in the story of goat's milk in North Carolina.

* * * * * * * * * * * *

Goats (*Capra hircus*) are an ancient food source, not native to the Americas. According to *The Oxford Companion to Food*, they were probably domesticated along with sheep in southwest Asia in the eighth millennium BC.

Goats conjure images of ancient nomadic shepherds, their flocks grazing in poor, scrubby land. Some cultures raise goats for milk *and* meat, and they roast kids for a celebratory meal. In fact, the word "butcher," which is *boucher* in French and *becaccio* in Italian, derives from the Old French word *bouc*, meaning "billy goat," and the earlier Italian *becco*, meaning "he-goat." But eating goat meat these days is apparently less popular than drinking goat's milk. Some 60 to 70 percent of the world's population drink goat's milk regularly. Goat's milk, which is mostly made into cheese in this country, is often lower in fat and higher in calcium than cow's milk. It's also higher in vitamins A and B, riboflavin, iron, and phosphorus and about equal to cow's milk in vitamins C and D, as reported by the American Dairy Goat Association. Because the fat globules in goat's milk are smaller than in cow's milk, it is easier for people to digest.

Raising goats has a gentler environmental impact, too. Goats are not factory-farmed, and they produce much less manure than cows. Of course, goats, being smaller, also generate less milk, but a single doe can produce around ninety quarts of milk every month for ten months a year. Thus, goat's milk and cheese are most often available as locally sourced foods and are produced in smaller batches than cow's milk.

As the Associated Press reported in 2015, "The nation's dairy goat herd climbed 2 percent in the past year to 365,000 animals, but producers said their annual sales are rising even faster — up by 15 percent or more." So goat's milk and cheese are increasing in popularity in the United States, but what does this trend have to do with North Carolina's food heritage?

* * *

I was surprised to learn that the American Dairy Goat Association is headquartered in North Carolina. Part of the reason for our state's prominence in goat farming goes back to a summer day in 1945 when Lilian Steichen Sandburg and her youngest daughter, Helga, came to the North Carolina mountains to look for land. They were hoping to find an existing farm with a house and barn large enough to accommodate their "herd," which consisted of 150 goats, the other two Sandburg daughters, two young grandchildren, and the patriarch of the family — the literary giant Carl Sandburg, who turned sixty-seven that summer. The family's move to a new home would also involve packing and shipping the poet's 17,000-volume library.

At the time, Carl Sandburg was between Pulitzer Prizes. He'd won the award for history for *Abraham Lincoln: The War Years* in 1940, and he would win the prize again, the next time for poetry, in 1951, after having comfortably settled into the rambling house that his wife and daughter ultimately found, along with 245 acres near Flat Rock, in Henderson County, which they bought for only $45,000.

Lilian Sandburg, who had studied broadly—the humanities, genetics, and economics, among other disciplines—at the University of Chicago, began breeding dairy goats in the mid-1930s. She named her herd Chikaming, after the township on the dunes of Lake Michigan where the Sandburgs lived at the time. Mrs. Sandburg, a brilliant woman who was a passionate political activist and linguist and had worked as a professional translator, proceeded to school herself further in the finer points of genetics, determined to improve the milk production of her goats by selective breeding. Originally she had hoped to add a cow to her flock of chickens as a means to provide most of the family's food, but her husband suggested that breeding cows would require complicated transportation for stud service. He told Lilian that she could carry a goat in the family car to the vet or to a breeder, and so her dairy began. As her goats became productive, the family enjoyed the rich butterfat flavor of the milk, and Carl became a vocal advocate of his wife's products. "If it tastes any different from cow's milk, then goat's milk tastes better," he would tell skeptics.

As time went on, however, rising before dawn during the harsh winters on the Lake Michigan shore became less and less appealing to the Sandburg women. In such fierce weather, the goats had to be fed in the barn and could not graze freely for several months of the year. Mrs. Sandburg sought to move the entire enterprise to a more benign environment, where she and her daughters might better manage the household and their goat-breeding business on ample pastureland.

Two of the Sandburgs' daughters lived with their parents their entire lives. The eldest daughter, Margaret, suffered from epilepsy. The middle daughter, Janet, was challenged from the effects of being hit by a car—probably a brain injury—and never left home. Helga, the youngest, married and left home for a number of years but returned with her two young children after her divorce. She joined the family in their move to North Carolina. An energetic and creative woman who wrote, painted, kept bees, raised dogs, and enjoyed the outdoors, Helga helped both her parents with their work, playing a key role in the goat dairy and typing her father's manuscripts.

Once the Sandburgs arrived at Connemara—the antebellum home

The poet Carl Sandburg; his wife, Lilian Steichen Sandburg; and their grandchildren, John Carl and Paula Steichen, gather for a family portrait at the Sandburgs' house near Flat Rock. The goatling is from Mrs. Sandburg's prizewinning herd. (Used by permission of the Billy Rose Theatre Division; New York Public Library for the Performing Arts; Astor, Lenox, and Tilden Foundations)

on the granite-faced mountainside that is not far from what is now the famous Flat Rock Playhouse — Mrs. Sandburg immediately set up the third floor to be an exact replica of the bedroom and writing space that her husband inhabited in the Michigan house, which she had designed. He often worked into the wee hours of the morning, finally going to bed about the same time that Helga and Janet would rise and head out to the barn to tend the goats. Throughout the Sandburgs' twenty-one years at Connemara, the house never had curtains. Lilian said, "Windows are for framing nature." She wanted the natural light and the splendid views of the ever-changing Blue Ridge.

● ● ● ● ● ● ● ● ● ● ● ● ●

Before we visited Connemara and watched the descendants of Mrs. Sandburg's goats cavort in the pasture, I was lucky enough to talk with Carl and

Lilian Sandburg's youngest grandchild, Paula, who still lives in Henderson-ville. Now in her seventies, Paula says her most visceral early memories come from the years at Connemara, playing with her grandmother's prize-winning goats and living by the daily rhythms attached to their caretaking, especially at kidding time, which usually began in February, when the newborns were immediately separated from their mothers.

The tender baby goats went straight to the cellar of the family home, where they were fed four times a day and kept warm by the furnace for at least ten days. A few of the feeding boxes are still there today, and visitors can see some of the equipment used in Mrs. Sandburg's goat operation, in-cluding the handsome Swedish Aga Stove that cost $1,000—a steep sum in the 1940s. With its two ovens and two grills, the Aga could heat water and keep it hot for twenty-four hours. In addition to serving as the feeding sta-tion for the baby goats, this area of the house was the summer kitchen, where Mrs. Sandburg and her daughters canned vegetables from their prodigious garden.

Granddaughter Paula and her brother, John Carl, would occasionally rise with their mother before daylight, carrying their bowls of dry cereal to the barn to watch the dams being milked. The fresh, raw milk would soon be added to their breakfast bowls.

Paula also remembered eating her fill of the delicious cream that was separated from the goat's milk by centrifugal force. "You could slice it with a knife," she said. In the summer, this pure white cream would be served over peaches brought fresh from nearby orchards in South Carolina. Other times it might be added to strawberries or blueberries that grew on the farm.

The cheeses, Paula said, were mostly consumed by the adults—Neufchâtel with pecans; Brie, her mother's favorite; and Kochkaese, a boiled cheese flavored with caraway seeds. Mrs. Sandburg's recipes for these and many other Scandinavian, French, and German-influenced dishes are de-scribed in *Cooking at Connemara: Carl Sandburg Family Recipes*, collected by Elena Diana Miller. Lilian Sandburg's parents had emigrated from Lux-embourg to the United States and Carl's family had come from Sweden, so their household cuisine often featured northern European flavors and prepa-rations.

"When I was a little girl, the scent in the springhouse was the most won-derful," Paula told me. The springhouse was where the Brie and Neufchâtel cheeses were cured. Later they would be brought to the house to be dipped in paraffin or transferred to cold storage. The Sandburg women also made buttermilk, yogurt, and butter.

Helga and her two children lived at Connemara until Paula was ten. Paula later wrote a graceful memoir, *My Connemara*, describing those idyllic times.

> The entire family was charmed by the goats — the playful acrobatics of the kids and the gentle friendly way of the milking does. Buppong [the children's nickname for their grandfather] often encouraged us to bring a kid to him on the front porch or front lawn where it would put on a show for the whole family. And we sometimes brought them into the living room after lunch, to play and explore the people and furniture. Any misbehaving was simply mopped or picked up from the rug — and the show continued.
>
> The older does were just as curious and affectionate as the kids, if not so active. My grandmother would walk about the barn discussing matters with Helga, an entourage of does following the two women, chewing intently on the hems of Gramma's dresses, already repaired carefully from previous attentions, and nibbling the buttons of coats, blowing softly into our faces and nuzzling our necks if we bent over or sat on the stone wall in the barnyard.

To this day, the goats, tended by National Park rangers, are a major attraction for visitors to the farm, along with the meticulously organized office in the house where Mrs. Sandburg kept index cards on every goat she raised, bred, and sold over the years. Next to this room is the less-organized downstairs office of the poet himself, who kept books and papers in open cardboard boxes from the grocery store, stacked everywhere on the floor and desktops.

Mrs. Sandburg continued her goat business for many years, winning top show ribbons for her goats' productivity, publishing her research in noted journals, and offering advice to other would-be goat breeders. For twenty years she served as director of the American Milk Goat Record Association. People came from all over the world to buy her goats, though she sold her dairy products only to local vendors.

According to the National Park Service, "The Chikaming herd grew in recognition with continual first and second place official United States milk production records from 1954 to 1966." A goat named Jennifer II achieved a world record for milk production in 1960, producing 5,750 pounds of milk, more than any other Toggenburg in the world, a record that held for twenty years. Jennifer II's half sister set a world record for butterfat production.

Of his wife, Carl Sandburg wrote to publisher Alfred Harcourt in 1953, "She is steadily reducing the herd but so long as she stays ambulant she will be breeding goats as her brother does delphiniums: it is a genius with her and the goat industry idolizes her for her knowledge and lighted enthusiasm."

Lilian Steichen Sandburg's brother was the eminent photographer Edward Steichen, who visited the farm often. It was Steichen who had originally suggested that the family consider relocating to North Carolina because of its hospitable mountain climate and long agricultural traditions. Steichen had stayed at the Grove Park Inn in Asheville in the 1920s to recover from a respiratory ailment. He had also served as an examiner for at least one photography student at Black Mountain College in the 1950s. Steichen made a stunning portrait of his sister, Lilian, with her Nubian doe named Brocade. The photo is still displayed in Mrs. Sandburg's office at Connemara.

* * * * * * * * * * * *

Photographer Liza Plaster first visited the Carl Sandburg Home in the 1980s, a trip she never forgot. "I saw Mrs. Sandburg's office with her detailed genetic studies of dairy goats, and I met the remnants of her herd, including the Saanen. Shortly afterwards, I went back for a lesson in hoof trimming and began a love affair with dairy goats," Plaster wrote in *The Dairy Goat Gazette*, a newsletter of the Piedmont Dairy Goat Association.

It would take two more decades before Plaster would realize her dream of creating a goat dairy. When I first met her in the 1980s, Plaster was director of the Caldwell County Arts Council in the Blue Ridge foothills. By then, her children, Jesse and Rachel, were teenagers, and they were all living in Liza's grandparents' charming stone house, fronted by giant magnolias. Behind the house, a lush pasture extends to the banks of the Yadkin River north of Lenoir, North Carolina. The farm, which has been in the family for six generations, is in an area known as Happy Valley. Liza's parents owned and operated Greer Laboratories, a roots and herbs business established in 1904 that depended upon local wild plant harvesters who were steeped in the mountain lore of using medicinal herbs to cure common illnesses and who knew where to find arcane botanicals. Today, the company produces immunotherapy products designed to treat human and animal allergies.

Plaster, a vivid woman with a soothing voice and manner, moved from leading the local arts council to working as communications coordinator for the family's business. Still, the romance of goat farming persisted in the back of her mind, and in 2000 she and her husband, William Early (then the resident photographer at the Bernhardt Furniture Company in Lenoir), began building sturdy fences in their twenty acres of pasture. Goats are hard to contain, but this pasture featured briar, honeysuckle, poison ivy, and other goat favorites. Liza apprenticed for a time at Goat Lady Dairy in Climax, North Carolina, south of Greensboro (another woman-owned goat farm), and then she toured France, visiting small goat dairies. In 2004 she bought her first four doelings, Saanens, from the Goat Lady. This breed of Swiss milk goat was one of the three productive breeds that Mrs. Sandburg favored.

By this time Liza's son, Jesse, was a practicing architect in Lenoir. After traveling with his mother to every goat dairy in the state, he designed a most remarkable structure that contains a milking parlor, cheese room, and laundry, while also providing an outdoor loafing area for the goats before and after milking. The building is filled with light and provides a safe and airy harbor. They named the operation Ripshin Goat Dairy, after the mountain ridge across the highway from the farm.

"I think I transferred my love of horses to goats," Liza said as we sat at the long wooden table in her dining room where the farmhands, family, and other guests have shared meals together for years. "And the kids! They are absolute whimsy.

"This table was always full during kidding time," she said, running her hands across the smooth, unvarnished wood. "We had interns, and they'd be up long before daylight. We'd keep a baby monitor in the house and listen for the sounds of kidding in the barn. The does like to kid when no one else is around. After a long night with the goats, we'd have big lunches with red wine."

When a doe gave birth, Liza would prepare hot water with molasses to give the dam for strength and energy after the delivery. The kids at Ripshin were allowed to nurse their dams for eight to ten weeks. For their own enjoyment, Liza and William also drank goat's milk every day — "raw, fresh, clean, and cold," she said. "After years of drinking goat's milk, cow's milk now tastes heavy to me. Saanens give a lean milk."

Liza and William have now retired from goat farming and cheese making after a decade of very hard work, in which they were confined to the daily routines of milking, feeding, mucking the barn, and selling their cheeses on

Liza Plaster poses with Polly, one of the first four doelings that she purchased for the Ripshin Goat Dairy, near Lenoir. Polly became the alpha goat— the acknowledged leader of the herd—for her entire life. (Used by permission of the photographers, Liza Plaster and William Early)

weekends. "I couldn't pay attention to the flowers, couldn't travel, couldn't even go out for supper," Liza said.

Though they did not show their goats in competitions, Ripshin doelings and bucklings were in demand from other goat dairies, and the cheeses were favorites with local chefs and at farmers' markets in Boone, Blowing Rock, and Hickory. Liza's daughter, Rachel, also a professional photographer, managed the cheese making operation for six years, and at its peak the farm was producing 5,000 pounds of cheese in a season. New Zealand's artisanal cheese pioneer Neville McNaughton helped the farm develop a special chèvre recipe that was designed especially for Happy Valley goats' milk. "He would ride up to the farm on his motorcycle and give us advice on everything from designing the dairy to the best rennet and cultures to use. I never tasted a chèvre that I liked better than his recipe," Liza said.

"Selling goat milk does not require all the labor of cheese making, and there's nothing better than fresh, raw goat's milk. We could have sold it, but we opted for cheese," Liza added. "To me, goat's milk makes the very best ice cream. It tastes like ice cream did when I was a child."

Nowadays William has taken up golf, and Liza is "trying to make the gardens more interesting." As a goat farmer, she admits that she was a different person, "really exacting. I was a hard-ass, a driven woman. I felt like it was all on me to make the dairy work since Willie had quit his job to help with the dairy. Now Willie and I can laugh together again. We created the dairy to have the best product we could, and in the end, I think we did it."

Liza's admiration and respect for Lilian Sandburg's life and expertise have never waned. "She's the one who figured out how to make the goat as productive as the cow. She studied the genetics and knew which buck and doe could create the most productive kid. She learned that you can judge a buck by his daughters' udders," Liza explained.

Ripshin kept bucks on the property but separate from the does except at breeding time. Bucks are the creatures with a smell that can turn off prospective goat's milk drinkers and cheese eaters. Many small goat farmers do not even keep bucks on their property and bring them in only for stud service when a doe comes into season, though as Liza pointed out, a doe will stand for a buck only in a narrow window of time—about eighteen hours at the peak of her cycle—so it is much easier to have the bucks at least in proximity.

These days, Liza and William have transformed the cheese facility into a mixed-use kitchen to be shared by local bakers, pasta makers, and jam and jelly makers. People still stop by to admire her gardens, walk in the enticing landscape, and gaze at the pastoral view toward the Yadkin River.

* * * * * * * * * * * *

At the Celebrity Dairy in Chatham County, February is the peak month when the goats deliver kids and begin milk production, also known as freshening. Visitors are welcome there for weekend barn openings to witness the birthing process among the dairy's Alpine and Saanen goats. The herd of approximately 100 goats shares 300 acres with several breeds of free-range chickens, a bevy of barn cats, and a team of fastidious caretakers who milk and tend the animals and make cheese, ice cream, and soap from fresh goat's milk.

For the past twenty years, Brit and Fleming Pfann have also been hosting once-a-month Sunday dinners that feature wholesome dishes dependent on the yield of their farm and garden. The recipes are often inspired, such as Celebrity Dairy Goat Milk Stir-Fried Kale, Chicken Pate and Chèvre Terrine, and Coffee Chèvre Truffles. The Pfanns also offer their dairy products at the weekly Carrboro Farmers' Market.

The annual cycle at the dairy basically goes like this: Goat-breeding takes place in the fall. (The gestation period for baby goats is around 150 days.) The does that gave birth in February have been "dried off" following ten months of lactation. For the dairy, this means closing out the milking season around Thanksgiving and preparing for the first arrival of newborns in the new year. By February they start coming fast — 150 kids or so are born each year. Visiting in February to see this new life stirring is a lift to the spirits and always energizing for children. The wobbly-legged kids are almost unbearably cute, and after a few days they are quite curious about the world around them, including the humans who come to visit. You can't help but wonder at the heaviness and wide girth of the expectant does. The imminence of additional births keeps everyone's attention trained on the barnyard. It's always a pleasant February distraction in an otherwise bleak month.

● ● ● ● ● ● ● ● ● ● ● ●

Several other goat cheese operations are thriving in the Piedmont, and at least one in the East also sells seafood. Meanwhile, western North Carolina dairy farmers have developed an official "cheese trail" that covers thirty-three counties. Some operations specialize in agritourism, offering hayrides, opportunities to pet and play with goats, and classes in cheese making and soapmaking, cooking, and goat husbandry. Others are more focused on cheese tastings and farm-to-table dinners. Some have overnight accommodations. Among these, a personal favorite is Mountain Farm, a sustainable, twenty-four-acre lavender, blueberry, and dairy goat farm in Celo in Yancey County, not far from Mount Mitchell.

The farm's small herd includes Saanen and Nubian goats that are raised free of hormones and antibiotics. The proprietors also rent out a renovated hundred-year-old, two-bedroom cabin for personal retreats in a pristine setting. Mountain Farm uses the milk the goats produce to make aged cheeses, handcrafted soap, and other body products that are often scented with French lavender, which grows in profusion around the farm in summer. As the smallest certified goat dairy in the state, Mountain Farm is open to the public only on a few special occasions a year, but it is especially delightful because of the unencumbered mountain views and the unusual combination of crops and products — a great destination if you're bringing children.

If, however, you are looking to buy a bottle of the first goat's milk of the season, as we were, there is only one farm that I could find in North Carolina that offers pasteurized goat's milk for sale. The Round Mountain Creamery, near Black Mountain, advertises itself as "North Carolina's Only Grade 'A' Goat Dairy." Grade A refers to a regulatory program for milk administered by the state's Department of Agriculture.

On a cold sunny morning in early February, Donna and I took the road less traveled to the dairy, meaning we drove in on Bat Cave Road from the east, a scenic, steep, and winding route through deep woods and gorgeous banks of rhododendron, which, I learned, is poisonous to goats. (The easier route to the dairy is Highway 9 South from Black Mountain.)

Round Mountain Creamery supports more than 250 goats in a valley bisected by a burbling stream and surrounded by steep hillsides. The two breeds here are the Alpine, which originated in the French Alps and can grow rather large, and the La Mancha, a breed originally developed in Oregon and known for its sweet temperament. It was startling to see that the La Manchas had no ear flaps, while the Alpines had stiff ears that stood out from their heads, neither of which was like the breeds at the Sandburg farm, where the animals' enormous floppy ears suggested a kind of joyful, puppy-dog personality. But these goats were friendly and curious, too.

On the morning we arrived at Round Mountain, the owner, whom I had talked to in advance, was off trying to get something repaired, so we were greeted by Adam Jernigan, a slender, studious-looking man in his thirties with cheeks and nose bright red from the cold. He explained that the dairy had 8 bucks, 138 milking does, and 8 pregnant does at the moment, with another 150 goats in the herd. "We also have three geese and two emus for yard art," Jernigan said with a mischievous smirk. He didn't look like a goat farmer to me, somehow. He then explained that they used milking machines to handle such a large herd.

"How long have you been doing this thing with goats?" I asked.

"I started in September helping in the milking parlor," he said. Jernigan is one of eight employees. "Now I have been promoted to herd manager."

"Wow, what kind of training did you have for this work?" I asked.

"I just finished my MFA in creative writing at Warren Wilson College."

We both laughed. He said the job allowed him to get some writing done since he lived only a mile up the road.

"Fiction?"

"Yep," he said.

"How do you know when a goat is about to kid?" I asked, going back into my reporter mode.

"The ligaments loosen and the udders tighten," he said. I did not ask the location of the ligaments.

"We'd like to buy some milk!" I said brightly, and we laughed some more while Donna roamed around shooting photos of the earless La Manchas poking their noses through the fence with, I swear, smiles on their faces.

Full disclosure: though I am a sometimes-reluctant fan of goat cheese, I had never tasted goat's milk in my life, so I wasn't sure what to expect. Jernigan went into the milk house and returned with a quart bottle printed with the logo of the creamery on the glass and topped with a plastic cap. He told us that goat's milk is best kept a little colder than the usual setting on most refrigerators. Thirty-five to thirty-eight degrees is the optimum temperature.

With tax, the quart was seven dollars and change. We put the bottle in a cooler in the car and wished Adam well in his writing and goat tending. I later found out that Round Mountain milk is also usually available at some grocery stores in Black Mountain and Asheville, including Earth Fare.

Back home from our adventure, I brought the milk to my mother's condo next door, and Donna and I set out three small juice glasses, all the while sharing stories from our adventure—the earless goats, the Sandburg herd's antics, the would-be novelist who milks goats for a living. My mother, at ninety-four, never remembered tasting goat's milk either, she said.

She did drink fresh cow's milk as a child at her grandmother's farm in summers and had told me the story many, many times of watching her grandmother fall asleep at the churn as she pumped up and down, gradually slowing until she finally nodded off in her chair, her hand still on the dasher.

I'll never forget tasting real buttermilk for the first time in the north Georgia mountains with friends who got it once in a while from a local farmer. The chunks of yellow, almost chewy butterfat were a surprise, even perhaps a little greasy, but I have always loved buttermilk, and the real, unadulterated product was no exception.

The Round Mountain Creamery bottle said to shake the milk before pouring because it can form little bits of solid on the milk surface. I figured this was like the country buttermilk, so I was not worried. I shook it hard and poured. The milk was as white as ceiling paint. Our half-full glasses before us, Mom, Donna, and I raised a toast to all the goats. We clinked and drank.

Mom, an increasingly picky eater over the eight years she lived next door to me in North Carolina, reminded us that she preferred 2 percent milk. But to our surprise she declared the goat's milk rich and tasty. She was soon ready for another pour. Mom always loved to travel and to try new things, though now she was confined at home.

"At least it's not chewy," I said.

I somehow intuitively understood how having this milk extra-cold made it better, though it is hard to say why. Perhaps the faintest goat scent might come out more if the milk were warmer. Donna, who hails from a family that can never have too much butter, called it delicious and was surprised by how much she liked it, too.

● ● ● ● ● ● ● ● ● ● ● ● ●

As it turned out, this was one of the last times we would sit together at Mom's table. For two months already she had been in hospice home care for congestive heart failure. Five days later, as we gathered around her bed, it snowed—small white flakes drifting like moths outside her bedroom window. They did not stick. She left us the next morning.

Like Mrs. Sandburg, my mother had a long, productive life. When the Sandburgs' granddaughter, Paula, had called me for our interview a few weeks earlier, I'd told her all about my mother's continuing determination to enjoy life, even in hospice care. Paula said she'd lost her mother, Helga, only two years earlier, at the end of January 2014. Helga was ninety-six. We laughed and commiserated, talking about our adventurous, brave, and picky mothers.

I will always be glad that Mom and I tried something new together that February day. Now goat's milk is my beverage of choice to toast her memory.

March

Shad

BRASSY LIGHT BORE DOWN THROUGH THIN AFTERNOON CLOUDS AS I crossed into Jones County on Highway 58 South—the road that runs from Kinston to the coast at Emerald Isle. A yellow highway sign warned "WATCH FOR BEARS COUNTYWIDE." I had to grin. Back then, in the early 1990s, this alert was posted at every major gateway into Jones County. As far as I know, the caution was never worded quite like that elsewhere in North Carolina. Jones County officials seemed to suggest that local black bears recognized their jurisdictional boundaries and were compelled to stay within them.

Bears are plentiful in this poor, sparsely populated county, where agriculture and timber operations dominate. I have caught glimpses of dark, furry figures foraging in fields of soybeans or silage over the years, but on this particular spring afternoon I had another focus. I was heading to my first-ever shad-fishing expedition. My host, the Honorable Walter P. Henderson, was a local judge and raconteur who loved literature and southern cooking as much as I do.

American shad (*Alosa sapidissima*) are to eastern North Carolina what salmon are to Alaska. The largest member of the herring family, these glittering, slab-sided fish make their home in Atlantic waters throughout most of the year and then suddenly turn inland in spring to spawn in rivers. Like salmon, their sense of direction is infallible. Their annual pilgrimage back to the waters of their birth is an astonishment of nature. Their capacity to adapt their metabolism to move between salt water and fresh is also nothing short of miraculous.

Shad are an ancient delicacy, first valued by native peoples when they began devising ways to catch them with loop nets, weirs, and spears. The environmental writer John McPhee confirms the old saw that native people taught the English invaders how to plant corn by placing fish in the ground along with seed to fertilize young plants. The lesser-known detail in the story is that the species most likely to be used for this purpose was shad, says McPhee in *Founding Fish*.

McPhee quotes a letter written by Edward Winslow on 11 December 1621, less than a year after the Plymouth landing: "We set the last spring some twenty acres of Indian corn, and sowed some six acres of barley and peas; and, according to the manner of the Indians, we manured our ground with herrings, or rather shads, which we have in great abundance."

American shad, alongside their smaller herring cousins, still scavenge the Atlantic from Newfoundland to Florida, swimming in schools with open mouths, constantly feeding on zooplankton, crustaceans, and small fish. Come spring, when shallow waters are nearing sixty degrees, they whirl into the estuaries of those freshwater rivers that have not been obstructed by dams or otherwise so polluted as to make reproduction improbable or impossible.

In the late nineteenth century and again between 1930 and 1960, shad stock were severely depleted by commercial overharvesting up and down the Eastern Seaboard. Today, increasing development and water pollution are still a threat to shad in eastern North Carolina's relatively unspoiled, wide-mouthed rivers, but the fish swim against the lazy currents of the Roanoke, Chowan, Tar, Pamlico, Neuse, and Cape Fear Rivers and spread out into the tributaries, too.

According to the North Carolina Wildlife Resources Commission, which has been working with the U.S. Fish and Wildlife Service to restock and restore shad populations, particularly in the Roanoke River, shad take to the middle of the channel to spawn at night. They prefer shallow water and moderate currents. Shad spawning farther south, below the North Carolina coastline, generally die after spawning, whereas in parts north of the Cape Fear River they can survive to spawn again the following year. American shad can live from five to seven years, the study found.

With their proportionally small heads and deep-bellied bodies, shad caught in North Carolina inland waters these days generally weigh from two to seven pounds, though early nineteenth-century accounts measured their upper weight at twelve or thirteen pounds. They are usually between four-teen and sixteen inches in length.

The Latin superlative *sapidissima*, which is part of shad's scientific name, means "most delicious," but shad are also extremely bony. More than one Native American tribal legend proposes that shad originated on the planet as porcupines that then turned themselves inside out and took to the water to live.

On the positive side, shad contain more healthy omega-3 fats than salmon. They can be deep-fried, roasted on a cedar plank (usually accom-panied by bacon), slow-baked, or pressure-cooked until the bones dissolve. Leftover shad can be made into hearty chowder with potatoes, celery, and onions. Some fancy chefs bake them in parchment, while others at home have been known to use paper bags and very low, slow heat. It seems that fishmongers who have conquered the challenge of filleting shad are few, and because of the labor intensity and scarcity of this talent, the deboned fish come at a high price in the marketplace. Regardless, recipes abound.

The smaller male fish is known as a "buck," and according to the late celebrated chef Edna Lewis, they have more bones than the female. The female shad, or "roe," as they are called, bear bright eggs that are considered a delicacy, often served in eastern North Carolina with scrambled eggs for breakfast.

Shad roe, however, are very fragile and a bit tricky to cook. Edna Lewis, who served for a year as guest chef at the Fearrington House Restaurant, near Pittsboro, North Carolina, offers definitive advice in her classic book, *The Taste of Country Cooking*. She directs that shad roe be cooked in a small skillet with one-third cup of cold water, which must evaporate completely before the roe are then gently sautéed with butter. "See to it that the roe does not become too dried out," she warns.

For generations in eastern North Carolina, the blessed arrival of shad has meant the end of winter's deprivations. Their appearance has long been a cause for celebration and a portent of the coming scent of spring blossoms and the cacophonous chorales of peepers and tree frogs who offer up the wetlands' first music.

In some places, the celebration of shad is undertaken in tandem with Easter, and because Easter moves around the calendar, this makes the catch less predictable than the party. In 2013, perhaps in an effort to honor all long-running shad celebrations equally, the North Carolina General Assembly passed a bill declaring Bladen County's East Arcadia Blue Monday Shad Fry, held annually for more than six decades, as the state's official *Blue Monday Shad Fry*. (Only in North Carolina is the day after Easter known as Blue Monday.) The same piece of legislation also designated the Grifton Shad Festival, running for more than four decades in Pitt County, as the state's official shad *festival*. That one occurs in mid-April.

Prime fishing time for shad, however, varies up and down the Eastern Seaboard. In the area of eastern North Carolina where I was headed, I was told that the first two weeks of March usually offer the best catch of incoming fish. Fisherfolk suffering from the cabin fever of winter eagerly prepare for shad's arrival, expecting a good fight to bring their prizes to shore. Shad are strong and swim deep, often causing anglers to lose their rigs in a tangle of roots and rocks at the river bottom. According to the *Carolina Sportsman*, catching shad successfully with a rod and reel requires some planning:

"The preferred shad-fishing technique is to use ultra-light spinning reels with 4- to 8-pound-test line and a spoon-and-shad-dart combination. Some anglers like tiny (1/16-ounce) leadhead jigs with white or chartreuse curly-tail grubs (crappie jigs) or No. 3 silver or gold spoons. Most use tandem rigs with a dart on the front dropper line and the spoon at the back. Fly-rod anglers often use small Clouser minnows in silver or chartreuse patterns with gold tinsel."

Ah, the poetry of lure naming! Curiously though, shad do not actually eat when they are spawning, so why will they fetch a shiny lure? Boredom perhaps? Or is it the familiar flash, which mimics their own luminous scales?

As a consequence of not feeding over the spawning season, shad lose serious weight. One study conducted by NC State University in 2014 electronically tagged 3,000 shad on the Little River. Researchers found that bucks may lose up to 30 percent of their body weight, while roe can lose as much as 60 percent. Best to catch the shad on the way upriver, then, which is just what my host in Jones County had planned for us.

* * * * * * * * * * * * *

I pulled into the town of Trenton just before dark. This village, one of only three municipalities in all of Jones County, is also the county seat. According to town officials, the historic dominance of large plantations as social and cultural centers during the era of slavery accounts for the absence of larger, long-established towns in the county.

Trenton has fewer than 300 residents today and is named for the Trent River—a pristine, tannin-dark tributary that winds in bold curves through the countryside before running into the Neuse River near New Bern.

Trenton proper encompasses several city blocks. There are historic churches; a hardware store; a café where locals gather for breakfast, lunch, and gossip; an old schoolhouse; a convenience store; a couple of gas stations; and a complex of county government buildings, including the Colonial Revival courthouse, built in 1939, and the old jail behind it, constructed shortly after the Civil War.

A portrait of Senator Furnifold Simmons, Jones County's most famous citizen, hangs in the courthouse lobby. Simmons was largely responsible for the creation of the Intracoastal Waterway and the establishment of Fort Bragg in North Carolina. He served as chair of the Senate Finance Committee during the Wilson administration. Before his service as a senator,

Simmons had been a leader of the white supremacy campaign that disenfranchised North Carolina's black voters at the beginning of the twentieth century. Simmons ran unsuccessfully for the Democratic nomination for president in 1920.

Trenton's proudest site, however, is Brock Mill Pond, protected on the National Register of Historic Places. The picturesque pond and dam provide a popular stop for picnickers headed to the beach. Giant cypress draped with Spanish moss surround the dark water that splendidly mirrors the trees. The millhouse, maintained now by a nonprofit group, was built in the 1940s. Earlier structures on the same site date back as far as 1776, according to local land records. Enslaved people built the original dam.

In his copious diaries, President George Washington writes about stopping in Trenton for a meal on 22 April 1791. He was in the middle of his famous southern tour, in which every town and country inn where he laid his powdered head recorded the event on a historical marker. (Trenton's marker is on N.C. 58 at N.C. 41.) Making his way from New Bern to Wilmington, Washington spent the night at Shine's Inn, a local tavern. He reportedly also met some men whom the president characterized as "indifferent members of the King Solomon's Masonic Lodge." His diary entry reads, "Friday 22d. Under an Escort of horse, and many of the principal Gentlemen of Newbern I recommenced my journey. Dined at a place called Trenton which is the head of the boat navigation of the River Trent wch. is crossed at this place on a bridge and lodged at one Shrine's 10 M farther—both indifferent Houses."

Visiting as he did in April, Washington was probably a bit late for the peak shad run in the Trent River, but as John McPhee confirms in *Founding Fish*, the president was a dedicated shad eater and a commercial shad fisherman before and after the Revolution. It was the spring shad run on Pennsylvania's Schuylkill River that allegedly saved Washington's troops from starvation at Valley Forge, McPhee recounts. I wonder if those Jones County Masons found a way to talk shad with the president?

Had he been on the scene, my Trenton host, Judge Henderson, would surely have brought up the topic of shad. The judge paddled the Trent all his life and committed to memory a raft of stories about the daring watermen who managed precarious, high-water log drives down the Trent River to deliver timber to the sawmills around New Bern. The judge also wrote a novel titled *Crazy Dream Horse*, about a ghost horse named Nightmare that would appear from time to time along the Trent where a disastrous Civil War skirmish had supposedly taken place.

In his late sixties at the time of our fishing expedition, the judge—or "Bud," as his friends and family called him—also claimed to have been Trenton's first hippie. He showed me a photo to prove it: scraggly-bearded and lanky in the mid-1960s, Bud was sitting outside the local café sporting tattered jeans, his feet bare. Now he was a bit thicker, with a head of thinning white hair, an aquiline nose, bright blue eyes, and surprisingly delicate hands. He carried himself with distinction and determination. He was proud of his Nordic lineage, so proud that he incongruously named his Jones County homeplace Yygdrasil, for the tree of life in Norse mythology.

After serving many years as clerk of court and then making an unsuccessful run for Congress, Bud was elected district court judge, presiding in the Jones County Courthouse, where his father, Leon Lassiter Henderson, had applied his carpenter's tools and self-taught aesthetics to decorate the stately rooms that encouraged reverence for the rule of law.

As a judge, Bud soon became known for his eccentric and often benevolent rulings in minor matters of traffic violation, nonviolent family disputes, and questionable public disturbances. Once he dismissed a drunk-driving charge brought against a local resident who had been ordered in a traffic stop to walk a straight line on the shoulder of the road as a sobriety test. Instead, the man remained silent and proceeded to pitch himself forward into a handstand and walk a straight line on his palms away from his car. Flustered, the highway patrolman wrote the ticket anyway, claiming contempt, and as Bud told it, the officer was still angry when the offender came to court.

After hearing the facts, Judge Henderson motioned the driver to the bench and whispered to him. The defendant then turned and hand-walked down the aisle at a nice clip toward the back of the courtroom, his feet completely steady in the air. As he reached the back of the room, Bud hollered for him to keep on going out the door. "Case dismissed," he declared as he rapped his gavel and eyed the red-faced patrolman.

In another story he loved to tell, Bud was called upon to rule in a sibling dispute over a piece of shared property. He patiently heard each party's complaints and then called them both to the bench and ordered them to "hug and kiss each other like you mean it." He then pronounced that each should pay their half of the taxes due on the joint property and vacate his courtroom so he could get on to more serious matters.

When we first met, Bud had been ready to retire from the bench, but Governor Jim Hunt had other ideas, offering him a lifetime appointment as an itinerant judge who would travel across jurisdictions statewide, relieving his fellow jurists when they went on vacation or took sick leave. Bud's quirky rulings thus spread across the entire state, sometimes resulting in local attorneys offering effusive welcomes home for the regular judges when they returned from leave.

Incredibly, Judge Walter P. Henderson had never earned a law degree and was the only judge in the state without such credentials during his tenure. Ever since his days as an undergraduate at the University of North Carolina, where he studied creative writing under the flamboyant writer Jessie Rehder, Bud was always working on some writing project or other — novels, philosophical musings, poems, historical essays. Words were his true passion. That was why we met. He took a noncredit writing class from me at Duke University.

No matter the genre, Bud's subject was always his home territory, its elusive beauty and troubled racial history. He fancied himself the Faulkner of Jones County, but in this little passage, which still appears on a website promoting paddling on the Trent River, Bud gives a nod to Whitman:

> I sing from the springs at the union of Duplin and Lenoir Counties on the property of Odom Futrell and have been doing so for fifteen thousand years. I tumble in erratic meanderings for more than 100 miles, ending in Craven County.
>
> My headwater is a meager five feet wide, yet my mouth is a mile wide where I end in the confluence in the Neuse River at Union Point in New Bern.
>
> I am the Trent River, named after the River Trent in England. In the early days of European settlement along my shores, it is said that I meandered by every major plantation in the county.

Next to these words is an old photo of the judge in a cotton shirt and ball cap, paddle in hand, ancient cypress trees looming dark and stately beyond his canoe.

Bud's love for the Trent River would buoy us that night as we celebrated the age-old ritual of pulling shad from the water that flowed just behind his sprawling brick home and well below the fanciful tree house he had built over the river as a studio to accommodate his writing habit.

Unbeknownst to me, Bud had already been out in his johnboat that

March afternoon to set a net across a narrow section of the Trent upriver from his house—a practice that was surely illegal at the time. Meanwhile his wife, Surena—"Rena" for short—had been preparing some serious eastern North Carolina comfort food for our supper.

Rena was the much-beloved legislative assistant for a string of senate and house members in the North Carolina legislature. Besides commuting to Raleigh for that work, she also launched a company, Inheritance Press, which published the judge's writings and her own volumes on genealogy and the history of the Tuscarora Indians, who once lived along the banks of the Trent.

When I arrived, she came out to the yard to greet me. We hugged hello. "We're having chicken and pastry," Rena told me as I unloaded my bag from the car. For me, the name of this dish conjured a vision of a crisp, brown, flaky piecrust atop something like chicken and gravy, but I was uninitiated. I soon learned that what eastern North Carolinians call chicken and pastry is the same chicken and dumplings my Georgia grandmother prepared with white flour dough rolled out with a baking pin, cut into squares, and then dropped into a pot of boiling chicken parts with a few bones to flavor and thicken the stew.

Once in the kitchen with Rena, I immediately smelled the collards she had been cooking all afternoon, plucked from her sandy side-yard garden. The scent of ham and peppery vinegar softened the tang of sulfur wafting from the pot of greens bubbling beside the stewing chicken.

On first blush, Rena seemed to be an unassuming country woman with deep rural roots, but the more time I spent with her, the more I saw her fiery side that sat like well-banked coals in a stove. Like Bud, she had strong opinions but measured them out more strategically. Bud was a bull to her fox. Her deep knowledge of history cultivated by a lifetime of reading and studying also shone through more gradually, probably because Bud took up so much air in most any conversation.

Bud and Rena's house backed up to the Trent River about a mile out of Trenton. Like Faulkner's house in Oxford, Mississippi, the approach to the residence was dramatic, but in this landscape, the long, tree-lined drive snaked through tall pines and across a small bridge that arched over the edge of a wetland that they had fronted with nonnative agaves. Their spikes seemed more menacing than the swampy thicket behind them. The house itself, still under renovation then, looked like a railway station, which it once had been.

Walter P. Henderson, a Trenton raconteur and local judge, and his wife, Surena Bissette Henderson, an amateur historian, take an afternoon rest on the patio outside the kitchen of their historic house on the Trent River in Jones County.

Bud had somehow finagled the purchase of a vintage train station near Kenansville, in Rena's native Duplin County. They had it moved to the Henderson family's extensive acreage in Jones County. The station was built in 1901 by Standard Oil baron Henry Flagler, solely for the purpose of bringing guests to town for a wedding that year — his third. Flagler, then seventy-two, was marrying the thirty-four-year-old Mary Lily Kenan at her ancestral home, Liberty Hall, in Kenansville. Wedding guests would arrive at the new station on a special train he'd commissioned. One car also carried a small orchestra and a team of Baltimore chefs for the festivities. Flagler arranged for carriages to meet the wedding guests and squire them eight miles through the countryside to Liberty Hall on a new road that he'd also built for the event. According to a contemporary newspaper account from south Florida where the couple would ultimately settle, the bride's wedding gifts from her new husband included "a $500,000 pearl necklace, a check for $1 million, and $2 million in bonds. For their honeymoon they left the steamy August heat of North Carolina for Flagler's summer home at Mamaroneck, N.Y."

Bud and Rena hired masons to painstakingly reconstruct some of the station's brickwork. A team of carpenters installed a two-and-a-half-floor, split-level layout inside, including wrought iron stairs and balconies connecting the three bedrooms. A woodstove heated an informal den on the first floor. Above, a formal living room sat at the house's front and center, festooned with federal columns, heavy moldings, and electric candle fixtures dripping with crystal.

They also dug out a basement for a playroom with a pool table and a library, where Bud kept his collection of first-edition Faulkners. Beyond the original structure, they added on a kitchen with an enormous bay window facing the front field that they leased out each year for tobacco. The kitchen, in turn, led into a three-car garage with a patio out back, constructed of heavy antebellum bricks in many shades of red, pink, and orange.

On the other side of the house, Bud was adding a broad deck overlooking the swampy section of land upriver, where Musselshell Creek meandered into the Trent. A narrow gangplank connected the deck to his tree house office, which hovered some thirty feet above the river. For several years Bud's frail railing meant that guests were always cautioned never to lean on the wooden balustrades while moving from deck to tree house, which itself was encircled by a deck with questionable railings. Eventually Bud found a carpenter who could retrofit the barriers to meet code.

He was a bit more successful in designing a sturdy, if steep, set of wooden stairs that plummeted down the riverbank to a small dock protruding out into the water. It was there that Bud kept his johnboat and sometimes a canoe, but on this evening, he had already parked the canoe upstream for our shad reconnaissance mission.

As I learned when the evening's first bourbon was poured, the plan was for the two of us to retire early and then get up at midnight, climb into his rusting truck, drive up a dirt road, launch the canoe, and, after filling the boat with shad, float back down the Trent the half mile to his dock behind the house. I didn't ask any questions. Captain Shad was in charge.

Sated by the heavy chicken and pastry and savory collards, we retired to catch a nap. At midnight, Bud rang a ship's bell and I rose in the guest room upstairs and threw on some jeans and three layers — turtleneck, sweater, and jacket. I came down the iron steps in my sock feet and laced on my hiking boots by the warm woodstove.

Outside, a silver veneer of frost covered the front lawn. Bud already had the truck warming up, spewing exhaust. I could see my breath, too. It didn't occur to me what we might need for this operation, but the bed of the pickup was cluttered with all manner of tools and coolers.

Once beyond the floodlights on the corners of the house, the gibbous moon took over. It was an oval kite trailed by a tangled string of stars. We could have traveled without headlights. We drove the distance to the paved highway and turned north but soon rolled off the pavement onto a sandy road flanked by deep stands of mature pines laid out straight as corn. "My father planted these trees," Bud said.

He offered me a sip of whiskey from a flask on the seat as we bumped along. We didn't talk anymore. I was still sleepy and full from supper, and it honestly never occurred to me that here I was headed into deep woods — the regular habitat of bears and cottonmouth moccasins. I was trusting a man twice my age to paddle me in black water through an obstacle course of cypress knees to some choice spot to catch fish I had also never seen or landed. That I was game could have had two meanings.

Soon, Bud stopped the truck and squinted once, then twice into the woods lit by his headlights and pulled the truck into an open space. He killed the rattletrap engine, which sputtered an extra beat. He handed me a big, boxy flashlight and took another for himself from under the seat. We opened and shut the truck doors as if someone might hear us. We headed into the brush. Ticks were not out yet, right? No. It was plenty cold.

It took him a little while, but Bud finally got his bearings and found the canoe pulled up on solid ground at the edge of the water. I noticed there was only one paddle in the boat. He dragged the canoe closer to the dark water and shoved it in. He put out his clean, chilled hand to escort me into the canoe as if I were some lady in a bustle and hat about to go on excursion. My boots clomped on the metal bottom, and the canoe shuddered. I sat unceremoniously. The cold from the metal seat soaked through my jeans like ice water.

Bud then settled himself in the boat, still holding a rope looped once around a skinny tree and tied to the canoe. We each put on life jackets that were stowed under the seats. Then Bud shoved us off with the paddle and pulled the rope from around the tree, throwing it to his feet. What had seemed to be very still water was suddenly moving faster than I guessed.

"I'll steer. You shine the light," he said.

He paddled with one arm, the spatulate end never leaving the water, stirring us silently forward. I shone my light straight ahead, downriver. He swept his light nearer to shore, finally confessing that he was looking for a pole that held one end of the net he had set that afternoon. Was that legal? I didn't ask. He was the judge.

When his light landed on something white protruding from the brush on the shoreline, he quickly forked the boat over toward shore. He pulled on a single glove and maneuvered the canoe toward the edge of the net. He lifted up one end, which bellied out beside us and somehow held the canoe in place. I pointed my light down into the water, but the river stopped the shine by inches, only giving up brown, like beer glass, then closer gold, like whiskey. As Bud pulled up more net, the water drops shone like opals, by turns persimmon and turquoise in the light.

"New weight here," he said, grinning, and pulled up another foot of net. At first they looked like a cache of fresh coins rising up, the scales catching light like lenses. Three shad, then six. Bud untangled them one by one with his gloved hand and threw them into the boat. They seemed huge, not unlike the overgrown shiners I caught as a child in my granddaddy's pond. Then an ugly, red-mouthed fish came up. Bud grabbed it and heaved it downstream with a loud splash.

Years later, I would find this passage in a piece by Joseph Mitchell, the *New Yorker* columnist who was born and raised in Fairmont, North Carolina, near the Lumber River: "Lifting a shad net is like shooting dice — you never get tired of seeing what comes up."

A trickle of blood soon coiled between our feet as the shad thrashed at the boat's bottom. We collected a total of ten, and then Bud let the net go. He realigned the canoe with the river. We floated back toward home in the moonlight, giddy with our success.

* * * * * * * * * * * *

The next morning when I came downstairs, Bud had already retrieved his vehicle parked upstream. He'd also strung the shad up on a line that swung from a frame in the back of the truck bed. He said we'd go down to the café to show off our catch and make plans for lunch with whomever could come out to the house. Rena was already in the kitchen chopping cabbage for slaw.

At the café, Bud introduced me around as "a shad consultant from Duke University." People seemed quite used to such proclamations from him and smiled patiently, offering me a hand or a nod in greeting.

We drank watery coffee out of gigantic Styrofoam cups at a booth near the window, where we could keep an eye on the fish in the truck. The café smelled slightly rank, of country ham and lard biscuits. The watery grits, which seemed to swim on every plate, looked thin, and I guessed they might have tasted a bit sulfurous as they often do in coastal areas because of the high water table.

The local gossip that morning concerned a school-bus driver who had not yet made it to the café on her usual schedule. There were many outrageous speculations going around the room as to why.

Many of the men were dressed in camouflage pants and well-worn canvas jackets or puff vests. Their wool hats and gimme caps dutifully came off in the flow of cold air at the door. Since everyone knew everyone, my reputation as a shad consultant spread quickly through the room. People stole glances our way and some followed us out to the truck to see our catch up close before we went back home. One enormously round, short, and red-faced man named Shug invited us to drive by his house to see the hog that he'd just killed, cleaned, and hung up in his toolshed that morning. Soon a group of men in suits came down the sidewalk headed for the courthouse. Bud called out to them to be at his place by "noon thirty sharp."

We'd be eating shad steaks, he told them. Then we got in the truck and went by to see Shug's hog for a minute, just to be polite.

●　●　●　●　●　●　●　●　■　●　●　●

Back home, Bud scaled and cleaned the shad behind the house using one of his inventions—a tilted table made of two-by-four scraps and a half sheet of plywood with a water hose affixed to the high end. As it turned out, there were three roes in our catch, and with these, he carefully removed the deep crimson egg sacks—two lobes per roe—and set them in a Pyrex dish he'd filled with water. Once he'd finished the extraction, he asked me to carry them into the kitchen, where Rena washed them again and placed them in another bowl of salted water that went into the fridge.

Bud removed the heads and tails and then sliced the shad into thick steaks, with the large backbone still in the middle of each piece. He scored the steaks "to help the bones cook," he said. One more washing in the kitchen and then they would be ready for salt, pepper, and a good roll in corn meal, he explained.

But first Bud was going to cook hush puppies in his new propane-powered deep fryer. These appliances had recently become popular for cooking Thanksgiving turkeys, and I had read about their hazards. I stood back a good distance when he lit the contraption, and soon Rena brought out the hush puppy mix to be dropped by spoonfuls into the hot peanut oil. The hush puppies cooked quickly, and I helped Bud spread them out to drain on a bed of fresh paper bags set atop a picnic table.

Food writers often warn that the oily nature of shad, which makes them flavorful, is also the property that makes cooking them indoors an activity that you will experience much longer than you want to. The smell is intense and lingering, which is also another reason to cook the hush puppies first, to avoid compromising their flavor.

The white men in suits arrived as arranged. They included the clerk of court, several lawyers, and the presiding judge of the day, all of whom were apparently involved in a juicy case back at the courthouse. The judge had called an extra-long recess to accommodate Bud's party. There was plenty of beer in a cooler on the patio, and Bud had also set out napkins, forks, and paper plates.

If I remember correctly, some of the men from the courthouse took a slug of bourbon before and after their beers. It all suddenly felt like a scene out of Faulkner. *Memory believes before knowing remembers. Believes longer than recollects, longer than knowing even wonders.*

The shad were delicious—buttery and crisp at once. And yes, there were bones, soft and worrisome. It was an eat-with-your-hands affair and thoroughly messy. Rena's coarse slaw, slathered with some slightly spicy pinkish dressing, helped balance the heaviness of the fish and cornmeal hush puppies.

I managed a couple of the shad steaks, filling a wadded napkin with teeny bones, and then excused myself to wash my sticky hands. The fish scent did not leave them for several hours. As I learned, fried shad is one of those meals, even if taken outside, that you will carry with you—a vague scent in your clothes and hair, an oily sensation on the hands, under the fingernails—and it takes more than one washing to let go.

And so it was in Jones County that day, where the past is not nearly so far gone as we sometimes think, for better or worse, as in many other parts of North Carolina and where shad fishing and eating are still a ritual, though depleted, like so many things, first by our collective enthusiasm for it and then by our neglect.

I would visit Bud and Rena many more times. Bud and I canoed the Trent River in much warmer weather. Before Christmas one season we spent an evening driving around Jones County in Bud's big sedan to see the holiday lights, which, I should have realized, would take us many, many miles between farmhouses to see. Our hunt for those rare bursts of color in the dark, strings of gaudy lights draped from gutters and flung around holly and oleander bushes, took up a whole evening.

We'd sometimes meet in Raleigh for oysters at the 42nd Street Oyster Bar when the legislature was in session and Rena had an evening off. The restaurant's dishwashing equipment often mysteriously magnetized the silverware there, and it became a perennial joke among us. We'd slide into a booth and Bud would unwrap his utensils from the heavy white napkin to see if they would stick together. If they were magnetized, he'd hoist a fork that magically clung by the tines to the butt end of his knife and declare it a consequence of his personality.

We ate shad together one more time after our fishing trip. By then, both Bud and Rena had begun to struggle with serious health problems — hers involved her heart; his was Parkinson's disease, which had finally forced him to give up his itinerant judging and his work with the local ABC (Alcoholic Beverage Control) Board. Still, Rena had managed to cook up a shad chowder for us, rich and heavy, with nary a discernible bone. The very next morning, she rose to make us all shad roe poached in bacon fat, scrambled eggs to the side. To me, they were not as delicious as promised in the recipes I have studied over the years. It might have been a matter of overcooking or of the Jones County bacon that was never as savory as the hickory-smoked varieties available in the Piedmont and mountains of North Carolina.

Or it might have been that everything seemed less colorful on that visit. Only seven months before, Hurricane Floyd had flooded Trenton, soaked Bud and Rena's basement and yard, and all but destroyed Bud's brother Bob's house in town. It was a fearful disaster — a 500-year flood. But the jumbled piles of indiscernible human property still waiting for pickup and disposal over great swaths of eastern North Carolina that spring didn't dispel Bud's enthusiasm as he drove us down to the courthouse. We were going to see a new oil portrait, recently completed, now hanging in his old courtroom. The image was totally Bud—a mischievous glint in his eye, promising the possibility of the unexpected. We stood close, admiring it for a long time.

The unexpected turned out to be nursing homes for the two of them—a few miles apart, each facility skilled at caring for the ailments that separated them. Rena died first, in April 2011, at the age of seventy-five. Bud followed her that August. He was eighty-three. Their gravestone is set on high ground in the Trenton Memorial Cemetery, well above the record high-water mark of the Trent River.

Naturally, Bud would have the last word, or many words in this case, carved into the stone: *Oh divine intervener, I bend in humble thanks for thou giving me me and ask what nimble fingers wove from the magic of marvel this peculiar piece of Quixotic flesh called man, this soul of being called spirit, this watchful heart seeking, finding and keeping love.*

Even better, though, was his obituary, in which his devoted nieces and nephews listed his passions as follows: *In his spare time, Walter enjoyed history, philosophy, politics, writing, and shad fishing on the Trent River.*

April

Ramps

THE LINGERING SCENT OF RAMPS AND SMOKE FROM A WOODSTOVE
is Yona Wade's most vivid memory of his visits to the house of his grand-mother Sally Wade, in the Cherokee community of Birdtown, on the banks of the glittering Oconaluftee River. "Grandma Sally was a basket maker, and she always had shavings all over the floor from the oak splits she used in her weaving. She had leather britches strung up around the house, too," Wade said. (Hanging and drying pole beans until they look like doll-size leather pants is a time-honored method of preparing meaty soup beans for later use in winter.)

"Of course, ramps and leather britches were considered poor folks' food," Wade added. "How ironic that ramps are appearing nowadays on up-scale restaurant menus all across the state."

Wade, known for his powerful singing voice, earned degrees in opera and arts management from the University of North Carolina School of the Arts. He then came back to the town of Cherokee to work in his home com-munity. He is director of the Chief Joyce Dugan Cultural Arts Center, at Cherokee Central Schools. Only in his mid-thirties, Wade has dark eyes that widen as he talks about the unmatched taste of wild ramps in spring—a Cherokee heritage food that, when cooked, is a little sweet, nutty, and gar-licky, all at the same time.

"When ramps come in season," he said, "I freeze them in gallon bags, but they don't last long. I can eat a whole bag in one sitting." Wade recommends putting ramps in any dish that calls for onion or garlic. "I put them in burgers or meatloaf, or just sauté them with olive oil."

Ramps (*Allium tricoccum*) are the first greens to pop up in spring in the Great Smoky and Blue Ridge Mountains of western North Carolina. Their narrow, flat leaves and white root bulb look like a cross between a lily and a spring onion, and their aroma is unmistakable—strong and sharp, like garlic on steroids. The Cherokee people of western North Carolina have been har-vesting ramps for more than 3,000 years. The plants generally thrive at eleva-tions above 3,000 feet and grow as far south as the north Georgia mountains, as far north and west as Minnesota and Missouri, and up the Appalachian chain through western New York, where they are called spring leeks.

Indigenous people still consider ramps a spring tonic and blood cleanser. They have antioxidant properties and contain high amounts of vitamins A and C. Ramps were also adopted as a folk remedy by the Scotch-Irish who later settled in the Appalachian Mountains.

"Ramps have sulfur compounds similar to what you find in garlic," explained David Cozzo, the only agricultural extension specialist in North Carolina who works for a sovereign nation instead of a county. He serves the Eastern Band of Cherokee Indians, holds a Ph.D. in anthropology with a focus on Cherokee ethnobotany, and works out of a single-story building set among a number of official tribal offices in the Cherokee town center. In recent years, the extension office has been active in research on ramps as a traditional Cherokee food while also working on the revegetation of river cane, white oak, and butternut trees for traditional basket making.

"The sulfur compounds in ramps are anti-cancer and anti–heart disease," Cozzo continued. "The Cherokee like to eat them very young. At their earliest stage of development, ramps have a chemistry similar to that of young garlic tips. People around here will harvest them out of the snow. The younger the bulb, the more intense the flavor."

According to another ethnobotanist, Lawrence Davis-Hollander, a founder of the Eastern Native Seed Conservancy, the name "ramps" comes from the Scottish word *ramps* or *ramsh*. Its use can be dated back to the seventeenth century to describe a species of garlic found in Europe. *Ramson*, a word that dates back to the fifteenth century, was used to refer to a kind of garlic (*Allium ursinum*) that grew in northern Europe and was a regular component of the diets of bears and wild boars. A garlic-flavored butter obtained from ramson-grazing cows was once a special delicacy in Switzerland. Scottish people chop and fold ramsons into a cream cheese made from heavy cream and soft crowdie, a type of cottage cheese, and call it *hramsa*.

Three variations of *Allium tricoccum* grow in North Carolina: the white bulb ramp, the red ramp (in which a tinge of red appears at the top of an otherwise white bulb), and the dwarf ramp. In the mountains, it is usually early April when the ramp plant develops its lily-like leaves. The leaves are definitely milder in flavor than the elongated root bulb, which, uncooked, is intense.

No matter what part of the plant you eat, however, the ramps you consume soon become ramp perfume, an unmistakable odor that begins to emanate from human pores. According to Yona Wade, Cherokee schoolchildren who ate ramps for breakfast back in the day would often be moved by their teachers out of the classroom and into the hallway so that they could "air out" for a while.

"I've heard of kids who eat them just to have the chance to miss their lessons," extension agent David Cozzo told me. When Cozzo comes home with ramps to cook for his own supper, he and his wife have a pact that both will eat them to avoid any olfactory offense to the other.

"I've had ramps for supper, crawled into bed, and then fluffed the sheets over me and caught a whiff. It's surprising how quickly they get into your system — kind of like asparagus," he said. And the strong scent can linger. One of Cozzo's coworkers in the agricultural extension office can always tell if he's had ramps for dinner. "I walk in the office in the morning, and she will ask first thing where I got my ramps," he laughed.

As a dedicated vegetarian, Cozzo said his all-time favorite meal is sautéed ramps with shitake mushrooms. He cooks them in a cream sauce made from almond milk and serves them over Japanese udon noodles. "It's my own invention," he claimed. "You sauté the mushrooms first, then add the ramps toward the middle — cook them a little, and then add the cream sauce and let it bubble while the noodles are boiling. I'm not even hungry right now, but talking about it makes my mouth water."

● ○ ● ◦ ◦ ◦ ● ◦ ▬ ● ◦ ●

As springtime fades, ramp leaves toughen and die back, no longer desirable to eat. By May or June, the female plants will send forth reddish shoots that are eventually topped by white blossoms that produce seeds — that is, if the ramps are allowed to mature.

As Yona Wade alluded to in his comment about restaurants serving ramps all across the state, the delicate ramp is no longer a little-known treat foraged by mountain folks who know how to spot them. In season, ramps command several dollars a bunch in places like the Western North Carolina Farmers Market in Asheville. They are also the celebrated accompaniment to fresh trout prepared at the Rainbow and Ramps Festival in Cherokee, usually held in late March or early April. Trucks loaded with bundles of ramps for sale begin appearing along North Carolina mountain roadsides come April.

"Why, you can even buy ramps at the *flea market*," said Marie Junaluska, a distinguished Cherokee tribal elder. Junaluska was born in Wolf Town and now lives in Paint Town, on the Qualla Boundary, which is the proper name for the Cherokee homeland in North Carolina. She is a writer, translator, teacher, and fluent speaker of Cherokee. Her deep commitment to preserving the Cherokee language and its many dialects is linked to her concern for the preservation of Cherokee foodways.

"We are no longer going to allow ramps to be sold like that, roots and all," she declared. "It has to change. It breaks my heart to see bunches of ramps pulled up with the roots still on them. This time of year you can go into the woods and see bare patches where people have come in and pulled up all the wild ramps they could find. The Cherokee have been gathering ramps in the Smokies for thousands of years, and they have never been depleted, because we know how to harvest them. But others do not. 'Dig' is the wrong word when you talk about harvesting ramps. We do not dig them. We cut them!"

Some environmentally conscious foragers have suggested that it is permissible to take the full ramp bulb from the ground in order to get the most pungent flavor, but it is necessary to limit the harvest to every fifth or seventh ramp to provide long-term sustainability for the patch.

By contrast, an article in the tribal newspaper, *Cherokee One Feather*, describes the method Marie Junaluska endorsed: "Cherokee harvesters have explained that the proper way of harvesting ramps is to gently scrape away the soil exposing a ramp bulb, then using a small pocketknife, cut the bulb in the ground above the roots, leaving the entire root mass in place. This is a tedious, time consuming process, but it is practiced by Cherokee harvesters of all ages."

The pocketknife must be very sharp and probably sharpened repeatedly in the field, because jutting a blade into the dirt can dull a knife pretty quickly, writes Eric Orr, a forager and blogger at *Wild Edible*. The good news is that ramps harvested with this technique of leaving the roots intact can survive for many, many years.

*　*　*

Historically, families in the Qualla Boundary and elsewhere in the Appalachians had their own "private" ramp patches. "You kinda knew who was picking where and didn't disturb another family's area," David Cozzo explained. The exact locations were jealously guarded secrets. Families still have their patches nowadays, but poachers are encroaching.

The Cherokee who survived Andrew Jackson's forced march to Oklahoma on the Trail of Tears in 1838 were so accustomed to spring ramps that

Pictured here at the tribal headquarters of the Eastern Band of the Cherokee Indians, Yona Wade (a cultural arts administrator) and Marie Junaluska (a tribal elder and native linguist) advocate the conservation of ramps.

they began looking for them in the new territory. They found only wild onions, which they decided to eat anyway, Cozzo told me. "Now the Oklahoma Cherokee who come back to visit in North Carolina have lost their taste for ramps and say they prefer wild onions," he said.

Lawrence Davis-Hollander suggests that a combination of factors — habitat loss to development, climate change that has amplified the presence of invasive plants, growth in animal grazing, increasing hiker and tourist traffic in the Appalachians, timber harvesting, and foraging by commercial vendors — are all working against the ramp. "We already know what can happen when wild species are over-harvested," he writes. "Wild herbs such as ginseng, black cohosh, and goldenseal were collected to the point of extinction in some regions before modern pharmaceuticals became the primary source of medicinal treatment." *Grub Street*, the food blog of *New York* magazine, came up with a timeline documenting the precipitous rise of ramps in high cuisine, which seems to be directly proportional to their increasing depletion in the wild. After languishing in culinary obscurity, ramps made their first appearance in a few cookbooks in the 1970s, the blog reported. By 1983, two recipes calling for ramps appeared in *Gourmet* magazine. By 1996, ramps had landed on the menus of several chic Manhattan restaurants. They became the leading ingredient in inventive dishes ranging from spaghetti and meatballs with ramps at P6 to a ramp brine martini offered at Momofuku to cod with a fondue of ramps and bacon at the Gramercy Tavern.

In the same period, a marked increase in the wholesale harvesting of ramps in Canada had already led Quebec officials to outlaw the sale and possession of ramps. By 2004, the taking of ramps from the Great Smoky Mountains National Park also became illegal. An avalanche of stories published over the past decade has touted the medicinal power of ramps, unfortunately promoting their value at the same time that environmental stewards have worried in print about their growing scarcity. The net effect of all this attention was an inflated price of seventeen dollars per pound for ramps at a New York City market by April 2013, *Grub Street* reported.

Most of the ramps being delivered to New York City markets over this period reportedly came from inside the state and from West Virginia and Michigan. In *Time* magazine, writer Josh Ozersky declared that ramps had become "the new arugula" among foodies. David Kamp, the author of *The Food Snob's Dictionary*, told Ozersky that the rush to taste the first green of spring had become something akin to the annual frenzy among baseball aficionados for an opening day game.

The rush for ramps continues. Today the demand in southern Appalachia is so high and the retail prices are so favorable that commercial collectors who have little or no experience in harvesting wild plants are entering the market. "They see ramp harvest as a relatively quick and easy way to diversify income and appear to have little knowledge or appreciation for the long term consequences of wild plant digging," writes Lawrence Davis-Hollander.

David Cozzo confirmed the trend in North Carolina. "I found this wonderful hillside full of ramps, and I went back the next year, and I didn't see *any*. That was just heartbreaking. I don't know if they will ever come back."

As Marie Junaluska pointed out, using a grub hoe and digging up every last ramp on a hillside is no way to perpetuate the crop for future years, so Cozzo's staff at the extension service is now conducting an experiment to test sustainable harvesting techniques.

"The bulbs are like little seeds in the dirt," he said. "And we think some of them may go dormant for a year, so that's another factor to study. We have established a bed of ramps and divided them into three groups. With one group, we took off the young tips when they first came up without disturbing the bulb, and we'll see what comes back. Later in the season, when another group in the bed was full-size, we cut the leaves off. And then we have a control area, where we didn't cut anything. We are trying to determine if cutting ramps rather than digging them up really can be more sustainable."

For more than a decade now, cooperative extension in Cherokee has been making ramp bulbs available to tribal members, one package per household, to plant at home. At Cherokee Central Schools, where Yona Wade directs the arts program, the science department is also focusing on ramps. "The students have built ramp cages behind the school so that the plant beds they've created won't be disturbed by animals. We will leave the roots and cut at the very top of the white bulb when we eventually harvest them," Wade said.

* * * * * * * * * * * *

After our April visit with the ramp experts in Cherokee, photographer Donna Campbell and I wound our way back up the mountain and over Soco Gap, where singer Johnny Cash and his friends once made snow cream. Before we got to Maggie Valley, we came upon a roadside grocery and farm stand called the Old Gray Mare. The proprietors advertised their offerings with only five words, composed in a random mix of red and black removable letters on one of those rolling signs that light up at night from within. The words caused our hearts to race as they proclaimed the day's fare:

OPEN — RAMPS

TOMATOES

HAM / EGGS

We rushed in and bought a bundle of ramps with clean, broad leaves, not at all wilted. "The first of the season," the man at the register said.

In the northern mountains of Yancey County a day later, we stopped by the Poplar Grove Food Mart, Campground, and Laundromat in the tiny Quaker village of Celo. We found freshly harvested ramps, roots attached, bundled in a box in a dark corner of the store. Though sad that the ramps had roots, we bought them anyway.

Both the Soco Mountain ramps and the ones from Celo were mild and delicious. We grilled a batch and ate them with beef filet for dinner at my mountain cabin in Little Switzerland. The next morning, another batch landed in a sauté with butter, which accompanied scrambled eggs and fried potatoes for breakfast. We saved back a few of the ramps with roots to plant within sight of my cabin, on the north side of an ash tree in heavy leaf litter. Time will tell if they survive.

The next week in neighboring Spruce Pine, at Mitchell County's acclaimed restaurant the Knife and Fork, Donna and I sampled chef Nate Allen's April menu, which offered a hearty ramp and potato chowder — outstanding, pungent, and very satisfying, for in late April a cold wind still blows of an evening in those rugged mountains. We also tried an appetizer of sautéed ramps that were lounging atop a smear of goat Gouda spread on a rather plain *ebelskiver* (a light Danish pancake). The dish was wholly dependent on the ramps for its punch.

Allen, a North Carolina native who pulled a ten-year stint as a private chef in Los Angeles, has also been known to serve ramps at the Knife and Fork with loin of lamb. His best innovation, however, is to dip ramps in a tempura batter for flash frying: the ultimate Appalachian/Asian-fusion onion ring — quite a savory surprise. Allen's gift for such combinations earned him the Small-Town Chef Award in 2011 from *Cooking Light* magazine.

Overall, the taste of this season's ramps was deeply flavorful but not overwhelming, unlike a previous encounter I had with them a few years ago. At my request, a friend ferried some ramps from Cherokee to Carrboro for us to sample. The ramps were so pungent that year that no amount of wrapping in multiple layers of newspaper and plastic bags could mask their presence in her car. I don't know if the intensity had to do with the time of harvest, the long travel, the particular soil in which those Jackson County ramps grew, or all of the above. But my friend Nancy Tom — an avowed foodie whose father is a gourmet chef from Shanwei, in the Guangdong Province of China — has never let me forget how long it took for the unmistakable stink to dissipate in the trunk of her then-brand-new Honda.

To me, a ramp's best and highest use is as an accompaniment to otherwise subdued and timid dishes that will benefit from the detonation of flavor that's set off, such as eggs, potatoes, white fish, or mild cheese. Ramp recipes are easy to find nowadays, and it seems that North Carolina chefs are doing quiet battle to see who can find the most novel application.

Nate Allen topped off his tempura ramps with andouille sausage and a savory waffle to win the Best Chef in Western North Carolina competition. In doing our research on soft-shell crabs, Donna and I ran into ramps at two other high-end restaurants. We sampled a crunchy rice-encrusted soft-shell crab served with a bright ramp remoulade at Vivian Howard's Chef and the Farmer Restaurant in Kinston. In Wilmington, at chef Keith Rhodes's establishment, Catch, we shared a buttermilk-and-flour-doused soft-shell crab that had been flash-fried and then draped with pickled wild ramps. (More on these dishes when we get to the chapter on crabs.)

How did those ramps get all the way from the mountains to the eastern towns of Kinston and Wilmington? Chef Rhodes told us he sourced his pickled ramps from Feast Down East, a local food co-op. (Pickled ramps preserved in jars are not ephemeral, of course, and are available from a few suppliers on the internet.) According to our server at Chef and the Farmer, Vivian Howard got her ramps for the remoulade from a vendor named George Patterson.

In her book *Cooking in the Moment*, Andrea Reusing, another celebrated chef, with restaurants in Durham and Chapel Hill, describes the ramps she gets every year from Joe Hollis, a forager and herbalist who now works out of Burnsville in Yancey County. Hollis has been a mentor to a number of aspiring plant propagators and is known for teaching sustainable methods for the harvest of rare and endangered native plants in North Carolina.

Nevertheless, in keeping with the tradition of secrecy around the location of ramps, it has not been easy to find out who actually might be trying to grow them commercially in our state. To do so successfully would seem to be a potential goldmine, what with all the chefs seeking ramps for their springtime menus.

My queries led me to North Carolina State University associate professor Jeanine Davis, who runs the Mountain Horticultural Crops Research and Extension Center in Mills River, near Asheville. Davis specializes in alternative crops and organics, helping small farmers learn how to grow medicinal plants, successfully coax black truffles and other mushrooms out of woodlands, raise hops for the state's expanding craft beer industry, and cultivate other forest-based products, such as ginseng and ramps.

With her coauthor, Jackie Greenfield, an agricultural research technician, Davis published the results of a North Carolina study that demonstrates some of the challenges in cultivating ramps from seed. Their research posits that ramps are best cultivated for commercial purposes in a natural forest setting. The study also showed that ramp seeds are most likely to germinate when planted in fall rather than spring and under the natural tree canopy rather than in an open field or under a built shelter. Consistent moisture is essential.

Ramps grow well in a neighborhood of trees that might include beech, birch, poplar, sugar maple, buckeye, basswood (linden), hickory, and oak. The authors offer the tip that if you plant your ramps in an area that hosts the native wildflowers trillium, toothwort, nettle, black cohosh, ginseng, bloodroot, trout lily, bellwort, or mayapple, the odds increase for successful ramp propagation. The soil must be rich and well drained and provide lots of organic matter. Hardwood leaves are the best mulch, they say—never a commercial product.

The study also showed that if you plant bulbs instead of seeds, growing ramps gets much, much easier. You might even have harvestable ramps within two to three years. Ramps thus require enormous patience and great care, which makes me wonder if there is any hope of being able to outpace the poachers in time to save the species.

●　●　●　●　●　●　●　●　●　●　●　●

Looking further at the online community of botanical growers that Jeanine Davis has fostered, it seems that rare-plant propagation and forest farming have been going on, at least around the Asheville area, for a while, though perhaps not at a scale that can stem the tide of overharvesting, commercial development, and other forms of damage to ancient woodland treasures like the ramp.

I found Sara Jackson's name and her company, Bat Cave Botanicals, on a web page that Jeanine Davis created to connect commercial growers to buyers of native herbs in the state. Of the several growers who had posted listings of their available plants that spring and summer, only Bat Cave Botanicals listed ramps among its current products.

As it turns out, Jackson and her partner, Martin Thaller, have focused primarily on "superior quality wild American ginseng roots," though they are expanding their offerings. They work on forty-seven acres that Thaller has owned since the early 1990s. Bat Cave is an unincorporated community in Henderson County, southeast of Asheville. The cave from which it takes its name is the largest known granite fissure cave in North America and is home to the endangered Indiana bat.

Some of the forestland that Jackson and Thaller "farm" is quite rugged, with a steep pitch that allows the frost to drain off well in bright morning sun. Thaller has been carving new beds slowly out of laurel thickets to make room for more native wild edibles and medicinals, adding to those already growing on their property. A stand of native persimmon trees beside their driveway provides fruit in late fall for hand pies and frozen puree, Jackson said. The couple is also working with a local land trust to establish a conservation easement, to ensure that the property remains a natural sanctuary.

Thaller, now in his fifties, grew up in eastern Tennessee in a traditional farming family and settled for a time in the Piedmont section of North Carolina, near Efland. Jackson, in her thirties, was raised in Wilmington. "I grew up with seafood, catching blue crab at the pier," she said. She has also studied Chinese medicinals with Joe Hollis, the ramp supplier for Andrea Reusing. "He's my hero, and an amazing resource," she said.

After several more minutes of conversation by phone, Jackson revealed that she was eight months pregnant with their first child. "My due date is Halloween!" she said and then chuckled. "And I live in Bat Cave. How's that for the granny witch tradition in these mountains?"

Even with the pending birth, Jackson and Thaller recently completed their annual chanterelle mushroom harvest. "You can't preserve them like a morel, which you can dehydrate and ship. Chanterelles are wild, fragile, and delectable," Jackson said. They sold their "found" crop to a few local restaurants for twenty-five dollars a pound. Their annual ginseng harvest will surely be even more lucrative. In addition to the wild plant business, Thaller supplements the family income by making art deco handmade furniture.

As for ramps, Jackson said they have yet to sell them in any quantity. In fact, she's been trying to build up their beds. "I was in a little store in Swannanoa last spring, and there were three crates of ramps, bunched with the roots on. I bought the whole lot for a dollar a ramp," Jackson explained sheepishly. "I know that's rewarding the bad behavior of others, but I brought them home and planted them right away."

The leaves dried up and the ramps went dormant. It would be a year before Jackson knew if any had survived. "You should have seen me doing my happy dance when those first green tips started coming up. Every one of them survived!" she said.

It seems crazy that ramp cultivation has become almost a game with people pulling up plants and selling them to others who plant them again. I asked Jackson what she would do when they begin harvesting: whether she'd use the Cherokee method of cutting the ramps just above the roots or whether she would harvest every fifth or seventh ramp.

"We'll do both," she said. "Cut them at the bulb and only take what we consider ethical: that is, selectively harvesting less than one-third of any mature population."

● ● ● ● ● ● ● ● ● ● ● ●

I still wanted to meet with the extension service's Jeanine Davis, but because of her busy schedule of lecturing and consulting, she sent me to Jean Harrison, a retired plant pathologist and former extension specialist who now runs her own wholesale operation, called Red Root Native Nursery. North of Asheville, near the tiny village of Barnardsville, Harrison and her husband, Christopher Rogers, a retired architect, have set up shop on two-and-a-half densely wooded acres nestled up against the wild old-growth forest of the Big Ivy section of the 500,000-acre Pisgah National Forest. Big Ivy is formidable, with some 3,600 acres that are as botanically diverse as any in North Carolina. The steep and rocky understory is thick with laurel and rhododendron and sheltered by a tall canopy of giant poplars and ancient hardwoods. We could see Big Ivy from the Blue Ridge Parkway when we looked northwest from the vantage point of the Craggy Gardens Visitors Center at Milepost 364. So precious are the features of this forest that local wilderness enthusiasts are championing an effort to get Congress to prevent the possibility

Standing in front of her potting shed in the Big Ivy section of Pisgah National Forest near Barnardsville, Jean Harrison, a plant pathologist, explains the complexity of raising ramps from seed.

of commercial logging and to declare the region permanently wild, hoping to save Big Ivy from any further encroachment, even as Asheville continues to expand in all directions.

Big Ivy is also home to native brook trout from the headwaters of Ivy Creek and forty or more species of endangered and rare plants, which are the focus of Jean Harrison's propagation work. She collects seeds and cuttings from her own land and buys others from reputable seed companies. Both the production and pest management of her plants is completely organic.

Now in her early sixties and with two grown sons — one an engineer working for Boeing in Seattle and the other studying for a business degree at the Wharton School at the University of Pennsylvania — Harrison, a Charlotte native, started her propagation work in Asheville several years ago with azaleas and rhododendrons. She later shifted her focus to rare and endangered species.

Her greenhouses and homestead in Big Ivy are not open to the public. Rather, with her husband's help, she ships her plants in quantity to nurseries, botanical gardens, garden centers, commercial herb growers, and landscapers across the Southeast and as far north as upstate New York. She sells retail to individuals twice a year at the Asheville Botanical Garden's spring and fall plant sales and, on occasion, at native plant conferences.

Jean and Christopher (who is originally from Marin, California) found their current property not so long ago while hiking in Big Ivy. The parcel was a rustic homestead occupied by a family and their thirty-year-old pet donkey, named Ivy. Ivy had free run of much of the property and had grazed most of the wild plants into oblivion. As far as she knows, Jean said, the donkey is still alive, probably from eating such fine botanicals all of its life. She now uses Ivy's little barn as her potting shed. A number of greenhouses of various sizes and densities of shade covering also occupy the immediate property around their cabin.

"We're letting everything grow back to see what's here," she said. Christopher expanded the original cabin, constructed from logs that were once a tobacco barn. The dwelling now includes an office loft and a forty-foot-long porch that wraps around two sides of the house. They heat with wood. One porch post has deep, menacing scars — the work, Jean explains, of a very large local bear that comes by once a year to mark the edge of his territory before heading higher up the mountain for the summer. Sadie, a brindle mutt with a graying muzzle, serves as the nursery assistant, following Jean around the property by day and sleeping safely inside at night.

Jean continues to perfect her technique for propagating ramps from seed, and she is not ready to share her secrets. Now that I have gotten to know her a bit, I suspect she will eventually take on an apprentice and publish her findings. She is a true scientist, with a master's degree in plant pathology from North Carolina State University, and she keeps faithful records of each crop and the weather cycles that affect dormancy and growth.

So far she has managed to grow thousands of ramp plants from seed, eventually transferring the seedlings to two-inch-deep cell trays, filled with a soil mix of her own concoction. She will nurture the plants for two years before selling them.

"I get the first two years over with for my customers," Harrison said. "The seed is very difficult to get started. It has a double dormancy, meaning that you have to go through a couple of cold spells to break the dormancy and get them to come up."

Harrison revealed that her ramp customers tend to be private landowners who want their own patch of ramps or who are more generally committed to putting natives back into a property they've recently bought. She also sells to growers who want to cultivate and resell the ramps at tailgate markets. She will sell every ramp that's ready by this coming March — usually a total of twenty trays, or 500 plants per year. She buys the ramp seeds from Prairie Moon Nursery in Minnesota. She has also been known to buy some of the ramps that appear at a crossroads market up the road. "We get them with the full roots still on and stick them back in the ground, to build up our own patch," she said. I nod and tell her about Sara Jackson's similar restoration project in Bat Cave.

Harrison also propagates ginseng, goldenseal, bloodroot, spicebush, slippery elm, partridgeberry, and dozens more perennial natives, some with whimsical names such as pussy toes and fairy wands. She admitted that because so many of the native plants here are fascinating and tempting to grow, it can be hard for her to restrain herself to a reasonable number.

"I could make a fortune growing and selling stinging nettles," she said, "but I don't want to fool with them." She shrugged. Stinging nettles have been trending lately with chefs who are turning them into a traditional dark-green soup that's long been consumed in Scandinavia, Scotland, and the Middle East. (This potage most recently earned a mention in the mainstream bestseller *Fifty Shades of Grey*, after having once received a loftier literary plug in Tolstoy's *Anna Karenina*.)

Jean hadn't planned this woodland life. She started out as a piano major at the University of North Carolina at Chapel Hill. Then she dropped out and returned later to study science. Max Hammersand (now an emeritus professor at UNC) was the botany instructor who kindled her interest in plants.

Already the demand for Jean's perennials is daunting. "I can't even meet the orders that I get," she said. Every year she has already promised all of her plants before they are ready to be shipped. Jean, who survived a serious illness in past years, is not interested in growing the business any further at this stage in her life. She wants only to preserve and propagate what she can at the current small scale.

When winter comes to this north-facing cove, the sun barely clears the ridge during the day. Come December, Jean and Christopher will drain the cabin pipes and close up tight, leaving the dormant plants under safe cover, waiting for more tending in March. The couple traveled to Europe this year and will spend the first months of the coming year in California. A trusted assistant will check on the greenhouses while they are gone.

Donna asked about the effects of climate change in this region. "This is a very diverse forest," Harrison said passionately. She mentions a distinguished colleague, Dr. Joe-Ann McCoy, who is the director of the Bent Creek Germplasm Repository at the North Carolina Arboretum. Botanists there are preserving the seeds and tissue of native plants in a storage facility south of Asheville. Recently the repository has also begun preserving medicinal plants treasured by the Cherokee people, who have given specimens to the facility because of their shared concern about the environment. The project is a defense against the worst scenario: the extinction of all of the wild botanicals that grow in the woods just beyond Big Ivy and right under our noses here in Harrison's greenhouses.

"I sometimes think this area may be the last stronghold for some of these species," Jean said.

We can only hope the growing popularity of ramps, with their unparalleled flavor and punch, can raise public awareness enough to prevent their demise. I know what I'm going to do the next time I see a bunch of ramps for sale with their roots on: I will follow the example of Jean Harrison and Sara Jackson and will plant them back in the soil in my patch on the Blue Ridge, setting aside maybe every fifth or seventh rooted ramp in the bunch to cook. With such a strong flavor, a few ramps should be plenty.

May

Soft-Shell Crabs

MURRAY BRIDGES, THE PROPRIETOR OF ENDURANCE SEAFOOD, IS IN his sock feet. He's sitting on a burgundy recliner in the den of his brick ranch house in Colington, near Kill Devil Hills, on the Outer Banks. Bridges, now in his mid-eighties, specializes in soft-shell crabs, but he won't be working on the water today. He's able to receive visitors on this mid-April afternoon because a nor'easter is pummeling the pollen-laden pines and blooming dog-woods outside. The sun is bright and the sky is crystalline blue, but the tem-perature is in the low fifties. Roanoke Sound is roiling with white caps all the way back to Mann's Harbor, on the mainland.

"We always get excited a little bit too early," Bridges said in his Outer Banks brogue that made excited sound like "ex*oited*." "I set out pots to catch peelers a couple days ago, but if we have any in there, they won't be shed-ding now." Bridges is referring to the coming season for soft-shell crabs, or "peelers," in the local parlance.

Usually in early May, North Carolina's blue crab population begins molting. These crustaceans — *Callinectes sapidus*, two Latin words meaning "beautiful swimmer" and "tasty" — outgrow their shells many times over their lifetimes. When the molting process starts, the crabs help it along by taking additional seawater into their bodies so that eventually their shells crack. Then they slip slowly out of their old armor and begin at once to grow a new, larger exoskeleton. In this soft-shell phase, the crabs are considered a delicacy. In many Asian kitchens, they will be prepared as sushi. In North Carolina, soft-shell crabs are more likely to be pan-seared or breaded and deep-fried.

In a report published in 1985 from a national symposium on blue crab, experts admitted that they weren't quite sure when the soft-shell blue crab was first harvested and sold commercially in North Carolina, but landings of the creatures are recorded as far back as 1897. In the biennial report of the North Carolina Department of Conservation and Development from 1937, the government stated that Carteret County was the only place south of Virginia that produced soft-shell crabs in quantity, employing "significant numbers of people during the months of April and May." Most of the crabs harvested in those days were sold to vendors in Maryland. The soft-shell business really didn't begin to scale up in North Carolina until some forty years ago, Murray Bridges said.

These days, North Carolina soft-shell crabs appear on menus statewide. Harvesting and shipping techniques have grown much more sophisticated.

For a long time, only coastal folk bothered to seize the moment of the crab's transformation and make a sandwich of it. Bridges said that people used to run across soft-shells in their crab pots or find them in the shallows and bring them home for dinner. Murray Bridges's wife, Brady, said that when she was a girl growing up in Colington, she would sometimes kick soft-shells out of the seagrass and sell them to Old Nags Head cottagers. But catching them in quantity did not become a practice until Bridges and others learned that their counterparts in Virginia and Maryland were turning an especially handsome profit on soft-shells in the month of May — normally a slow period in the sea-food cycle, when fishermen are waiting for the shrimping season to begin.

"I learned about soft-shells from the government's Sea Grant program," Bridges said. "They were going round to different communities to show fishermen better ways of doing things. I went to meetings, and I even went up to Virginia and Maryland to see how they'd come up with this method for shedding crabs. I seen where it was a good thing. Price-wise, too. They could sell a soft-shell for three times what we'd get at the local market."

Bridges was raised in Wanchese, at the southern tip of Roanoke Island, and spent more than twenty years on the water as a merchant marine. He had settled down with Brady in her hometown of Colington, which sits near the convergence of Currituck, Albemarle, Croatan, and Roanoke Sounds — the perfect site to launch a seafood business.

Bridges learned about grading soft-shell crabs according to size, which is a different system from grading hard-shell crabs. When he began, the very smallest crab was called, curiously, a "medium." Four additional categories, each increasing in size, were hotels, primes, jumbos, and whales. Initially, only male crabs could be classified as whales; the largest females could only be placed in the jumbo category. "That was the way they graded up north," Bridges said, shaking his head, "so we had to follow that until the number of males fell off. Now females can be graded as whales, too. Go figure."

Bridges devised special crab pots, smaller than the traps used for blue crabs the rest of the year. During soft-shell season, he puts a small male crab — known as a "jimmy" — inside these smaller pots for bait. "We don't use a big rusty crab for bait. A little jimmy's got the stuff," said Bridges, grin-ning. Because molting occurs during what is also the mating season, the traps lure hundreds of females, and then males follow them into the traps. Mating happens immediately after the female has shed. Once caught, these peeler crabs are placed in tanks, called shedders, for a few hours — only long enough to finish molting and to firm up sufficiently to be handled for shipping. Once a crab has shed its old shell, the new, larger shell will harden in a mere twenty-four hours if the crab stays in the water. A live soft-shell must therefore be taken out of the water and sent to market very quickly. Or it may be cleaned and frozen.

In the early years, Bridges began to scale up his operation with float shedders — tanks that actually rode on the surface of the creek behind his house. They were rigged to circulate water as the crabs inside began to shed their shells. But the process was cumbersome. The peelers had to be watched around the clock and pulled from the water quickly, once they molted. Bringing the peelers to shore once they had shed was also tricky.

"One night I went out to check on my peelers and got tangled up and fell in the shedder!" he said, chuckling. "Right then and there I decided I was going to do better, and I came home and fixed me six or seven shedder tanks on solid ground with electric lights strung up so I could watch them at night."

As his soft-shell business grew, Bridges eventually built by hand 150 four-by-eight-foot tanks. They are lined up outside the processing warehouse that flanks his ranch house. Each is outfitted with overhead lights. A complex grid of white PVC pipes is connected underneath the wooden and fiberglass tanks to carry water pumped from the creek to overhead spigots that shower the crabs and freshen the water. The water pressure can be adjusted above each shedder. Drains in the bottom of each tub circulate the water back out into the creek on the other side of Bridges's spit of land. Moving water provides the molting crabs with oxygen.

"We try to bring them into the tanks just before they start shedding," Bridges said. "When they first shed, though, they're too soft to work with. We have to wait a bit before they're ready to be handled. They need to firm up so they can live for at least two or three more days after we ship them. But if you keep them too long in the shedder, they'll weaken and die."

Bridges still sets his own crab pots and buys thousands of additional peelers from many of the other ninety-some Dare County crabbers who have shedding permits. He was among the first to master the technique of properly packing and shipping the crabs to maximize their freshness. When the creatures reach the best possible moment after molting, they are carefully packed in waxed cardboard cartons, layered with parchment paper and a scrim of ice on top. Depending on the grade, the cartons hold seven and a

Veteran waterman Murray Bridges surveys the soft-shell crab
shedders along the creek bank behind his house in Colington.

half dozen to fifteen dozen per box. At the peak of the season, which usually
lasts a week to ten days, six members of the Bridges family will work day and
night monitoring the water temperature and the condition of every single
crab, which sheds on its own timetable.

At the peak, the family actually handles 4,000 to 5,000 dozen crabs per
day. Their record shipment of crabs at one time, says Bridges, was fifteen pal-
lets. A single pallet holds 216 dozen. The quick math on that figure translates
to a little more than 38,800 crabs processed by hand in a single day.

"My daughter, Kissy, gets all hepped up this time of year," said Bridges.
"Once we're into it, though, it gets a little rough. We don't get much rest or
eat regular."

It takes a seven-figure credit line and the seasoned eyes of the Bridges
family team to pick and purchase the peelers that are within days of molting.
Murray Bridges explains that the telltale sign is on a crab's back paddlers,
where a fine white line runs along the little hairs at the end of a section of
leg. "That line will go from white to pink to blood red when the time comes,"
Bridges said. He pulled a blue crab out of the cooler to point to the precise
spot.

Though some crabbers will show up at his dock with their day's catch, hoping to pass off peelers that are far from shedding, Bridges can always discern the degree of readiness. "And we don't let the crabbers grade their catch. We do it ourselves," he said.

Even before the crabs start shedding in earnest, Bridges and his competitors watch the weather and their traps intently. They will get "clamlipped," he said, as the race to collect peelers draws near. In his warehouse on this day, more than 2,000 waxed boxes have been assembled and stacked, at the ready. Out in the yard, some of the thousand peeler pots that Bridges's daughter, Kristina—known since childhood as Kissy—has made in the off-season are waiting to be deployed.

Though he sells some of his catch locally and some to a couple of Japanese markets, most of Bridges's soft-shell crabs leave his operation packed in tractor-trailer trucks that travel up the East Coast. The bulk of his live crabs end up at the famous Fulton Fish Market, which operated from 1822 to 2005 in Manhattan and now is at Hunt's Point in the Bronx. If there is a glut of crabs at a certain point in the season, Bridges might also send some to Handy International in Crisfield, Maryland, the largest crab processor in the world. At Handy, a hundred-some employees clean crabs around the clock and then freeze them. While soft-shell crabs are prized, because diners don't have to pick the sweet meat out of the claws and shells and can instead eat the body whole, it is still necessary to remove the mouth, eyes, gills, and abdomen in the cleaning process.

Bridges said negotiating price is among the most stressful parts of his business. Kissy generally handles that. "Sometimes," he said, "they'll call us up from New York and say, 'We can only pay you ten dollars a dozen for these soft-shells.' They take them on consignment, see, and we might be thinking we'd get thirty dollars a dozen when they try to give us ten. Or they'll say, 'Half your crabs are dead.' We have no way of knowing if they are trying to cheat us! They can get so many crabs coming into the market up there that they'll cut the price right out from under you." Once Bridges rode the freight truck all the way up to the market to see the situation for himself.

For most of the past century, the Fulton Fish Market was known to be influenced by one or more Mafia families at a time. Federal racketeering charges were brought against the market and upheld in 2001. Now the business is regulated by the City of New York. More than a billion dollars' worth of seafood comes through the new location at Hunt's Point these days, making it the second largest seafood market in the world, surpassed only by Tokyo's Tsukiji fish market.

Feather and Willy Phillips, longtime friends of the Bridges family, own Full Circle Crab in Columbia, North Carolina, an hour's drive inland from Endurance Seafood. In the early years of their shedding operation, Willy, who is almost twenty years younger than Murray Bridges, would go out to check his pots while Feather stayed home with their young son, Jake. Feather monitored the shedders at their homestead at Old Fort Landing, on the Alligator River in Tyrrell County. She has witnessed the seasonal vigilance and tension build among crabbers for decades now. There is no set date for the start of soft-shell season. It all depends on the moon, tides, and water temperature.

"When honeysuckle sweetness fills the air, the shedders will be full," Feather said definitively. "Some crabbers here use potato plants, watching for the flowers as the sign. Of course, the full moon is always a sign, too."

In 2016, a full moon came toward the end of April and put all the crabbers on high alert. "It seems like the molting usually starts about a week before the full moon in May, but the April moon was so late this year," Murray Bridges declared. "Seventy-five percent of all the soft crabs we harvest will usually come in May, not April." But the mysteries of nature keep fishing families guessing.

Willy Phillips was four years old when he first saw battalions of small fiddler crabs coming out of the salt marsh and marching toward his childhood home on Hewlett's Creek in New Hanover County. Those crabs were not responding to the moon, however. They began climbing the exterior walls of his parents' house to find purchase on the roof. In that fall of 1954, long before Doppler radar and sophisticated weather prediction was possible, the surge of crustacean refugees was the only sign the Phillips family had that Hurricane Hazel was barreling toward Wilmington.

"When they came back again in the late fifties and sixties, it was always a bad sign," Phillips said.

Sixty years later, Phillips represents the generation behind his mentor, Murray Bridges. He sells thousands of dozens of soft-shell crabs each year through his wholesale and retail seafood market on U.S. Highway 64 in Tyrrell County.

Phillips speaks passionately about the current state of the soft-shell crab harvest in North Carolina's northernmost waters of the Albemarle Sound and the challenges created by global economic forces and environmental degradation.

"The blue crab sheds thirty-two to thirty-seven times during its lifetime. They shed all summer long and are the bedrock of our ecosystem here, which is the second largest lagoon system in the country," said Phillips. "The soft-shell crab are helpless when they shed, so they are food for trout, flounder, croakers, spot, red drum, striped bass — all the other seafood that we harvest. Beyond their importance to us, they are essential to the health of the whole system."

Though I have visited his operation many times, on this day Phillips was talking to me on the phone from his retail seafood shop. It was 8:30 in the morning, and he had been up for hours. This was his busiest season. He stopped the interview midsentence and apologized for the sudden interruption. He put down the phone, but I could hear him talking to someone who was about to leave the store: "No, no charge. I don't want you to pay me for anything. That's for Miss Libby. You tell her that's for all the years she's been buying my crabs and making my crab pots."

Phillips's retail store is small compared to the massive coolers and the spread of shedders that stretch out back, under the roof of his Butler building, behind the storefront. His is one of the largest businesses in Columbia (population 850), and he's a generous member of the community. He supplies free ice for weddings, funerals, and other local celebrations. He has also been known to store wild game — bear and deer — for local hunters in his walk-in coolers.

Finally, Willy came back to the phone. "So . . . soft-shell crab actually shed all summer long," he continued, "but it's that first taste of spring, kind of like shad used to be, that causes the frenzy among fishermen and seafood lovers. It's the signal of the start of beach season nowadays."

Unlike Endurance Seafood, Full Circle works with a Wanchese trucking company on Roanoke Island to ship most of its catch to a New York wholesaler that serves a number of upscale delis in Manhattan and the Hamptons. Phillips's standards are extra-high, he said. He insists that all the soft-shells he ships must have two claws and legs on both sides. Others may not hold to this standard, but Phillips is adamant. In addition to the high-end New York markets for live crabs, he also sells to wholesalers and individual restaurants on Maryland's eastern shore — establishments in Annapolis and St. Michael's, home of the Chesapeake Maritime Museum. "People know our product, and now they ask for it by name," he said.

Beyond the tens of thousands of live crabs he ships, Phillips also freezes a portion of his soft-shells and has been able to sell the frozen stock in the off-season to maintain cash flow, especially around Christmas and before the new season for soft-shells begins.

"But hundreds of dozens of frozen soft-shells are flooding the market now from Indonesia. It's a cheaper product with value added," he said. "The Asian crabs are often already breaded and cooked. They only need to be heated. We used to be able to hold our frozen crabs back as a way to cash out in winter, but the market is definitely changing with imports. We are still in a better position with the live market, because of our proximity. You can't ship live crabs all the way around the world from Asia — at least not yet."

When I asked Phillips how he likes his soft-shell crab prepared, he was definite: "We always remove the mustard." Mustard (also known as to-malley) is the yellow substance in the middle of the abdomen. "Some save it and use it for extra flavor in deviled crab and crab cakes, but we don't. We also take off the 'back' — the paper-like shell that is just beginning to form there — because it gives an off flavor and it's easier to clean the water out that way. When you fry a soft-shell in hot oil, too much water left inside will cause splatter. My mom used to bake them with a slice of butter under each wing, so to speak. You can also marinate and grill them, but it doesn't take much heat to cook a soft-shell on a grill. A light brown color on the crab is sufficient."

As for size, Phillips said, "The tourists always want to see whales on their platters. But I think the best size is the prime — the four-and-a-half- to five-inch crab. The smaller ones taste sweeter and cook easier. To cook through a larger crab and get the middle done, it means the legs get too done."

* * * * * * * * * * * *

Exactly a month has passed since Donna and I first visited Endurance Seafood. It has rained more than usual, and Willy Phillips told us by phone on our way east that cool temperatures have made the soft-shell harvest spotty. At four o'clock in the afternoon on the twelfth of May, temperatures are warmer than any so far this year on the Outer Banks — in the high seventies with gusting winds. As we cross the William B. Umstead Bridge, Roanoke Sound is the color of Elizabeth Taylor's eyes — violet and worthy of a double-take.

When we arrive at Endurance, Kissy Bridges is shoving a heavy push broom back and forth over soapy concrete floors where the latest shipment of crabs has already gone out for the day. A seeping water hose curls on the floor behind her boots.

We already know that Kissy is famous for her hard-edged negotiations with the New York seafood wholesalers. "She can cuss like a sailor," Willy Phillips said, "and she won't back down if they try to drop the price when the Endurance shipments arrive in the Bronx."

Donna asks Kissy about the day's catch. "We only shipped 1,600 dozen today," she says and stops her scrubbing. "I wish it was more like 5,000 dozen — that's our usual by this time of the season."

Her father, who had apparently been resting back at the house, comes up behind us. "I'm afraid it's not going to pick up this year, Kissy," he says.

"Don't say that, Dad," she answers and turns back to shoving the broom.

Bridges invites us to follow him through the warehouse and out back to the shedders. About half of the shedders are populated with crabs that have not yet molted. He points out the freshest ones, a dark mass moving underwater. He pulled them from his pots this morning. He says they usually limit each shedder to about 300 crabs. "Every day we have to move them around to different shedders based on how they're coming along. These caught today" — he moves toward a full shedder where an occasional claw breaks the surface and the water is violently stirring — "they are wild acting. We have to put them off by theirselves. The ones that's been here for a while have calmed down. But these wild ones will hit or damage the calm ones."

Bridges moves his hand over the water, and the crabs reach out as if to high-five him. "Yep, these is still wild. They'll get in a fight and will throw a leg off to get loose. A nub will form and eventually the limb will grow back. We call them false biters," he says. "That's why you see some crabs with one claw bigger than the other."

As he walks and talks, Bridges is now picking out empty shells where several crabs have recently molted. He drops the shells into a basket. He pitches the occasional broken limb and dead crab out into the creek beyond us. A small circular corral made of hardware wire sits in the middle of each shedder. Bridges gently lays the just-molted crabs into these "pens," where they will be protected from the other crabs. As we make our way down the aisle of tanks, I marvel at how he can discern, despite slightly murky water, the difference between an empty shell, a just-molted crab, and the rest of the circus that is clambering along the shedder bottoms in every direction.

I look closer. The crabs are eerily animated in their "faces." They track us with their eyes. Their mouths open and close in a silent, underwater diction. They bring their big claws forward as if to rub their faces. The tiny parts that flank their mouths clap together at times like the pouting lips of a fervent child. One crab will seem to wave a big claw to another across the way. They clown around, pile on, pick at each other, bunch up, leapfrog, and race sideways to new destinations in the shedder. They stare back at us with, what— menace, amusement?

When we come close to another shedder that's full, Bridges moves his hand above the water and the crabs again raise their claws and break the surface, reaching as if to pinch their captor. "These are all males," he says. Their legs are a lovely peacock blue. (Willy Phillips later told me that he thinks of the crab color as Richard Petty blue—the precise hue of the racecar once driven by North Carolina's most revered NASCAR celebrity.)

Now Bridges pokes his hand into another shedder, pulls out a crab, and turns it over. It's a female with the telltale red line on the paddler. "She'll be shedding before dark," he says. "We have to separate the males from the females. It takes the males longer to calm down. They're like lions. They'll fight you until they get used to being kept."

Murray Bridges rose at five this morning and was out on the water by six. Working with "another feller," as he put it, he checked every one of his 400 crab pots in the sound and creek, returning for lunch before one o'clock. "The crabs out there are looking for a shady place to molt, where they might not be seen by predators," he tells us. "We paint the pots black, and they crawl right in."

He points out several "busters"—crabs with shells that are visibly cracking. Donna rushes over to shoot video of the entire event up close. This process is obvious, even to the untrained eye. The shell opens at a seam along the hind edge of the buster, and its grayish insides are pushing out. We wait, the hot sun bearing down. After the shell fully cracks, the crab begins expelling water, trying to make itself smaller. It takes about ten minutes for the crab to work its way free. The final thrust involves pulling its limbs out of the old claws, much like an elegant woman might remove an elbow-length evening glove.

"Sometimes," says Bridges, "if a feller gets stuck, another crab will come over and help pull him out. See there?" We watch a buddy crab holding a buster, grounding him, almost like a spotter for a gymnast about to perform a dangerous maneuver. "Soon as he's out, he'll start rocking side to side to fill himself back up with water," Bridges says. Another buster nearby seems stuck, his seam only halfway open at one end. "He might not make it," Bridges adds.

When the crab that Donna has been recording with her camera finally breaks free, I look away for an instant and then back into the tank. Now I'm confused. Which is the live crab that's come out, and which is the shell? The translucent one doesn't move. Somehow, though, my mind believes that the ghostly figure is the new crab — the pale soul disengaged from its earthly shell, its see-through self holding still, exhausted. But it is the darker twin that suddenly moves. It looks more like the others that have not yet shed.

How Murray Bridges can spot the soft-shells at the precise moment of their transformation and then transfer them to the safety of the corral is a wonder of the universe, as is the sight of a molting crab.

Brady, Bridges's wife, has come out of the house and is starting her shift, pulling the just-shed soft-shells from a row of tanks behind us. She has been tackling this chore for more than forty years. During the same period, she has also developed a hobby and fascination parallel to her husband's. In the ranch house living room where we first met, every wall is given over to floor-to-ceiling glass cases chockablock with porcelain figurines: a thirty-two-year collection of Hummels, worth many thousands of dollars — as pale, fragile, and pristine as a just-shed crab shell.

Other members of the family will come out after dark to monitor and sort the busters at nine this evening and again at three in the morning. It's a tough pull in the dead of night, best left to the junior members of the family. "They shed better at nighttime," Bridges explains.

To service all the tanks — removing the empty shells and dead crabs, moving the newest soft-shells into isolation — takes about an hour, given the size of the harvest right now. Come daylight, the group will start packing a new shipment while Murray Bridges goes out for another round with his pots. Other crabbers will begin bringing their peelers in for Murray to select from when he gets off the boat.

"You have to pay a crabber enough to make the catch worth a day's work. That's how I govern myself," says Bridges. That means sometimes paying fifty dollars per dozen, sometimes twenty-five dollars a dozen when the quantities pick up. "Before we lost the medium grade, we could shed a couple weeks earlier and go for the smaller sizes."

In Virginia and Maryland, some crab houses heat the water in the shedders to expedite the molting process and extend the season. "They'll come down here early and get our crab and take them back up there to the heated water. Heck, they'll go all the way down to Florida for peelers. Some crab-bers heat the water in their shedders in North Carolina, too, around Swan Quarter. I've tried it," says Bridges, "but it didn't really pay off."

He says the best soft-shells to eat are the hotels (pronounced *HO-tels*) — the smallest grade. "They are all virgin females," he notes, "and the best eating size, because they're so small, perfect for a sandwich."

I wonder whether Bridges eats the mustard — the pasty, dark-yellow substance in the middle of the abdomen that some people think of as fat. The organ is actually the hepatopancreas, the main part of the crab's diges-tive system. According to local columnist Rosie Hawthorne of the *Outer Banks Voice*, the mustard "acts as both liver and pancreas. It serves to pro-duce digestive enzymes and is also responsible for filtering impurities from the crab's blood." Like Willy Phillips, Hawthorne says she won't eat this part of a soft-shell. Research has demonstrated that the mustard is where "color-less, odorless, and tasteless chemical contaminants such as PCBs, dioxin, and mercury accumulate." Though some consider the mustard a delicacy, Haw-thorne always removes it before cooking.

So do Brady and Kissy. "They wash it out of the ones we eat," Bridges told me. "It has a bitter taste."

* * * * * * * * * * * * *

That night, Donna and I head out to dinner. Though it is two more weeks until Memorial Day, when high season begins at the beach, the Kill Devil Grill, on Virginia Dare Trail at Mile Marker 9.75, is already surrounded with dinner patrons waiting for a table on this Thursday evening. A local favorite, fourteen years on this site, the Grill is attached to a 1939-vintage diner, which now serves as the restaurant's bar and is listed on the National Register of Historic Places. We step through the crowd to get on the waiting list. Thanks to a pair of bar patrons who are leaving and point us toward their seats, we get lucky. We must be telegraphing our hunger. We sit down and ask if they have any soft-shells left. It is 7:30 and the sun has not set.

"Nope," says a passing bartender over his shoulder. He turns. "This is the last pair we have." The plate he is carrying is mounded high with a nest of shredded cabbage and lettuce, topped with two soft-shell crabs fried to a warm golden brown. He passes the platter like a slow punishment in front of us and then gives it to a couple down the bar.

"We buy our crabs from just one guy every morning," says another bartender, noting our craned necks and longing looks. "Fresh today and gone when they're gone."

That one guy, we know, is Murray Bridges. We order beers and stare blankly at the menu.

A few minutes later, bartender number two returns with a single flash-fried soft-shell with slaw and fries on the side. "The very last one. Not a full order," he says. "Okay?"

"Absolutely," Donna says, "and thanks!" We order some shrimp to round out the meal. I cut the crab down the middle and scoop away the mustard.

The temperate sweetness of the slaw is a perfect foil for the crust on the crab, which we soon learn is the same breading the Grill uses for its fried chicken. It is nothing like the thin dusting of flour that covers the restaurant's fried shrimp, which the chef has butterflied to provide more real estate for the batter.

The crab breading is much thicker, saltier, and laced with red chili powder, which gives it a surprising lift. The dressing supplied is pink — a cross between tartar and cocktail — an unexpected hybrid that also works. There are no hush puppies on the side, or on the menu, for that matter, but the fries are first-rate — no old, overused oil here. We are happy.

Our neighbors at the bar — a contractor and his wife from Virginia Beach who tell us that they come down to their cottage at Kill Devil Hills and eat here at least once a week — report that the crab cakes are also exceptional.

It's a satisfying end to a long day, but when the intelligent and comical faces of the crabs we saw at Endurance Seafood flash in memory, I am suddenly grateful for the breading that hides them a bit. The crab taste is there, but it is only one element in a medley of flavors. It will turn out to be a good standard for comparison with the other soft-shell crabs we will sample tomorrow.

As we depart Kill Devil Grill, a smaller group of would-be diners is still clotted around the restaurant, but darkness has come. On impulse, we drive back out to Colington Island, passing beyond Endurance Seafood to see the shedders of Murray's competitors dotting the shoreline. As the road winds through the island, we can see their operations lit up like Christmas and reflected in the surrounding water. These hundreds of shedders pay homage to Bridges's pioneering effort forty years ago and are a testament to the ongoing profusion of blue crab that still mate and molt in North Carolina's ever-churning waters.

The next morning, Cheryl Wiggins, who runs the nautically appointed, two-guest-room Roanoke Bungalow in Manteo, is making our breakfast. We tell her about our visit to Endurance Seafood the day before. We've stayed with Cheryl several times but usually in cooler weather. Her inventive breakfast menus are special, as is the working fireplace just outside the guest rooms on a covered breezeway, where the Carolina jasmine is just beginning to bloom as it twines in profusion along the porch posts and railings. The water feature in the garden burbles as we sit down to baked blueberry pancakes and fresh fruit. Sumptuous.

Wiggins tells us that she and her two grown sons have a Mother's Day ritual of feasting on soft-shell crabs — as many as they can get for deep frying outside in her yard. Just a week before, Cheryl's friend Cowboy paid fifty-six dollars a dozen for the soft-shells he picked up fresh from Murray Bridges. "They were worth every penny," Wiggins said.

After dillydallying on the bungalow porch, we head back inland on Highway 64 to Willy Phillips's Full Circle Crab market in Columbia. We arrive just ahead of the lunch crowd and order a single soft-shell crab sandwich. Melissa Ruiz, the chef, dials up the heat in a small fryer and opens the refrigerator, which holds a bowl of Moss Seafood Breader mixed with Full Circle Crab Company Seasoning (both for sale in the market). She pulls out mayonnaise and hamburger buns. This makeshift kitchen is right inside the market, just behind the iced rows of smoked mullet, fresh flounder, bay scallops, and red snapper in a long glass case. The crab comes from the shedders out back — fresh and just cleaned. Ruiz dips one side and then the other into the breading mix and drops it into the fryer. Three minutes later, the crab is done. She breaks the body in half at the midsection to tuck both pieces more handily into the now-toasted bun. She also adds lettuce and a dollop of mayo. The whole affair is only $6.95, including a bag of chips and a soda (and two dollars less if you order the sandwich only).

Donna and I split the sandwich. Breakfast wasn't that long ago. Each bite is light, flavorful, simple. It could hardly be fresher, all crab, nothing else but the crunch of the lettuce and the slight, cool sweetness of the mayo. So very satisfying.

Now we turn south toward Wilmington — not an easy destination, given all the water between here and there. If we were flying in a straight line, we'd aim ourselves over Lake Mattamuskeet (the state's largest freshwater lake), the Pungo and Pamlico Rivers, the Neuse and the New Rivers (with the constellation of lakes in the Croatan Forest in between), and then the White Oak River and finally land in Wilmington. As it is, by car we have to take a wide berth to the west to get around all those wide-mouthed rivers. Our first stop will be Little Washington, where the Tar River meets the Pamlico and where the Washington Crab and Seafood Shack runs a restaurant and catering operation and sells seafood both raw and cooked. In the log building with a screened side porch, cheerful staff are bringing oysters by the bucketful to midafternoon diners, who sit on the benches of shellacked pine picnic tables. Each table is outfitted with a roll of paper towels and the Shack's cocktail sauce, which is both sweet and heavy on the horseradish. The sauce would make an outstanding Bloody Mary starter. But we are here to try the grilled soft-shell crab — not something you find everywhere. In fact, full disclosure, this will be my first-ever *grilled* soft-shell crab.

The creature, darkly striped from the grill, comes split down the middle with the "lid" off, meaning most of the mustard has been cooked off. It's a rather pitiful looking thing — small, which is good, but perhaps made smaller by what must have been the intense heat of the grill. It has a nice aroma and is doused in smoke, butter, and Old Bay, but it's quite chewy — too chewy. I should have known better.

Andrea Reusing, the chef at the Lantern Restaurant in Chapel Hill, makes a mean salt-and-pepper shrimp, which, according to Asian tradition, are not peeled. The peels are supposed to cook off. But they don't quite. The texture of the grilled crab is roughly the same. Willy Phillips's caution to marinate and grill quickly on low heat has not been applied here, apparently.

But I won't condemn Amy and Tony Tripp, the proprietors of this establishment. After all, the place is packed this rainy afternoon. Most folks are eating oysters or fried soft-shells and seem to be regulars at this rare relic — the old-fashioned kind of seafood shack you'd find only at the beach several decades ago. I will be back, but next time I will order my soft-shells fried or try the frog legs. That's not something you find every day on a menu, either.

For now, I buy a mesh cap with a handsome image of a crab above the bill as a souvenir, and we're off.

⁂

A gargantuan rainstorm ushers us the rest of the way to Wilmington, hail-stones ticking against the car and waves of water flung up by trucks, slapping against the windshield. At last, before dusk, the sun emerges. We plan to dine at Catch, where Keith Rhodes was voted Best Chef in Wilmington each year from 2008 to 2013. On Market Street, in a modest strip mall, the restaurant is not overly elegant but plays more to the concept of a comfortable sushi shop.

Tonight, soft-shells are on the menu, served on a bed of scented grits that stay creamy even as they cool. The crab is bejeweled with red Russian kale and outstanding pickled wild ramps.

On first bite, the ramps carry a tart sweetness, something like pickled peaches. Then the true ramp flavor kicks in — sharp and savory. The crab itself is elegant — crisp, small, and tender: a hotel, perhaps? Its oceanic flavor is brought out by a bacon-sherry vinaigrette, sparingly applied so as not to overpower the taste of the crabmeat. This soft-shell is as easy to chew as the one we had at Full Circle earlier in the day.

When Rhodes — the staff simply calls him "Chef" — finally comes out to meet us at the bar, a cacophonous crash rolls like thunder from the kitchen. Chef says, "They've got it," and offers us a warm handshake.

We get right down to it. Rhodes tells us he sources his soft-shells from "Uncle Phil" Smith in Kure Beach, a crabber whom he's known for more than twenty years. He drenches the crabs in buttermilk before dredging them only once in a combination of flour and cracker meal. Each crab cooks in hot oil for four minutes.

I tell Chef about our grilled soft-shell earlier in the day. He grins and suggests that roasting or grilling soft-shells requires a larger grade to keep its size and avoid desiccation. Good idea, I'm thinking.

Wilmington-born, Rhodes is a formidable presence, and he's unreservedly passionate about his work. He's made appearances on the *Top Chef* television show and was a James Beard semifinalist for the best chef in the Southeast award. Though his culinary profile is now national, he easily admits that he dropped out of Wilmington's Laney High School in the tenth grade and meandered a while before finding his way to a degree in nutrition.

Now, Rhodes has become an evangelist for local food. He's had offers to go elsewhere, but he says he's dedicated to his hometown culture and to cultivating culinary talents in the next generation.

His wife, Angela, manages their food truck business, while his daughter, Kristen, serves as the dessert chef for Catch. "There's lots of talent in this town," he says. Looking for what he calls "the flame of inspiration" when hiring staff, Rhodes aims to leave a lasting impression on staff members, no matter how long they work for him.

Rhodes refuses to apologize for a menu that might price some folks out of his restaurant. "Good seafood ain't cheap, and cheap seafood ain't good," he says. "We push a higher-end product. You know, I love Calabash style as much as anyone else, but I guess I'd say that Catch is for everyone, but everyone might not be for Catch. We don't want to copycat, and we try to create our own flavors."

A few days later, we manage to arrive early enough at the Chef and the Farmer Restaurant, in Kinston, to be seated at the bar without a reservation — nothing short of a miracle. On this night, PBS celebrity chef Vivian Howard's crew was making soft-shell crab topped with ramp remoulade (a fancy name for tartar sauce), a garlic leek velouté (a broth thickened with roux), and charred collard slaw on the side. The most significant aspect of this dish was the breading on the soft-shell. It was made with rice flour, which is almost always gluten-free and produces a very crunchy crust on the crab.

Initially I was skeptical. I once sampled a Korean fried chicken leg that was encrusted with rice flour. Unfortunately in that dish, the batter actually separated from the chicken to create a hard shell that reminded me of those beetles that would leave their exoskeletons attached to the pine trees in my grandmother's front yard. Not so appealing.

But Howard's rice flour coating clung fervently to the crab and created a successful mask for whatever degree of shell formation had already been under way when the crab was cleaned in Beaufort — its provenance, we were told — and packed to travel fresh to Kinston.

This dish was a revelation. As Murray Bridges explained, the peelers, once shed of their old shells, do start forming new ones immediately, and as long as they are in water, the formation continues. This might explain why the soft-shell crab we had at Full Circle — literally from shedder to table —

Keith Rhodes, chef and owner of Catch restaurant in Wilmington, offers up a plate of his delicate soft-shell crabs, which are drenched in buttermilk and lightly dredged in flour and cracker meal before frying. (Used by permission of the photographer, Ali Morrow)

seemed so fresh that no new shell was perceptible. The grilled soft-shell in Little Washington, in contrast, was probably farther along in its new shell formation and then lost its plump under fire.

Vivian Howard's rice flour, however, was the perfect jacket for the crab, making a new edible shell and masking whatever chewiness the crab might have started to form on its own. To my taste, the only negative in the preparation was the presence of the crab's mustard, which was bitter, unsightly, and especially unwelcome, now that I know what it might contain.

After closing out our month of research, sad news came to us in June that Willy Phillips had discontinued his makeshift kitchen at Full Circle Crab. He decided to focus on his primary business of getting delicious soft-shells out into the world, up and down the East Coast. The good news is that he still sells all the ingredients to make that simple soft-shell sandwich we had and which I plan to try at home when the soft-shells return next season.

I also now know not to be fooled by the presence of soft-shells on a winter menu. They might even be those breaded and cooked crab that come frozen from Asia. I am willing to wait for the scent of honeysuckle and the sight of blooming potato plants to tuck into my next soft-shell sandwich. Fresh is by far the best.

June

Serviceberries

IN CARRBORO, WHERE I LIVE, IT HAPPENS IN JUNE. IN EARLY MORNING, when I take my dog Nebo for a walk, I hear them arriving, feeding on the plump mulberries across the meadow on the far side of the driveway. Their high, metallic whistles are shrill, sometimes hard to ferret out amid the whoosh of distant traffic and the beep and grind of garbage trucks lifting dumpsters behind the restaurants on Main Street. But once you've heard a group of cedar waxwings gathered in a tree or flying overhead, it's easier to pick up their unusual voices, the *brzeeee* that accompanies their foraging expeditions in pines, cedars, junipers, and fruit trees.

On one morning walk this year, an unruly flock exploded out of the high pines. Struck by sun, they blazed orange, like fireworks going in all directions overhead.

The cedar waxwing is like no other bird. Both male and female are multicolored, with soft gray tail feathers that come to a blunt end like a flat paintbrush dipped in bright yellow paint. Their gray wings, trimmed in white, are also marked with luminous red chevrons. A feathery brown crest curls over their heads, and a black Lone Ranger mask surrounds the eyes and beak. The upper back is a warm brown, while the breast in front fades from brown to yellow to a washed-out white toward the underside of the tail.

The first time I ever came close enough to see the bright details on these shy birds was a few years ago in June, when a dozen or more cedar waxwings descended to feed on the small red and purplish berries of a young tree not thirty feet from my front door. They were pulling the berries into their beaks in a frenzy, performing acrobatics to sustain their purchase on limber branches and swinging themselves in all directions to pluck fruit.

I was curious. What were those berries on the small tree that had been planted by the landscaper when the condos were built, almost a decade ago? I wasn't yet familiar with the *Amelanchier arborea*, the common serviceberry. I picked a few berries that had turned from red to purple and tasted them cautiously. They were sweet, pleasing—something like a blueberry but a bit sharper, with a note of raspberry—and so began my research.

⋅ ⋅ ⋅ ⋅ ⋅ ⋅ ⋅ ⋅ ⋅ ⋅ ⋅ ⋅

As it turns out, serviceberry trees are native to North Carolina. They are everywhere and unheralded, often propagated in the forests by birds that eliminate the undigested seeds. The berries are not really berries at all but pomes. *Amelanchier* is a member of the *Rosaceae* family, as are apples and pears.

Serviceberry trees have become increasingly popular with landscapers, it seems. They are shapely, understory ornamentals that bloom very early in spring—on the cusp of February and March where I live midstate. Their showy white blossoms are composed of narrow petals that unfurl well before the leaves on the tree develop. In fall the leaves—which are small, saw-toothed, and symmetrical—turn a warm apricot color and tend to linger on their branches into November.

"I design serviceberries into gardens any chance I get," said Caroline Siverson, a longtime landscaper who works out of Chatham County, in the North Carolina Piedmont, and who confirmed that my Carrboro tree is a serviceberry. "I buy nursery-bred selections rather than the straight species seedlings, mainly because that is what is most easily available at any size," she said.

Nowadays, many varieties of serviceberry trees are available. One, known as Canadian serviceberry (*Amelanchier canadensis*), is also sometimes called chuckleberry, currant-tree, Juneberry, shadblow, shadbush, and sugarplum.

Observant readers might connect the names "shadbush" and shadblow" to the seasonal migration of the shad—the fish considered in chapter 3. In many areas when the tree blooms, the fish are running at the same time. To those who know these signs, both tree and fish are happy harbingers of the end of winter.

Writing about the serviceberry trees that grow in the forests of New York State's Hudson Valley, the arborist and former *New York Times* columnist William Bryant Logan offers this explanation for the name: "The *amelanchier* ... [is] also called serviceberry, because its tasty fruits set in spring just about the time that the ground thaws enough to bury the dead." Serviceberry, then, as in funeral service.

Another explanation for the moniker, posted on the discussion board of a blog sponsored by the Washington [State] Native Plant Society, suggests that the name "serviceberry" originated with farmers in the northwest United States who took the tree's blooming to be a sign to call in the stud service for their cows.

Long before the settlement of Europeans, Native Americans across the continent gathered serviceberries to eat. They also used them when available as an ingredient in pemmican, the portable "energy bar" of the era, made from pounded and dried meat, fruit, and fat.

In Canada, the serviceberry is usually called "saskatoon" — a Cree Indian word that means "the fruit of the tree of many branches," according to the Saskatoon Berry Institute of North America. The City of Saskatoon, in the Saskatchewan Province, was named for the tree. This variety grows from Alaska to Maine, where the fruit is sometimes called "sugar pea." A number of commercial fruit growers in Michigan and a few other states and Canadian provinces actually cultivate the northern berries, which to me look more like blueberries in the photos I've seen than do the serviceberries that grow in North Carolina.

In our mountains, the serviceberry is historically known as "sarvisberry" or "sarviceberry," spellings that reflect the Appalachian pronunciation. The popular western North Carolina journalist John Parris offered an explanation in a 1967 *Asheville Citizen* column titled "How 'Sarvice' Got Its Name":

> Back when folks were opening up the wilderness and putting down their roots, the hand of woman was still a stranger to the soil.
>
> As cabins were grooved together and the land cleared, the womenfolks planted their flower seeds and waited for blooming time.
>
> But while they waited they looked to the appearance of wildflowers for their funeral wreaths and wedding decorations.
>
> But in a land where winter was long and spring came late the wildflowers were late in coming, too.

Parris credits those hardy Scotch-Irish women as the first to notice "the spring-heralding flowers of the high-mountain forest trees for which they had no names. They gathered them and carried them to church services and funeral services." Hence the name "sarvis" or "sarvice" in the local parlance.

Storyteller, naturalist, and herbalist Doug Elliott of Union Mills, just north of Rutherfordton, told me another sarviceberry legend from western North Carolina. This version claims that it was the circuit-riding preachers who divined that the blossoming sarviceberry tree was a sign from heaven to resume their preaching duties with their far-flung congregations. Until the sarviceberry tree bloomed, the clergy (and their flocks) knew that it was too perilous to travel across rugged mountain roads in icy winter.

The popular naturalist and *Reader's Digest* columnist Donald Culcross Peattie was first brought to the North Carolina highlands as a boy because of his poor health. Thereafter, throughout his life he often visited the town of Tryon in Polk County. His mother, Elia Peattie, a novelist of some note, eventually settled and was buried there. Her son the tree expert likely had a hand in the inscription on her tombstone: "She ate of life as if 'twere fruit."

Peattie conducted many botanical forays in North Carolina, especially in the southern mountains. He writes of the Sarvisstree (his spelling) in *A Natural History of Trees of Eastern and Central North America* — his best-known work, first published in 1948 and last issued in 1991.

"It is from the fruits that the Sarvissberry takes its name," Peattie writes, "for the word is a transformation of the *sorbus* given by the Romans to a related kind of fruit. Sarviss is a good Shakespearean English form of the most classic Latin, whereas Serviceberry is meaningless as a name, or is at least a genteel corruption of an older and more scholarly form." *Sorbus* is the Latin word for "tree."

Peattie also gives us two other notable facts about the serviceberry: its wood is the fifth hardest among trees that grow in the United States (the persimmon is the hardest), and it "takes a beautiful polish, so that it would be a more valuable cabinet wood than White Oak if only the trees grew large enough for lumbering."

Peattie also explains that François Michaux, the son of the eighteenth-century botanist André Michaux, accompanied his father on his botanical research in the United States, including the mountains of North Carolina, and once observed serviceberry fruit for sale in the markets of Philadelphia, but he said that only children were buying it. Peattie then adds his own editorial comment, arguing that the serviceberries seemed mostly to "find favor" with "ever-hungry youngsters," something Peattie may well have witnessed firsthand on his forays in the hollers and ridges of the North Carolina mountains.

Zetta Barker Hamby was born in 1907 and lived in the Grassy Creek community along the border between Ashe County, North Carolina, and Grayson County, Virginia. She was a teacher and school principal. Her book, *Memoirs of Grassy Creek*, is a recollection of mountain life early in the twentieth century, including foods, celebrations, farmwork, and home remedies.

Hamby died in 1997, at the age of ninety, just before her memoir was published. Her daughter, Gayle Winston, still lives in the area and runs the

River House Country Inn, set on 170 acres at the North Fork of the New River, one of North Carolina's oldest waterways. Gayle, now in her eighties, is a gourmet chef and former Broadway producer. Her dinner guests enjoy fresh ramps in March and pickled ramps year-round. Gayle also serves fresh native greens, local apples, and mountain trout to diners. When I called to ask about serviceberries, Gayle said she'd have to do some homework. The local fruit is not part of her mountain menus these days. No surprise: her mother's recollection of having to climb a tree for berries so small you could not find them if they fell in the grass might be the first clue as to why River House does not serve them. As Zetta Hamby wrote:

> In early spring a tree could be seen in full bloom with dainty white flowers. After the bloom was gone, tiny green berries could be seen where the flowers had been. About August the fruit had grown to the size of a peppercorn and turned a deep red. They, too, were sweet and tasty to eat raw after someone had climbed the tree and gathered them. They were so tiny they could hardly be picked up from the grass underneath the tree. My brother would climb a tree, break off a few branches and hand them down for us to eat while he picked some to take to the house. Sometimes we would stir up cake batter and put the service berries in, just as we use nuts or some fruit in cakes today.

It seems that in North Carolina, serviceberries are hardly eaten at all any more. In my informal survey of Tar Heels who are familiar with the fruit, most have told me they rarely bother with them. Canadians, however, still use them liberally in "pies, tarts, scones, muffins, bread, coffee cake, jams, compote, sauces, salad dressing, trail mix, and other snack foods. They can also be used in wine, cider, and a variety of liquors," reports the Saskatoon Berry Institute. The institute also cites a study published in the *Journal of Food Science* indicating that the berries have high antioxidant properties and "appear to be an excellent source of manganese, magnesium, iron, calcium, potassium, copper and carotene. Saskatoon berries are considered a better source of calcium than red meats, vegetables and cereals. Saskatoons are high in natural sugar, rich in Vitamin C, and also contain more than three times as much iron and copper in the same weight as raisins."

So what is our problem with this healthy, natural food source that comes ripe in June or a bit later at higher altitudes in North Carolina? To learn more, Donna Campbell and I visited a tree nursery.

Hollis and Jay Wild live on nearly thirty acres off Idlewild Road in Ashe County, not far from the South Fork of the New River. Their tree farm, now mostly devoted to growing herbs, sits in a low spot, relatively speaking. The Wilds say they usually experience the first and last frost in the county.

"That first year when we moved up here in 1980," Hollis said, "the New River froze solid. People were driving trucks on it!" In subsequent years, the river froze and thawed, heaving huge ice floes up on the banks and bridges. These days, with climate change, such frigid weather is rare. "We haven't had a September frost in several years, but we still have forty-degree nights in July and August," Hollis said.

She is a small woman—thin and strong with thick silver hair and a healthy complexion that belies a life of work outdoors. Her husband, Jay, whose passion is photography, also has a farmer's tan and a build that suggests plenty of dirt work with hand tools and tillers.

After being raised in Reidsville, Hollis took an elective course in field biology in the early 1970s with Dr. Hollis Rogers at the University of North Carolina at Greensboro. The fact that the professor and his student shared the same first name was only a coincidence but perhaps a sign that the two would come to share academic interests, too. Hollis remembers the professor's field trips, the class sitting in campsites and on picnic tables in various parts of the state, listening to Rogers describe the surroundings. "He told us about the sarvis or shadbush and how it was the first to bloom on the mountain slopes, way before any other deciduous tree," she said.

Though Hollis had begun college as a music major, her biology teacher held sway, and she changed her focus to land-use planning. She soon found herself working at Pilot Mountain State Park, supervising a pack of thirteen- to fifteen-year-olds whose parents had signed them up for Youth Conservation Corps camp. She met Jay on the job that summer as they both helped lead the young conservationists in clearing new hiking trails.

After Hollis and Jay married, he took a job as a ranger stationed on the peak of Mount Mitchell, North Carolina's highest mountain. It would be a three-year stint that included one long January in which ninety inches of snow fell within the month. When the snowplow broke, Jay had to take welding lessons over the phone to fix it. They could not possibly get down the mountain without the plow.

The winds howled. Hollis remembered how crystals of ice would form *inside* the windows of their cabin, and she would paint the ice with antifreeze to be able to see outside. "The wind was so fierce that the cups blew off the Mitchell wind meter," she said. "And the couch in one room of our house and the bed in the other would slide away from the walls as the rafters bent and the walls bowed from the sheer force of the wind." When spring finally came that year, Jay brought Hollis the first bluet he found growing on the mountain — the start of a tradition he keeps to this day.

When the Wilds launched their nursery business, Hollis ran it at their new Ashe County homeplace while Jay served as the superintendent of Mount Jefferson State Natural Area and New River State Park, both in the county.

"When we started, there was not much of an interest in native plants," Hollis said. Instead, tree buyers wanted cultivars with a branded name. Thus among serviceberries the *Amelanchier grandiflora* "Princess Diana" — a cross between the *A. aborea* (downy serviceberry) and *A. laevis* (Allegheny serviceberry) — was much in demand. According to the Missouri Botanical Garden website, this trendy hybrid was "noted for its yellow flower buds, abundant white flowers in spring, deep bluish purple fruits, wide-spreading branches and red fall color." No mention was made of the fruit's flavor, though we do know that the Allegheny serviceberry is a variety known to be especially sweet when eaten right off the tree. The plant developers opted instead to emphasize how the tree was useful in attracting birds to the garden.

About the same time (1993), the *Amelanchier laevis* "Prince Charles" or "Prince Charles" Allegheny serviceberry was given a name in the royal family for marketing purposes. The University of Florida Institute of Food and Agricultural Sciences described it as follows: "The purplish-black edible berries are sweet and juicy but are soon eaten by birds. The fall color is orange-red. It is well-adapted for planting beneath power lines." Some selling point!

Next came the "Prince William" — another variety in the "Royals" group. According to the J. C. Raulston Arboretum in Raleigh, "the 'Prince William' is the shrubbiest of the three."

Hollis explained that gardening magazines at the time these brands were launched were full of recommendations for named plants, shrubs, and trees (as they still are). "But they got ahead of the growers in their promotions," she said. "People came asking for these new brand-name plants, and we were always playing catch-up. The breeders and big nurseries like Monrovia had people breeding plants for them to meet the demand. Then tissue culture came along, and plants that were hard to graft or bud, such as redbuds, and plants that were hard to start from seed, like the native fringe tree, began being cultured from tissue."

Tissue culture is a process by which small pieces of a plant are cultured in sterile conditions on a nutrient medium. This method, known as micropropagation, actually produces clones of the starter plant. The development of micropropagation techniques led to many new and unusual varieties that were named, branded, and marketed to the public across the country, often without regard for their native habitat. Instead, they were simply sold by hardiness zones.

The Wilds, however, kept on planting seedlings and hand-digging their trees for sale. "We found that with each housing slump in the economy, the nursery business was also impacted, so we finally decided to switch to produce. If we couldn't sell produce, we could still eat it. We couldn't eat the trees that didn't sell," Hollis said, smiling. They sold their produce at the local farmers' market. "Now we just do herbs," she said.

Hollis and Jay (who has now retired from the state park system) took us on a tour of the landscape and greenhouses behind their house with their dog, Taffy, in the lead. We wandered through an arbor of young trees along one side of the property, including a row of serviceberries easily ten feet tall.

"Do you harvest the berries?" I asked Hollis.

She shook her head. "I find that the birds like to eat them about two days before I think they are perfectly ripe for human consumption."

* * * * * * * * * * * *

Sadly, my own serviceberry tree was unproductive this year. I noticed early on that the fruit was swelling up and turning orange. The berries then developed little horns all over the surface of the fruit. It was an ugly Halloween nightmare in June. The berries looked like flails, those balls with spikes that were attached by chain to a rod and swung at attackers in the Dark Ages. As usual, the cedar waxwings made their way to the neighborhood, but they fed only on the mulberry and cedar trees far from my door.

Caroline Siverson, the landscaper, diagnosed the disease as cedar apple rust, which—to put a fine point on it—was probably a related rust called *Gymnosporangium globosum* that affects serviceberries in particular. Basically, this bacterial fungus takes hold on a juniper or cedar and overwinters there. When the warm rains of spring come, spores germinate and travel by

Hollis Wild, a horticulturalist in Ashe County, examines the fall foliage on a mature serviceberry at the tree farm she launched years ago with her husband, Jay.

wind to the leaves and/or fruit of a nearby broadleaf plant—in this case, my serviceberry. With the right temperatures and moisture, the infection multiplies and is eventually carried back on the wind to the host plant. I suspect the host plant was the juniper tree planted beside another nearby condo, which has since been removed because it was unsightly and getting too big. Maybe the serviceberry will recover with the juniper now gone.

In the meantime, I was able to sample serviceberries elsewhere this season. The Knife and Fork Restaurant in Spruce Pine—mentioned earlier, in the chapter on ramps—has a bar, appropriately named the Spoon. One hot afternoon in June, the bartender was muddling serviceberries for a cocktail of his own invention that also involved bourbon and mint. It was something like a cross between a julep and an old-fashioned. Very satisfying.

But there are other ways, I learned, to enjoy spiked serviceberries. Following the multitude of formulas for a drink known as the blueberry smash, you can substitute serviceberries for blueberries. Serviceberries muddle well with lime juice, mint, or basil. Rum or vodka also works with various mixers that might be added, such as a splash of simple syrup, orange liqueur, or St. Germain. The whole enterprise can be topped off with club soda or sparkling wine. Handily, the Knife and Fork has a small but healthy serviceberry tree growing in its courtyard, so these experiments will likely continue.

Other mixologists have been known to cook down a cup or two of serviceberries with sugar to create a syrup that can be refrigerated and then added to a flute of chilled prosecco or cava to make a colorful aperitif. You can also make a thicker syrup to serve on pancakes or blintzes.

Toward the middle of June, I visited the North Carolina Arboretum, in Asheville, and meandered among the formal gardens, enjoying the blooming glory and hoping to see a serviceberry tree labeled, as are most of the specimen plants there. Finding none, I ended up in the education building and asked the staff at the desk how to find them. They all smiled knowingly. "The closest serviceberry trees are planted in an island—it's where the circular driveway out there meets the main parking lot," the young man at the desk explained, pointing out the window.

"Any berries left?" I asked.

"You might find one or two," another staff member said. She explained that arboretum employees make a practice this time of year of bringing

Tupperware containers to work and harvesting the serviceberries on their way into the building in the morning. "Between staff and birds, they are probably all gone," she concluded.

Ten healthy trees — a veritable arbor of handsome serviceberries of the Princess Diana variety, all about the same size — were, as promised, in the parking lot. But no berries.

On another trip to the far-western part of the state later in June, I asked my friend Annette Saunooke Clapsaddle, a Cherokee novelist and teacher at Swain County High School, where I might find a mountain-hardy service-berry tree to buy and plant at my cabin. (This effort would be a hedge against the fungus on the tree back home in Carrboro.) She knew immediately: Country Road Farms and Nursery near Dillsboro, a big operation with a number of *Amelanchiers* — all of the "Autumn Brilliance" variety. This cultivar is redder in the fall than the variety in Carrboro is. I looked it up on the same Missouri Botanical Garden website that covered the Princess Diana. Finally, here was a description that actually listed the edible berries as a primary asset for human consumption, promoting the fruit for "jams, jellies, and pies"!

My four-foot-tall "Autumn Brilliance" is set at the edge of the yard in Little Switzerland. There were some berries on the tree when I planted it. Even Nebo, the dog, seemed interested in them, as she is in my blueberry bushes nearby. Still, I had yet to find someone who cooks with them.

Peyton Holland is a fourth-generation Chatham County native whose family expertise in trees is featured in the upcoming chapter on persimmons. It occurred to me to ask Peyton whether his family ever harvested serviceberries.

"I love Juneberry pie," he said, his face lighting up. Peyton immediately checked with his mother and sent along her instructions:

> If it is a regular-size pie crust, wash berries and fill the bottom crust.
> Then sprinkle a half-cup of sugar over them and drizzle a little
> Parkay. Add the top crust and poke a few holes in the top with a fork.
> Bake at 350 until crust is brown. If it's a deep dish, add more berries
> and put in 2/3 cup of sugar.

Peyton, who is a history buff in his twenties, ruefully added in his email message, "We are getting so very close to many pieces of our culinary culture being lost because a lot of those traditional recipes that stemmed from local agriculture and access to resources around the home are not being passed down or are being replaced by modern convenience."

Of course, Peyton is right. Our lives are too busy and complicated to pick a fight with birds over some ephemeral fruit. At least, that is what I heard over and over from those who actually know what a serviceberry looks like. We just let the birds have them, people said. It's not just the exotic cedar waxwings that want them, either. Bluebirds, robins, catbirds, mockingbirds, and thrushes will go for serviceberries, too. According to one source, some thirty-five species of birds will eat this delicate fruit, but the cedar waxwings apparently love them the most, and if you want to see these elusive birds, planting a serviceberry is sure to draw them, according to the bird books I consulted.

If you're willing to fight the birds for the berries, you are in for some work, but I think the payoff is worth the effort. The taller the serviceberry, the more challenging to protect the fruit. Nets can be difficult to put on and take off and are not always effective. But I also learned this key fact: service-berries will continue to ripen after they are picked, so Hollis Wild might re-consider her situation and simply pick the berries before she thinks they look completely ripe and before the birds get to them. I will try the same in Little Switzerland, and in Carrboro, too, if the fungus there is cured.

Serviceberry trees are gaining status in North Carolina among those who worry about invasive, nonnative trees and shrubs that have been planted here. North Carolina State University has officially recommended the serviceberry as the preferred substitute tree for the nonnative Bradford pear, a supposedly sterile ornamental that began being planted extensively by developers in subdivisions across the state in the 1980s or thereabouts. The Bradford pear is beloved for its showy early blooms — an asset that, as the university points out, the serviceberry also can provide.

Unlike serviceberries, Bradford pears, however, have a notoriously weak branch system and are prone to shattering in ice and windstorms. They have a short lifespan (twenty to twenty-five years) and, contrary to their descrip-tions, will cross-pollinate with other pear trees, which can create an over-abundance of them. Cross-pollination can also cause the offspring trees to revert to the characteristics of their forebear: the Callery pear. The Callery (an ancient Chinese variety of which the Bradford is a later cultivar) can produce long, tire-piercing thorns that are devastating to mowers and other machinery. These pears often grow into forest thickets that tend to choke out North Carolina natives: pines, maples, dogwoods, and oaks. Callery blossoms also have a smell that has been compared to rotting fish.

"Callery pear grows very fast and can spread by rhizomes, which allows it to colonize areas very fast and exclude native plants," Johnny Randall told Amy Dixon, a special correspondent to the *Winston-Salem Journal*, in 2016. Randall, director of conservation programs at the North Carolina Botanical Garden in Chapel Hill, was spreading the alarm. "It is also an incredibly hardy tree that can grow in a wide variety of soils and moisture conditions. I have witnessed acres of callery pears in fallow agriculture fields and miles of callery pears along roadsides."

• • • • • • • • • • • • •

Thanks to Evalynn Halsey, a writer and serviceberry eater in the mountains, I was able to track down one more enthusiastic serviceberry expert who learned on family camping trips as a girl how to forage for and cook these berries. Rhonda Walls is a retired nurse and member of the Rugby, Virginia, Rescue Squad. She lives a mile from the North Carolina state line and went to high school at Grassy Creek, where Zetta Barker Hamby lived. "Grades one through seven in my school were in Virginia," she said, "and when you walked down the hall to the classrooms for grades eight through twelve, you were in North Carolina."

Rhonda grew up camping and hiking in what is now Grayson Highlands State Park, in Virginia. Her grandparents Luther and Bertha Kilby Richardson owned the 200 acres that became the first land transferred into the care of the park service. Earlier generations of Richardsons and Kilbys lived on the New River in Ashe and Alleghany Counties in North Carolina. Their forebears had migrated up to the mountains from Wilmington on the coast. Rhonda's grandparents' home stood where park headquarters sits today, and she says there are still serviceberry trees close by.

As a girl, Rhonda would ride her plug horse Twinkles into the woods and fasten an empty lard can onto the horn of her saddle. The horse was content to stand still and provided enough height for her to pick the biggest and best sarvisberries (as Rhonda has always called them), which her family used to make a campfire cobbler. She continued the tradition with her husband when they were first married. He would fish for trout to fry up for supper to go with the cobbler. Later, her own children gathered sarvisberries, "eating about half of all they picked," she said. Here is Rhonda's old-fashioned recipe for sarvisberry cobbler, cooked over an open fire:

> Use a heavy iron Dutch oven with a lid and put it on the campfire coals after breakfast has been cooked. Put in two cups of sarvisberries, two cups of sugar, and two cups of water. Let the mixture boil while you mix up a cup of self-rising flour and a cup of milk. Cut a stick of butter into the flour. Spread this mixture over the hot berries and juice and cover with the lid. Don't stoke the fire any more, just let it sit.

"We'd go hiking once this was cooking, and by about four o'clock, the cobbler would be ready," Rhonda told me. She also remembers that if her uncle was along on one of these campouts when she was a child, "he would go out to his land and lasso one of the cows and milk her so that we'd have fresh milk with our cobbler."

Rhonda offered one word of warning: "Be sure that you know what sarvisberries look like." As a nurse on the local rescue squad, she has seen people who misidentified wild plants. Mostly she's treated cases of eager foragers who mistook skunk cabbage for branch lettuce (an early-growing form of watercress in the mountains). Skunk cabbage can cause extreme digestive distress. Though Rhonda has never had a victim who mistook the wild cherry trees that grow around Grayson Highlands for serviceberry trees, she warned that wild cherries will kill a cow that eats them, and probably a human, too.

My advice is to plant your own serviceberry tree and be prepared to harvest the berries ahead of the birds.

July

Cantaloupes

POOR CANTALOUPE! IT'S EVERYWHERE—AS AN ORANGISH GARNISH
for bacon and eggs in chain restaurants; cubed in plastic fruit cups and
tucked into catered box lunches; slabbed alongside honeydew melon
(a close relative), grapes, and strawberries on buffet trays; and even promoted on hospital menus as a "super-fruit," because it's safe for diabetics
and full of potassium, beta-carotene, and vitamins A and C. But rarely, oh so
rarely, is cantaloupe delicious. More often it is tough, pastel pale, and barely
scented or sweet. Why?

When ripe, cantaloupe is fragile. According to the George Matjelan
Foundation—a global nonprofit dedicated to healthful eating—a ripe, uncut cantaloupe can be stored safely only for three or four days at the optimal
temperature of thirty-six to forty-one degrees Fahrenheit—a range that is
best accomplished in the crisper bin of a home refrigerator.

Cantaloupes that land in major grocery stores have usually been picked
for shipping quite prematurely, and unripe cantaloupes don't ripen much
more after they're picked. It's a long haul to North Carolina from California, where more than half of the cantaloupes in the United States are grown.
Other big producers are Arizona, Colorado, Georgia, Indiana, and Texas.
U.S. food suppliers also buy great quantities of cantaloupe from Guatemala,
Honduras, Costa Rica, and Mexico. So unless you grow your own or a dedicated farmer is raising melons for your local fruit stand, the true taste of a
ripe cantaloupe—sun-warmed from the field—is elusive. Most American
children today have probably never tasted a vine-ripened cantaloupe.

What we call cantaloupe in the United States is actually a muskmelon,
Cucumis melo. This species of fruit has been cultivated around the world
and transformed into many varieties. Contrary to myth, it does not cross-
pollinate with its cousins the squash, cucumber, or watermelon, which can
be planted in proximity.

Botanical historians believe that the first melons grew wild in Egypt,
Iran, and northwest India. After the fall of the Roman Empire, Arab civili-
zations began to cultivate melons with enthusiasm. Columbus reportedly
introduced melons to North America by bringing seeds to Haiti in 1493.
Melons arrived in England in the sixteenth century. Today by far the largest
producer of melons is China, but experts suggest that Afghanistan grows the
finest melons on the planet.

The North American cantaloupe or muskmelon (sometimes also called
nutmeg melon or netted melon) has a distinctive raised network pattern on
the rind. The seeds are edible, and the rind may appear segmented or not.

The flesh is usually orange. Though the name derives from the Italian town of Cantaloupo, due north of Naples and southwest of Rome, the variety on this side of the Atlantic differs significantly from the melons that were first grown in Italy.

In North Carolina, two very small communities more than a hundred miles apart share a century of colorful cantaloupe history, and they still produce legendary fruit. The village of Ridgeway, in Warren County, northeast of Raleigh near the Virginia border, is sadly on the sunset side of its cantaloupe fame. The crossroads known as Rocky Hock, in Chowan County, near the Albemarle Sound town of Edenton, is in ascendance. Both are prime destinations in July for travelers who want to experience fresh cantaloupes that are allowed to ripen on the vine to a perfumed perfection.

Wait, you might say, *I have to go get them? Don't they ship them around the state?* Alas for North Carolinians, many of the state's best cantaloupes are shipped north, out of state. That's also a tradition that goes back to the beginning of the last century, as is the shipping of soft-shell crabs and other seafood to points North.

* ● ● ● ● ● ● ● ● ● ● ●

Richard Holtzmann Jr., which is how he always introduces himself, lives in the same farmhouse he grew up in on U.S. 1 in Warren County. The homeplace is shaded by century-old oaks and pecans and surrounded by outbuildings essential to the farming operation. Holtzmann raises cattle, soybeans, watermelons, corn, tomatoes, and cantaloupes. He is the last in his family still farming here and the only major producer of the original Ridgeway cantaloupe.

The Ridgeway, a historic melon, is now celebrated annually on the third Saturday in July with a fund-raiser to benefit the local fire department. The Ridgeway Historical Society, the festival organizer, must depend on growers from other communities to supply enough cantaloupes for free samples, which are not, unfortunately, genuine Ridgeways.

"It's not like I can hold them back and store up enough for what they need in one day," Holtzmann says. He has no refrigeration for his crop, and on principle he won't pick the melons any closer than two or three days from full ripeness. This year, Holtzmann's cantaloupes are coming in late, but the fruit stand across the road and a quarter mile up from his place is already selling cantaloupes more than two weeks ahead of the festival. Donna Campbell and I stopped there on our way to meet Holtzmann, and I asked immediately about the melons' provenance.

"Georgia," said a pale boy with peach fuzz on his chin. "They're the same as the locals and just as good." I was not convinced.

Pulling into Holtzmann's driveway, we were ambushed by a wild-eyed border collie, who dodged and danced around the perimeter of the farm-house, barking constantly. Holtzmann came out and introduced Ralph, the dog, who backed away suspiciously. We headed into the house through a screened porch to the kitchen.

With the exception of Ralph, Holtzmann, fifty-eight, lives here alone, surrounded by his mother's decorative Avon bottle collection, which fills a china cabinet and continues around the room. Miniature glass cottages, cars, trucks, lighthouses, and human figures are set high along shelves just below the ceiling. A cross, a thermometer, a collection of arrowheads, and a picture of Jesus are hung in a narrow space between doorframes. The house has the timeless smell of many meals cooked and vegetables canned.

"My father is eighty-eight," Holtzmann tells us. "He farmed until he was eighty-four, still drove the tractors and combine. He started with signs of dementia and was diagnosed with Alzheimer's. My mother died five years ago, and the first year after, he seemed to go down real fast. They had been married fifty-nine years. Everything was changing. He went into the nursing home for rehab after a knee replacement and his Alzheimer's deteriorated. My sister is a registered hospice nurse, and she told me, 'You know, Richard, you can't take care of him and farm.' So he is still in the nursing home, and sometimes he doesn't really know anybody."

Holtzmann is soft-spoken, with a charming Virginia border accent—no hard *r*'s. "Farm" is pronounced "fahm" and the words "out" and "about" sound more like "oat" and "a boat."

He is a gentle presence, a wiry man with deeply tanned arms and a pale forehead from the cap he always wears in the field. He says he came right out of high school and picked up farming with his father. He's never traveled farther north than Chicago—a 4-H trip he won as a teenager—and he once visited New Orleans. He never married but eventually assumed leadership among his farming peers, serving as secretary/treasurer of the now defunct Ridgeway Growers Association, a collective that ordered supplies together each season. Out of habit, Holtzmann still buys a few extra pounds of canta-loupe seeds each year for others in the community.

"This year, my neighbor, a ninety-six-year-old black man who still plants

Richard Holtzmann Jr., the last major grower of the famous
Ridgeway cantaloupe, sells melons at the roadside produce
stand on his farm near Norlina in Warren County.

a few cantaloupes to sell, came by and asked me if I had any seeds, and I gave him some," Holtzmann says. "So he's growing cantaloupes. I'd say there are three or four other folks growing them around here besides me. They might sell a few on the road when they have extra. But nothing big."

Richard Holtzman's great-great-grandfather Diebold Holtzmann, a native of Alsace-Lorraine, came to the States in 1867 and moved his wife and children from Pennsylvania to Warren County in 1884, settling on 264 acres not far from Richard Holtzmann's current spread. The Holtzmann clan was one among many hardy families of German and French origin who came to the area before the turn of the twentieth century. They had heard about this region, which was apparently promoted as a fertile land of opportunity. What they found, however, were vast tracts of plantation land once cultivated by enslaved people and soil that had been drastically depleted from years of growing cotton and tobacco.

"What I always heard was there had been a lot of washing and erosion back then," Holtzmann explains. "The soil was not what they expected. They were used to good, productive soil in Germany. They had a lot to do to improve it. They planted clover and cowpeas — any kind of legume they could turn back into the soil to enrich it. The locals said, 'Look at those dumb Germans. They're plowing all their clover down instead of cutting it for hay!'" he laughs.

Diebold Holtzmann's three sons — George, Philip, and Henry — helped establish the St. Paul's Lutheran Church in Ridgeway in 1898. George and Philip were also among the farmers who helped to cultivate the Ridgeway cantaloupe in the early years of the new century.

According to local historian and author Barbara Sinn Bumbalough, by 1922 the brothers were among the shareholders in a new mercantile company in town, and they were also among the group of local farmers who organized a producers' cooperative called "The Pride of Ridgeway Growers Association." Most of the co-op farmers were of German descent and attended St. Paul's, but the organization also included a few non-German families.

By the 1930s, Ridgeway growers had begun shipping their distinctive melons north, to be served in top restaurants in Washington, Philadelphia, Boston, and New York, including the stylish Waldorf-Astoria Hotel. In 1932, the co-op shipped 13,000 crates of cantaloupes by rail from the Ridgeway depot. The enterprising growers registered and patented their cantaloupe as "The Pride of Ridgeway" and had an appealing image of a half melon drawn up for the label. North Carolina State University extension specialist George

Hughes told a reporter for the Associated Press in 1983, "It was said that if you went to a parade in Boston or Philadelphia [back then], half the people would be sitting on Ridgeway cantaloupe crates."

In her local history, *Come with Me to Germantown: Ridgeway, North Carolina Revisited*, Barbara Sinn Bumbalough describes the taste of the Ridgeway melon she remembered from her youth: "Unlike the American muskmelon, the Ridgeway cantaloupe was more akin to the European melon, which originated in Italy. Smooth-contoured and smaller in size than the native melons, its rind was thick and heavily netted. The deeper-colored orange flesh was succulent and sweet with a delicious, delicate flavor — noticeably different from the fruit grown elsewhere."

Thanks to this melon, prosperity had at last come to Ridgeway, even in the middle of the Depression. By the end of World War II, the local farmers were shipping some 80,000 crates in a single season. They commissioned special train cars during the peak of the harvest and loaded them up with melons day and night. In a single summer, a record 110 railcars full of cantaloupes left the Ridgeway station bound for points north.

Then a wilting blight nearly obliterated the Ridgeway melon, and growers increasingly turned to tobacco and soybeans to secure their livelihoods. The Ridgeway depot closed in 1951. Meanwhile, the demand for eastern melons fell off as western growers took over the market, with their drier climates and irrigation methods more reliable than the rain patterns that sometimes overwhelmed the crops with moisture here. New seed stocks were being developed to favor the western climate, too.

Still, Richard Holtzmann's father kept going. In the AP story from 1983, the senior Mr. Holtzmann, then fifty-five, told the reporter that he was one of only two producers left. He expected a yield of 20,000 to 25,000 melons that year, but he admitted that he was depending on soybeans for most of his income.

●　●　●　●　●　●　●　●　●　●　●　●

Probably the most common cantaloupe found in North Carolina groceries today is the hybrid Athena, which is wilt- and mildew-resistant, has a tough rind, is tolerant of shipping, and is unlikely to split. "Good shelf life, even when harvested ripe," as one seed purveyor described it in a catalog.

Holtzmann plants some Athenas these days, but the melon he considers closest to the original Ridgeway comes from a seed called Resistant Super

45s. "It's basically a western shipping cantaloupe. You can buy the seeds in Texas. We special-order them. You don't find them around here. Ridgeway has used several varieties over the years—Hale's Best 36 is one, but we went to the 45s."

More important than the type of seed, apparently, is the soil. "My dad always said it was an eight-square-mile area where the soil was right for cantaloupes," Holtzmann says. "U.S. 1 and the railway were built on the ridge that gives Ridgeway its name. The waters to the south go into the Tar River and the waters to the north flow into the Roanoke River. Basically, you go three or four miles either side of the ridge, from right here up to Manson, and the soil is kinda unique. Anything beyond that is not the Ridgeway area," he says with certainty.

We ride out to his cantaloupe field, about half a mile from the house. Acres of corn and soybeans are planted along the way. Ralph, the dog, races through the field while Richard steers us onto a paved road. In about a quarter of a mile, we turn off the pavement into a dirt driveway and approach a farmhouse older than the one Richard lives in. "This was my grandfather's," he says. "He planted all these ash trees here." The trees have created an enormous, lush canopy—a fine respite from the bright fields in every direction.

We get out of the truck as manic Ralph arrives with a muddy golf ball in his mouth. He wants us to throw it for him to retrieve. Now he is my best friend. As we walk along the rows of lovely bluish-green melons half-hidden under thick leaves, I hurl the golf ball down the dirt rows that divide one melon patch from the next. The dog is quick and relentless.

The soil is rocky, red dirt: part clay and part loose gravel, which drains well, Holtzmann explains—an essential factor in growing a good melon. He's also vigilant about watering. "You can overdo the water easily," he says. "More than you realize. Some folks give them too much water and wash the sweetness out of them."

He continues, "We've got mixed soils here in Warren County, but the red gravelly soil makes the sweetest cantaloupe. You can tell; the netting is tight." Holtzmann leans over and pulls back leaves to reveal the rough, corklike pattern on the outside of a ripening cantaloupe. A patch on the surface of the melon where the netting has not formed is called a half slick. "Don't want that melon," says Holtzmann.

He is proud of the innovations his family brought to the growing of melons in Ridgeway. "My grandfather was the first in the area to lay down black plastic to surround his early plants. My uncle Willie went to State College [now North Carolina State University], and that's one thing he picked up there in the fifties. He brought that technique back to his dad and my grand-father."

Plastic helps hold moisture and warmth in the soil for young plants early in the growing season. It also helps prevent weeds, so the melons get off to a good start. Holtzmann sets his first slips—which are started indoors—in plastic sheeting and then staggers the crops thereafter, seeding subsequent patches with a push planter and no plastic.

"I start planting around the thirtieth of April and go on planting every two weeks. I put in my last melons this year around the tenth of June," he says. Just as his father did before him, Holtzmann covers three and a half acres with cantaloupes. "They used to say that 300 crates for an acre of melons would be an exceptional harvest. I've never seen it that good," he says.

"How many go in a crate?" I ask.

"That depends on the size," he says. "It can range from eighteen [very large] to forty-five [very small], but twenty-three to twenty-seven canta-loupes in a crate used to be the standard around here."

Holtzmann drives us back up to his house, and Ralph again races the truck through the bean field. We head to the cantaloupe shed to examine the eighty-year-old grading machine Holtzmann still uses to sort melons along a conveyor belt outfitted with slots of increasing dimension. The cantaloupes roll along the belt and drop through the slots by size. It's an ancient-looking contraption that works as it did in his grandfather's day. "The grader knocks some of the dirt off," Richard says. "We don't wash them."

Washing cantaloupes, I later learn, can increase the probability of dan-gerous bacteria. Salmonella and listeria can gain purchase and grow in the crannies on the rough rind of the fruit. Experts urge consumers to wait until they are ready to cut a cantaloupe before scrubbing it thoroughly with a brush and water. Only then should a knife go into the rind.

Old wooden slat crates, nested market baskets, and heaps of bags made of plastic netting surround the grader. Holtzmann points to a pile. "As kids, we assembled and put the Ridgeway label on those crates. I remember nail-ing them, and I remember nailing my thumb, too." He laughs. "The last crated cantaloupes went out from here in the early 1970s." Now he mostly hauls them in boxes and baskets up to the highway to sell.

When the harvest begins in earnest, Holtzmann will work fifteen- to eighteen-hour days, first in the fields and then at the fruit stand out on the highway, where he sells his melons and other produce in the evenings. He has three other people who help him harvest, including his cousin, who works in the Warren County Sheriff's Department. "I have some other folks from the community who help me out. I'm lucky," he says.

The pickers hang the net bags from belts around their waists and drop in melons until the bag is nearly full. Until a few years ago, the 1926 Model T parked in the shed was still in working condition. His grandfather used it to carry melons from the field. Now Holtzmann uses his dad's 1955 Chevy truck and a 1965 red Plymouth Fury to haul the harvest. The culls — those canta-loupes that are not good enough to sell — go to his cows.

His sister, Linda Seeley, her husband, Bill, and Holtzmann's uncle, Willie Kilian, from Lynchburg, Virginia, pitch in on some weekdays and weekends at the roadside stand, which is actually a wagon with partitions that Richard rolls out to his front yard, right on Highway 1 about a mile beyond the Ridge-way Post Office and the Opry House.

The melons he sells on the roadside go from $1.00 for a softball-size Ridgeway to $3.50 for an extra-large one. Holtzmann also delivers melons to King's Red and White supermarket, about an hour's drive southwest, on East Club Boulevard in Durham. It's a relationship his dad established more than twenty-five years ago, after he had been turned away from the farmers' market in Raleigh.

"Nobody wanted small cantaloupes by that time," Holtzmann says. "They wanted those big hybrids in Raleigh, but Mr. King told my dad he'd take ours. I'm still working with his two sons who run the store now."

Holtzmann also delivers his produce to other fruit stands. One is on Dabney Drive in nearby Henderson, and another is in South Hill, Virginia. He sometimes sells produce to local restaurants, too.

Holtzmann says his father used to go to the grocery store in the early spring each year and bring home a cantaloupe. Sometimes he would even save the seed. "He'd try them — from Mexico or wherever — just to see if they were any good. We had a cat that loved cantaloupe worse than anything in the world. That cat — he was black, and his name was Smut — would eat cantaloupes and leave the cat food alone. All our cats ate cantaloupe, but that one was just wild for it. Sometimes we'd buy a melon just so he'd have one. Or when we'd go to Golden Corral, we'd bring him a piece home." Now, Holtzmann, like his father, periodically checks the melons at his local Food

Lion. "Most of them are as green as they can be. Probably picked two weeks early, but once in a while you can find one that's worth eating."

As for pests, Holtzmann mostly has to contend with crows on his cantaloupes. "I string up string and put out scarecrows," he says.

It's been a good morning, and Holtzmann tells us he has some watering to do. Donna and I bid him goodbye and head on down the road. We'll be back when the Ridgeways are ripe.

              • • • • • • • • • • • •

To travel from Ridgeway to Rocky Hock, our second melon destination, you continue northeast a short distance on U.S. 1 and pick up U.S. 158 in Norlina. U.S. 158 is a major state artery that runs 350 miles, from Mocksville, on the western side of Winston-Salem, all the way to Elizabeth City and then across the Currituck Sound and down to Whalebone Junction, at Nags Head, on the Outer Banks. But to reach Rocky Hock, you don't go that far. You must turn south on Alternate 158 in Gates County, passing through the county seat of Gatesville, a charming village near Merchants Mill Pond—a primeval swamp with cypress and tupelo that tower over the alligators and brave kayakers. In Gatesville, you pick up N.C. 37 to N.C. 32, which rolls by Rocky Hock on its way to Edenton, the historic port on the Albemarle River, which was the site of North Carolina's first permanent English settlement and served as the capital city for twenty-one years, beginning in 1722.

On the long ride, we first stop at a fruit stand in Littleton, near Lake Gaston. The cantaloupes for sale there are from South Carolina. We pass on them and continue through bean and tobacco fields and an occasional solar farm, virtually the only nod to the future on this route. Queen Anne's lace is growing madly in the ditches, the flat white crowns bobbing in the wind, waving us on. In town after town, there seem to be more funeral homes than fruit stands. It is July, so front porches are festooned with American flags. Rocking chairs facing the road sit empty in the noonday heat. In the little town of Conway, on the far side of Roanoke Rapids in Northampton County, the corn rows run all the way into town and up to the sidewalk on Main Street. Only handsome white farmhouses and storefronts interrupt the dominance of crops in that town.

This part of North Carolina still holds so many traces of the past, seen in the architecture of the houses and churches and in the roadside offerings: chair caning, peanuts, fresh rockfish (the local name for striped bass). Historical markers appear every few miles telling tales of past travelers — soldiers, Indians, revolutionaries, horse breeders, and civil rights leaders.

After driving for more than two hours, we finally arrive at Jasper Evans's spread in Rocky Hock. Three inches of rain fell the night before, and puddles are still glinting in the afternoon sun around his outbuildings. The Chowan River is close by, though the lay of the land prevents a direct view of the water. Evans's biggest crops, we learn, are cotton, soybeans, and peanuts, but he has also planted twenty-five acres of sweet corn, twenty-eight acres of watermelon, and ten acres of cantaloupe for this season. He grows the hybrid Athena cantaloupe; the soil here, he says, is what makes his melons extra-sweet. The dirt is black, with veins of sandy white minerals interspersed.

Inside Evans's office, purple crepe paper hangs from a ceiling fan and twirls as the fan turns. Black balloons that have lost their lift drift around the edges of the room on the floor.

"Excuse the decorations," Evans says. "My wife, sister, and the kids surprised me the other day. It was a big birthday." He shakes his head, sheepish. "I just turned fifty."

His son, Spencer, wearing racecar-driver sunglasses, comes in behind us. He grins with pleasure as his father recounts the party. At twenty-two, and two years out of North Carolina State University's Agricultural Institute, where he studied applied agricultural science, Spencer represents the fourth generation of Rocky Hock melon growers in the Evans family. His sister is studying at Wake Tech in Raleigh, with hopes of eventually earning a veterinary degree at N.C. State.

Jasper's grandfather Zachariah Trotman Evans bought land and built a house here in 1900. He and his wife, Effie Louise White Evans, had twelve children — six boys and six girls.

"Daddy was the baby and ended up with the homeplace," Evans says. Jasper's father, Alvin Jasper Evans Sr., is gone, but two of his sisters are still living, one in Virginia and the other ten miles down the road. "Aunt Eleanor is in her late eighties and still drives," Evans tells us. "I expect she'll be pulling in the driveway to get her cantaloupes any day now. We're just a few days away from the start of the harvest."

Like Richard Holtzmann, Jasper Evans will not pick his melons until they are ripe. "The net has to be thick — no bald spots," he says. "The tighter the pattern, the better. We wait until they're breaking yellow to pull them, and if they're ready, the vine will pop right off. You don't have to cut them loose."

Evans works six days a week, never on Sundays. As a result of that one day of rest, the beginning of each new harvest week has come to be called "Yellow Monday" by his crew. They pull the most melons on Mondays. During the three weeks at the peak, they will harvest 4,000 to 5,000 cantaloupes per day, he says. Evans started the seeds in a greenhouse and planted the first crop on 18 March. The second crop he seeded a month later directly into the field.

"We can't do this without bees," Evans explains. He rents sixteen hives for $1,000 and puts them at the far end of his field. "The bees pollinate the crops, and then the beekeeper comes and gets them and takes them somewhere else to keep working."

Out in the yard we meet Evans's crew chief, a man who has worked with the family in these fields for fifty-two years, even before Jasper was born. Edward Earl Leary, or Eel as he is fondly known, is a tall, dark-skinned man who wears bright gold jewelry around his neck, even in the field. He has a flamboyant and youthful presence. His nine children and many more grandchildren have all taken a turn working on his crews over the years. Eel sells used cars in the off-season, and, ever entrepreneurial, this year he is launching a fruit stand on N.C. 32, not far from his house. "Come see me," he says.

Eel shows us the "crow cannon," a four-foot metal tube attached to a propane tank. A timer sets off an electric spark that ignites the propane to make an ear-splitting boom about once an hour. "You got to move it around the field or the crows get used to it," Eel says. "A crow will peck a hole in a melon and then leave it. That will ruin a cantaloupe, but if they peck into a young watermelon, that melon will heal itself back up!"

Evans says he is one of the last farmers in the area to hire local folks exclusively for the weeding and hand-harvesting of his melons. He does not want all the paperwork and regulations that come with hiring migrant workers. He is proud of providing jobs for his neighbors. "Everybody in this area at one time or another has worked in the fields. It's a rite of passage," he says.

Lifting melons, especially watermelons, is backbreaking labor. "One thing about it," Evans says, "whatever job a young person gets after doing this work is going to seem like a breeze."

It takes twenty to twenty-five people to handle Evans's melon crop at harvest. "Eel gets a few older people for wisdom, and the rest are young

Edward Earl Leary, Spencer Evans, and Spencer's father, Jasper Evans, prepare to lead the team that will harvest the Rocky Hock cantaloupes on the A. J. Evans and Son Produce Farm near Edenton.

people for strength," he says. Eel explains that the crew works in teams of three — one to pull the melons, one to pass them, and one on the edge of the row to load the melons into the field wagons. Evans grows all his melons on black plastic.

"We start harvesting at seven in the morning, and we all work until dark," he says, "sorting and crating. I'm about the only one around here that don't run the melons through a washer."

Evans's melons are GAP (Good Agricultural Practices)-certified, meaning that he periodically submits to a voluntary audit of his production, handling, packing, and storing practices by the U.S. Department of Agriculture. "You know, any time there is a health issue with cantaloupe, they come back to the farmer first," he says. He is always mindful of food safety and the potential for bacteria.

Once a wagon is loaded in the field, the cantaloupes are brought back to the shed. They are graded, put in bins, and stored in the air-conditioned barn, which he shows us on the way back to his much cooler office. Each cantaloupe is given a lot number, he says, but there is no way to tell if the melons will be cared for properly when they leave his farm. Commingling cantaloupes from different farms at the point of sale is illegal, but it does happen, even in grocery stores, he says. And because of the growing buzz about the flavorful melons from this part of North Carolina, there are cantaloupes already on the market labeled "Rocky Hock," but they are not authentic, Evans says.

"There are melons with that name out there right now, and nobody's started pulling them here. The season is late this year." Evans smiles and wrinkles form around his striking green eyes. Unlike the Ridgeway farmers, the growers in this area never got around to registering the Rocky Hock name, which derives from a nearby creek. The name, Evans believes, is of Indian origin.

Some of Evans's neighbors and relatives ship their Rocky Hock cantaloupes and watermelons to "Lib City," as he calls Elizabeth City, less than thirty miles east. Some ship to produce stands along the Outer Banks. Almost all of Evans's cantaloupes, however, go to the Wholesale Produce Terminal Market in Baltimore.

"We have reliable customers who wait there for my truck to pull in. They know ours by history and taste," he says.

He also gives a good many cantaloupes away. "My father always said that for every melon you give away, you'll sell two tomorrow. That's how we operate."

For his own consumption, Evans prefers the medium-size cantaloupe. "When they get too big, they lose flavor," he says.

I ask him if he ever salts his melons to enhance the sweetness. (This was something my aunt used to do with watermelon, and I later discovered that putting salt on the sourest grapefruit will also sweeten it dramatically.)

Evans admits he does apply salt once in while "for something different." It was not a practice he grew up with but something he learned from the truckers who take his crop up the coast to Maryland. I also learned that some people in North Carolina grew up applying black pepper to cantaloupe, and it's possible to find internet recipes that call for the application of pepper on the fruit. That was totally new to me.

Though the cantaloupe season is relatively short, Evans's cotton and peanut harvest will keep him busy until Thanksgiving, he says. Then he gets a break to pursue his other passion—bow hunting. Several enormous bow cases sit next to the filing cabinets in his office. A collection of turkey tails, fanned out, is sitting in a corner. "I never pick up a gun any more," he says. Bears, deer, and wild turkeys are plentiful in the area.

We say goodbye and thank Jasper Evans, promising to return to sample his melons before the end of the harvest.

* * * * * * * * * * * *

The sixteenth of July is festival day in Ridgeway this year. Traffic cones were set out early in the morning to discourage parking along the main highway. Instead, visitors are directed down a side road to a parking area behind the festivities.

An enormous slice of cantaloupe carved from wood and painted bright orange sits in the grass like a clown's oversized grin. Children are already jumping in an inflatable playhouse. Large cardboard cartons of cantaloupe are set out on slats in front of the fire station. Food tents are going up all around the perimeter of the grounds. We pass it all by.

Down the road about a mile, cars are parked on the shoulder, bumper to bumper, in front of Richard Holtzmann's produce stand. We park and cross the busy highway carefully. People—mostly older folks—mill about asking after his dad, and Richard repeats the story he told us about his father's continuing decline. They thump and sniff the melons, then chat with Richard's sister, Linda, and Uncle Willie. The harvest has finally started in earnest, and those in the know are here to get the first taste of the short season, clearly a significant ritual imprinted on them early in life.

We buy three Ridgeway cantaloupes—small, medium, and one a bit larger. Richard tells us to wait a couple of days on the bigger one. He is busy, moving back and forth to refill his stand with melons and making change. He introduces us to his family. More cars stop. The crowd grows.

Back home, the Ridgeway melons chilled, we scrub the medium-size one down and slice into it. The rind is surprisingly thin, the flesh deeply colored, the seeds plentiful in the middle cavity.

Oddly, at first bite the taste reminds me of a banana Popsicle—my favorite treat as a child. Tasting it is like stepping into a time machine, as if I just got off my bike at the little store we used to visit at the beach. I would reach deep into the cooler and bring up the wax-paper-wrapped chunks of ice with the two wooden sticks to hold onto while eating. Fishing among the orange, grape, and cherry, I'd pray there would be a banana one. If I got lucky, when I peeled off the icy paper, the yellow Popsicle itself would frost up in the warm air before it began to melt. Then the first lick and the first bite. So impossibly sweet and cold. All of this comes back in a flash.

Returning to the present moment in the kitchen, I realize that maybe it is the degree of sweetness in this cantaloupe that almost seems unnatural, as it surely was in those Popsicles. The melon melts between my teeth, turning to liquid. I swallow, and the aftertaste is profoundly earthy in the best possible way.

Now I am seeing Richard Holtzmann's bright green plants, the yellow blossoms, the red dirt. This melon is fundamentally of the earth and sun, which, with just the right amount of water, is miraculously spun into a meaty sugar.

It will take several of the small slices to satisfy the infatuation. I vow never again to eat the pale cantaloupe on a restaurant breakfast plate or settle for the hard, chewy crescents on a buffet spread.

It's another Yellow Monday in Rocky Hock—maybe the last one of the season, because it is actually the first day of August. Donna can't come on this quick trip today, so I am traveling alone. After a drive of several cloudy hours, a gentle rain begins to wash the windshield of the car right when I pull off N.C. 32 onto Rocky Hock Road. As far as I can see in one direction, the cotton is blooming, waist high. Peanut plants on the other side of the road are low and lush in their mounded rows. A line of crows flies overhead, scouting the crops. A big-wheeled truck up ahead is rolling alongside a small phalanx of watermelon pickers, who seem oblivious of the rain as they make their way up a wide row, hefting and pitching green-striped melons the size of well-fed toddlers into the waiting arms of workers in the truck.

When I finally pull into Jasper Evans's yard, I park in front of an open wagon with a couple dozen nice-sized watermelons in view—a tacit sign to passersby that he is selling fruit today—but nary a cantaloupe is in sight. I throw on my raincoat and Evans comes out to meet me halfway across the yard. He is more deeply tanned than he was on our last visit. The crew behind him is just now heading out to the melon shed, Eel in the lead. Eel is wearing his usual gold chains and white undershirt. A broad-brimmed straw hat is cocked back on his head. The men and women with him look fit and are elbowing each other, laughing. Evans explains that they are all giddy from the rain. Even he is relieved. He had set up the tractor to spray the peanuts this morning, but the big green John Deere sits idle beside the garage. It is eleven o'clock in the morning, and the rain feels like a whispered blessing. We step under the roof of the garage.

"I came for some cantaloupe to sample," I say, a little nervous that I might be too late.

"We've still got a few," Evans says. "A man came earlier this morning wanting thirty. We had to go down a whole row to get that many." He tells me how brutal the week before had been. Every day, the heat index—the combination of heat and humidity—was hovering around 110 degrees. "We pulled every day until real late," he says. "For a good three weeks up to now we pulled close to forty bins a day—exactly 110 count per bin. They were really good-sized cantaloupes."

Working six days a week with more than 4,000 melons pulled in a day, the crew must have harvested some 72,000 cantaloupes, I figure.

We step into the outer office and Evans's son, Spencer, is sprawled in a rolling chair, his long legs stretching under the desk, his back nearly parallel to the floor. He looks tired. He bolts upright as we enter and grabs a Pepsi can on the desk. He takes a long swig. A friend about Spencer's age is also hanging out, avoiding the rain outside. Evans asks the two of them to take his truck and go find a couple of cantaloupes for me. "You might have to go all the way to the other end of the field," he says. Spencer hurls himself out of the chair, all gangly limbs, and grabs the truck keys. I smile at him and shrug, sorry to send him on such a mission in the drizzle.

Evans warns me that the cantaloupes that are left really baked in the heat last week. "They began to ripen very quickly," he says. "I'm not sure they're quite as sweet as they were a couple weeks ago. Everybody has said the taste is good, though. No complaints."

"How is Eel's produce stand coming along?" I ask. "I think I passed it on the way in on N.C. 32." It looked like a brand-new metal shed with tilted boxes of produce set like an apron around the building.

"Yep, that's it. He's done well," Evans says. "He gets just enough produce from me for the day, not too much — corn and melons — and he sells out every afternoon."

I ask Evans if his aunt Eleanor has been by to get her melons. He grins. He says she comes by in her big car and doesn't even get out anymore. They have a routine. "She just pulls in the yard, leaves the engine running, and pops the trunk from inside the car. I load in the melons, close the trunk, and then she lets her window down and hands me a pie. She always feels like she has to give me something."

"What kind of pie?" I ask.

"Lemon," he says. "She knows that's my favorite."

•　•　•　•　•　•　•　•　•　•　•　•

Three hours later, back home in Carrboro, I wash one of the three cantaloupes Evans gave me and put the hefty seedless watermelon he also loaded in my car into the fridge to chill. I could smell the cantaloupes from the moment Spencer approached us from the field. Driving home, they perfumed the car, nestled together like giant yellow eggs on the back seat with the watermelon beside them, steady as a rock.

Ripened Athena melons are intensely yellow, unlike the Ridgeways, which have a rougher netting that stays brownish and raised on the surface of the rind. The Rocky Hock cantaloupes are twice the size of the Ridgeways. They thump like a gallon jug of water. The rind is similarly thin to the Ridgeways — definitely ripe to the very edge.

I slice up a half of the Rocky Hock into crescents. Its perfume is intoxicating. The slices seem so big compared to the dainty Ridgeway portions we consumed two weeks ago. The satisfying sweetness of this melon, however, is more in the finish, not in the first taste. To me, the water and earthiness seem to precede the sweetness that emerges at the back of the palate. I refrigerate the other two melons for tomorrow. Jasper Evans may be right that these melons cooked a little too long in last week's sun — hence the perfume but not quite the intensity of taste.

The next day, for good measure, I run to King's Red and White grocery in Durham to buy a couple more of Richard Holtzmann's Ridgeways, which, as he promised, are there, set out in three rickety old cantaloupe crates at the entrance to the store's exceptional produce section. The little melons look battered compared to the larger and more pristine Athenas (also from a local grower) that are mounded up in a cardboard bin down the way. Watermelons circle the edges of the linoleum floor with bright orange price stickers. King's even has early-crop scuppernong and muscadine grapes (the subject of chapter 9) from down east. This store sells everything: pig's feet, chicken gizzards, chitterlings, streak o'lean, liver mush, and old-fashioned hoop cheese. It is a marvelous throwback to the mom-and-pop grocery stores I remember from forty years ago in Durham.

I select two Ridgeways, a bag of fresh-shelled lady peas, and a bag of local pink-eyed peas that were sitting on crushed ice in a portable cooler. Arms full, I head for the checkout. It is time at last for the ultimate taste comparison.

Side by side on a plate, the two cantaloupe slices look like Mutt and Jeff — the little Ridgeway and the muscular Rocky Hock. Tasting both, my first impression stands. The Ridgeway seems sweeter, but with successive tastings I realize that it is more about the melons' size. The Rocky Hock has so much more real estate. It is thicker, so there's more melon. It seems less sweet the farther away you get from the melon's interior. However, when I take my spoon and scoop out the first quarter inch of the Rocky Hock slice, right where the seeds had been nesting, it is definitely sweeter than a whole bite of the Ridgeway. The most intense sweetness seems to lie in the very middle of the melon. Because they ripen from the center outward, Richard Holtzmann's contention that smaller melons are sweeter makes perfect sense. This taste testing could be a good activity with children, having them sample the cantaloupe from the middle outward toward the rind and judge the degree of sweetness.

My friends Dawn and Jim Shamp agree to taste the two kinds of cantaloupes before our dinner together that night. I do not tell them which is which. Jim is intrigued by the Rocky Hock's perfume. "If you blindfolded me and put my nose in this melon, I'd swear it was a watermelon," he says.

Dawn says she thought she'd prefer the small one — the Ridgeway — but ultimately favors the Rocky Hock for its "pockets of sweetness and clean texture." With a straight face Jim calls it "smoky and complex." We catch ourselves standing around the kitchen island, passing melon slices and sniffing them deeply, a tableau of would-be gourmands acting like we're on some food show. We burst out laughing.

Either melon is a winner. On the one hand, the Rocky Hock is firmer — almost crisp, you might say — and yields a serving large enough to handle a wide blanket of prosciutto draped over each wedge to make a beautiful platter. On the other hand, you could eat an entire Ridgeway melon in one sitting while imagining yourself in the chic, 1930s elegance of the Waldorf-Astoria, that foodie paradise that was famous nearly a hundred years before the term "foodie" was coined. Sadly, the birthplace of Waldorf salad, veal Oscar, the Rob Roy cocktail, and eggs Benedict is now being transformed into condominiums, its restaurants closed, at least for a time. But you can still taste the little Carolina cantaloupe — the Pride of Ridgeway that the Waldorf once served. Try one while you still can and make your own judgment.

August

Figs

LEARNING TO RECOGNIZE A PARTICULAR SCENT IS LIKE LEARNING TO read. When you see words on a page, you can't avoid reading them once you know how. So it is in late spring when I round the corner of the condo where I live. I smell the fig tree, but I didn't always know what that subtle, sweet fragrance wafting through the garden was. I didn't even notice it for several years, but now I do.

I learned the fragrance of fig after my friend the old-time music legend Alice Gerrard posted her recipe for fig leaf tea online. It's simple: Pick some fig leaves, cut them into strips, pour boiling water over them, let them steep, and strain. The elixir is delicious. The leaves have their own unforgettable scent and flavor, long before and after the fruits ripen. What I still didn't know, however, was that even though my particular fig tree makes a most pleasant tea, not all of them do. More on that topic to come.

Every time I've moved to a new house as an adult, I've put in a vegetable garden and planted a fig tree. The gardens have always done well, but not until I landed in Carrboro had a single fig plant survived in my care. I bought the little twig in a gallon pot at the Carrboro Farmers' Market. I planted it close — too close — to the southwest corner of my two-story condominium. To say it has been happy there is an understatement.

Of course, now I discover from the agricultural gurus of Clemson University that I must not have been paying attention all those other times I planted figs. "When it comes to growing homegrown fruit," their website says, "nothing could be easier than figs. Cultivated for thousands of years, figs have few demands on their caregivers."

Embarrassing. But at least I finally got one planting right. Over the first four days of August this year, I harvested all the figs I could reach, pulling the higher limbs down toward me with a boat hook. I've gathered five gallons already, with probably twice that quantity yet to ripen on the lower limbs.

I cede the highest branches to the birds and squirrels, and they've already made a mess under the tree. Shredded, sticky fig pieces are strewn on the ground and all over the nano-patio, as I call it — the four-by-six-foot rectangle of concrete pavers where a breakfast table and two metal chairs are now quite amply shaded by the fig.

My fig is in its tenth year. It's nearly twenty-five feet tall, and its spread is equally wide along the south side of the house. My friend Jim Harb took one look at this fig tree two years ago and said, "Oh, no. No!" Harb is a former chef who has cooked in two well-known French restaurants, including Chapel Hill's La Residence. Though he was born in Tennessee, he is from a long line of fig-growing sages from Palestine and Syria. He just kept shaking his head, staring up into the branches of my tree.

"I have pruned it and pruned it again," I told him. He was aghast at the amount of fruit that is so difficult to reach.

My *Ficus carica* is of the "Celeste" variety and is hardy in Zones 7–10. It is not meant to be a shrub. The plant guide I consulted says this variety will grow from fifteen to twenty feet in height and spread, so I'm not *that* far off. I begin each season by harvesting no more than a handful of figs in June. These early figs are called the breba crop, which forms on old growth limbs. The main crop comes in the heat of August, on new growth.

My fig's expansion over the years has limited the view from my living room window when the leaves fill out, but I can also monitor the lower limbs from indoors when they shake with the weight of a squirrel, crow, or catbird. If the critters come too low in the tree, dipping into what I consider my share of the fruit, I rap on the window, which also gets Nebo barking. It's our August routine.

I have learned that figs also attract turtles, foxes, and, a few years ago, a scruffy little pocketbook dog I immediately nicknamed Figaro. (I gave him a bath while Nebo stayed with my mother in the condo next door, unaware of the presence of any canine competition. Then Figaro's people came looking for him, and it turned out his real name was Schwartz.)

A while later, still smarting from Jim Harb's assessment that I'd let the tree grow too tall and was surrendering too much fruit to the birds, I tried to rig an aerial fig picker. I used the special telescoping pole that I have to change the recessed light bulbs in the high ceiling of my kitchen. I clipped a single-edge razor blade — sharp side facing inward — onto the lip of the small basket that is designed to keep the burned-out light bulb from crashing to the floor once unscrewed. I thought that if I could raise this contraption and position the basket under one fig at a time, a swift twist to the pole would slice the fig at the stem. The fig would then gently drop into the basket for easy retrieval. Voilà!

It worked only once without the razor blade either coming loose and flying down into the mulch perilously close to my bare toes in flip-flops or slicing into the wide middle of the few figs that I successfully managed to wrangle into the basket. I hate to think what it looked like to my neighbor, Jaime, who might have seen me from his upstairs window that Sunday morning: me jousting at the fig tree with a twelve-foot pole painted safety yellow.

Apparently, the only fruit more perishable than the fig is the raspberry. But figs, says British food scholar and literary historian David C. Sutton, are far and away the most succulent and tempting of all fruits. Fresh figs, because of their fragility, were seen in ancient societies as a rare luxury, worthy of religious worship. Dried figs, then and now, are considered the food of the masses. They keep well and are good nourishment in desperate winter. Dried figs in great heaping piles are usually sold in street markets around the world at a price much, much lower than fresh figs. Sutton claims that only 3 percent of the global consumption of figs is eaten fresh. The rest are dried, canned, or bottled.

Figs are prehistoric. Fossil figs that date back more than 2.6 million years have been found in France and Italy. Archeologists have also found intact figs left as funerary food in Egyptian and Turkish tombs. Near Jericho, in the West Bank, figs were discovered in an 11,400-year-old house, leading a Harvard anthropologist to posit that this fruit was cultivated centuries before humans began planting grains for bread.

Before their domestication, however, wild figs — which depended on pollination by a special wasp — flourished, and communities grew up around them. When people observed that fig branches, stuck into the ground, would sometimes develop into new trees, they began breeding the trees and taking the fruit with them as sustenance as they migrated to Africa, Asia, and beyond. Figs will also sprout from seeds, and so they spread worldwide through the dung of mammals, including humans. Alexander the Great's marching army reportedly carried dried figs in their pouches as a substitute for bread.

Figs figure prominently in Greek and Roman mythology. In one Greek story, mother earth Gaia turned her son Sykeus into a fig tree to protect him from the lighting bolts of Zeus, giving rise to the belief that fig trees could protect us against lightning. According to historian Christopher Cumo, figs ranked second only to the grape in the wild parades that honored Bacchus, the Roman god of agriculture and wine. After celebrants carrying grapes and figs led the parade, all the other fruits followed in lower status. The Romans believed that the fig was a gift from Bacchus, and ever since, figs have been pressed into service in the making of wines, brandies, and liqueurs.

Figs are often depicted in ancient Egyptian imagery. Cleopatra committed suicide by snakebite, and the asp was supposedly delivered to her in a basket of figs, her favorite fruit.

The prophet Muhammad said, "If I should wish one fruit brought to paradise, it would certainly be the fig." In Judaism, sitting under a fig tree is associated with the devout study of the Hebrew Torah. Buddha obtained enlightenment under the bodhi tree, a sacred fig (*Ficus religiosa*). A number of biblical authorities have even argued that the forbidden fruit in the Genesis story was actually a fig, not an apple.

"The Bible is clear that there were fig trees in the Garden of Eden; apples are not mentioned," David Sutton argues in his excellent global history of the fig. "Figs are the fruit of temptation, lusciously alluring." While apples do grow in the cradle of civilization, Sutton concludes, "they are rare, small, and untempting." (Others have suggested that the forbidden fruit might have been a pomegranate or a citron.)

The first figs to arrive in North America came with the Spanish conquistadors to the Caribbean in 1520. Greek immigrants planted figs in Florida as early as 1763. Later in the same decade, Spanish missionaries brought figs to California, where they are still grown in great quantities. It was in this same general era that newcomers to North Carolina's Portsmouth Island, a settlement authorized by the Colonial Assembly in 1753, likely began planting figs. Portsmouth was "the first and for many years the largest settlement on the Outer Banks," writes University of North Carolina botanist C. John Burk, who also reports that locals at the time of his investigation of island flora in 1959 "believed the *ficus* to be a native."

The founders of the United States were proponents of both wigs and figs. George Washington planted fig trees at Mount Vernon. Thomas Jefferson was so enamored of the figs that he sampled on a trip to France that he brought home several plants of the Marseilles variety. According to Peter J. Hatch, a former director of the gardens and grounds at Monticello, Jefferson planted his figs alongside a terrace below a south-facing wall adjacent to the kitchen garden. The terrace became, Hatch writes, "a popular site for Jefferson-escorted tours of the landscape. It also created a warm microclimate that, when compounded with the unusual hardiness of the Marseilles, gave the Monticello figs a reputation for unusual fruitfulness." Some of the descendants of the original fig trees planted at Monticello, Mount Vernon, Williamsburg, and Jamestown are still growing, Hatch says. (Though vulnerable to weather damage, fig trees can survive a long time, rising out of the ground after being laid low by extreme cold spells.)

Despite the enthusiasm of early planters in the United States, the love of figs has never been universal. The once-popular expressions "I don't give a fig" or "That's not worth a fig" likely came from those who viewed figs as a lowly fruit. Other evidence suggests that the fig had a salacious connotation. Peter Hatch reports that Jefferson's friend and frequent guest at Monticello Margaret Bayard Smith, who was a prominent novelist and biographer living in the nation's capital, told her staff that she wanted to serve figs to her guests for dessert one evening. A prominent waiter in Washington told her, "Oh no, ma'am, they are quite vulgar." In the same era, says Hatch, the publication *The American Farmer* found it necessary to counter such claims by using the adjective "wholesome" as often as possible when describing the fruit.

Figs are actually flowers that grow inward, and their insides are usually a deep red that's quite juicy. Their texture is fleshy and laced with seeds smaller than a poppy's. D. H. Lawrence wrote about their sensual appeal in the poem "Fig" in 1924, calling them "a fruit like a ripe womb." But figs unopened can also suggest male parts.

Coarse gestures have a long association with the fig. In Italy, poking a plump thumb between two fingers and raising the fist abruptly is a fig-inspired salute that is apparently comparable to giving someone the finger on this side of the Atlantic.

In my experience, picking figs does lead the mind to wander and make associations. Figs are elusive. It takes time to find them. To see all of the ripe figs on a given limb, you must approach the tree from many angles, almost like looking up a skirt. The fruit hides, nestling up under the big leaves like the private parts that the fig leaves in the Bible were used to cover.

At the time of full fruit, fig leaves are large, and their undersides are hairy, even scratchy. Picking figs is hazardous. They can make the skin itch, and though a fig's limber branches will bend handily, they'll also slap you in the face if you're not careful to let them go gently.

The ripe fruit is usually sticky with latex—a milky substance that is difficult to wash off and can cause an allergic skin reaction. Fig latex, or ficin, is a protein-degrading enzyme that discourages worms by literally dissolving them! Fig latex has been said to be effective in removing warts and boils and can even be used to curdle milk for the making of cheese. This same property can cause discomfort to the hands as the latex works on the protein in the skin, at least in those who have this allergic reaction. The degree of allergy may also be determined by the variety of fig, some say. Both my thumbs at this moment, after several days of fig picking, feel hot and sore, almost as if I had poked splinters under my nails.

Nevertheless, harvesting figs this time of year must go on at least once and sometimes twice a day to secure the fruit at the best possible moment. In the case of my Celeste, I have found that the figs can be picked almost at first blush—when a pink wash tints the skin and the surface texture of the little bulb wrinkles as if there might be blood vessels just beneath the skin.

If they are hard to the touch, I leave them, but if they have begun to soften and droop downward, curving at the stem, I will pick them. Letting figs go to their most extreme ripened state—which is manifest as a deep purplish/brown hue in the Celeste fig—runs the risk that they'll turn to a mushy jam in the hand.

Jim Harb rejects my preference to pick them a little early. He believes that not letting a fig go to its fully ripened state is "akin to a sin." But others will tell you that the harvest can be war. In their full color, figs are prone to the pecks of predators. My Celeste is assaulted daily. Harb says this is not necessarily true with other varieties of figs. He claims his Kadota fig is never bothered. Perhaps that is because Kadotas stay green even when they are ripe.

My Celeste figs will also split from the battery of a heavy rainfall—not good because of the possibility of bacteria forming in the cracks. Too much rainfall can also lead to a watery taste, says Harb.

Regardless of the timing, figs can be harvested only one at a time. The work is arduous and rather Zen-like—a contemplative practice that cannot be rushed. Figs demand that each be handled individually. Trying to hold one fig in the palm while pulling another with the free fingers of the same hand will usually damage both figs.

I have experimented over the years, picking my figs soon after the latex starts weeping from the fat end of the little punching bag with its pink eye on the bottom. Picked in this state and given a day to rest, they will be near perfect to eat. However, letting them rest on the countertop also leads to a bit of shrinkage: the Celestes seem to lose discernible mass and sheen over twenty-four hours.

Figs can last in the refrigerator for several days, but the notion of refrigeration horrifies Jim Harb. He argues that figs are best consumed immediately or frozen on a tray for about an hour and then bagged in the freezer for later use in smoothies or to make preserves. They can also be thawed and cooked down as a topping for yogurt or pancakes or as an ingredient in breads or cakes.

But how many fresh figs can one person consume? The best solution to me is to give some away in the moment, which is especially gratifying when I'm sharing with neophytes. My stepsister, for example, is a child of the convenience foods fifties like me. By age sixty, the only figs she'd ever tasted were in Fig Newtons. When she came to visit last year, she finally tried the real fruit, plucked fresh from my Celeste. "Who knew?" she said and asked for more.

                •   •   •   •   •   •   •   •   •   •   •

To make fig preserves you need only figs, sugar, lemon juice (some use the zest, too), and the patience required for slow cooking. Whatever else you add is up to your imagination. Today Donna Campbell is in the kitchen making two batches of fig preserves—one with rosemary and the other with thyme. The former is quite pungent, great on pork roast or on biscuits with ham at breakfast. The addition of thyme for the second batch is an experiment. I planted two kinds of thyme this year—one in a pot and the other in the ground near the fig tree. I kept stepping on this ground cover and brushing by the pot while pulling ripe figs. The scent of thyme and figs was seductive, and as it turned out, it conveys well in the preserves.

Now I discover in Sutton's fig history that the Sumerians had a medical prescription calling for a combination of figs, thyme, and pears from around 2750 BC. Whatever health benefits may accrue from this year's preserves, I welcome.

At my request, my mountain neighbors Alvis Smith and Dennis Williams whipped up some fig ice cream from this year's crop that was subtle and satisfying, though I think I could have given them a few more figs than the two cups called for in their recipe.

Besides eating them fresh, however, my favorite preparation involves figs sliced in half, stem to bottom, and laid out in a Pyrex dish, each topped with a tiny rag of prosciutto, a sprinkling of fresh Parmigiano-Reggiano, and a port wine reduction drizzled over all. Broil them until the cheese is melted and the prosciutto is crispy, and you have an elegant appetizer.

Jim Harb, however, goes me one better: He mixes goat cheese and basil to stuff inside his large brown turkey figs and tops them off with a drizzle of Cointreau and honey. He then wraps each fig in a thin strip of Benton's Tennessee bacon with the excess fat trimmed off. He enfolds each fig in a grape leaf, secures it with twine, and grills the little packets until the grape leaves are charred and can be unwrapped and removed. Sublime.

My Celeste figs are simply not big enough for stuffing. At a recent gathering, I brought some for Harb to sample. He confirmed that they are too small for his recipe, but I didn't understand how very small they were until I went to Ocracoke Island, a popular destination in the chain of North Carolina's Outer Banks. There I realized how much I still have to learn about the amazing variety and sizes of figs.

● ● ● ● ● ● ● ● ● ● ● ●

Donna and I spent the night on the mainland in Beaufort on our way to catch the Cedar Island Ferry to Ocracoke. We managed to get a table at Aqua, a restaurant with one of the most interesting menus in the village. In the midst of our supper, I asked the restaurant's manager, Kim Hopper, why there were no fig dishes on the menu that night, explaining that we were headed to Ocracoke the next morning for the fig festival. Hopper was un-certain about sourcing figs in Beaufort, but in her neighborhood across the bridge in Morehead City, she said, the fig bushes were thriving. She had al-ready helped herself to more than a few samples this season.

Filching figs when they are plentiful is a time-honored if somewhat risky practice in these parts. Hopper lives in the Promise' Land, a historic water-front neighborhood of about four square blocks near the heart of Morehead City's restaurant district. In 1899, after a hurricane nearly destroyed the Outer Banks fishing village of Diamond City (now part of the Cape Lookout National Seashore), the Bankers moved their homes piece by piece on boats to the Morehead mainland. Their modest cottages, many now beautifully re-stored, are landscaped with fig bushes of the same vintage as Diamond City.

This phenomenon of early coastal residents migrating with fig cuttings also likely occurred on Ocracoke, when ship pilots and their families, some from Portsmouth Island—the aforementioned earliest settlement—began relocating to Ocracoke to engage in the emergent shipping trade, in the late 1700s.

The next morning it was hot as a griddle on the deck for the two-and-a-half-hour ferry ride from Cedar Island to Ocracoke. The breeze was fickle—starting and stalling. We sweated our way across the miles.

Unincorporated Ocracoke Island occupies nearly ten square miles and has about a thousand full-time residents. According to Ocracoke oral historian and author Alton Ballance, the name comes from the Woccon Indians, a tribe that lived near the Neuse River but came to hunt and fish on the island they called Wokokkon.

The first English people came ashore on the island after hitting a sandbar in Ocracoke Inlet (as the ferries still do occasionally). Much is still made here, mostly for the benefit of children, of the pirate Blackbeard's fondness for the marshy hideouts along the sound side of the island. Blackbeard met his grisly end in Ocracoke Inlet in 1718.

Tourism and commercial fishing are the main activities of the present day, and in an effort to promote one of its most unusual assets to visitors, Ocracoke recently created an annual August fig festival to celebrate the fruit that grows like gangbusters here.

"I've been a plant person all my life," Chester Lynn told an audience of a dozen souls brave enough to bake in the afternoon sun to hear his fig talk outside the Community Store on the first day of the 2016 festival. "I grafted a rose of Sharon when I was ten years old. Later on, I took to potting some of the figs we have here to see if I could sell them. They went fast, so I kept selling them." (Some 300 plants a year, he later told us).

"Then what I done," Chester continued, "I took some paper and set down what's on Ocracoke. I counted fourteen varieties of figs—some fruit early, some now, some late."

In his late fifties, Lynn is an antiques dealer and one of only two florists on Ocracoke. He has also earned the distinction of being the island's foremost fig expert. He drew laughter when he explained that the late figs are a serious hazard to islanders. "If they don't ripen until October, you got to get through hurricane season with them." (Spoken in his island brogue, "hurricane" sounds like "herricun.") "If we have a storm, you got to worry about them little green balls flying off the bush and through your windows," he said.

Lynn is the grandson of George O'Neil, who captained the island's legendary mail boat, *Aleta*. Working with the Ocracoke Historical Society, Lynn has verified the long presence of fig trees, both here and on Portsmouth Island. He told the audience about a letter he came upon, written by John Gray Blount to John Wallace, the co-owners of Shell Castle Island, a trade and shipping enterprise established at Ocracoke Inlet in 1789. During the company's startup phase, one man wrote to the other to report that he would not be able to return to the area "until fig season" — proof enough, says Lynn, that figs were important here from the beginning of postcolonial commerce. Lynn also said that on Portsmouth Island, the residents tended to prefer their fig preserves flavored with cloves; Lynn prefers cinnamon in his. (The last inhabitants of Portsmouth left the island in 1971.)

"My mother would roll fresh figs in a bowl of shaved chocolate or coconut and call it candy," he went on. "That's what we got on the island when we didn't have any other kind of sweet." He recalled one fig tree that was large enough to have a porch swing hung from its branches. "We'd push that swing and shake it to get bombed by the figs." He took on a mischievous look. Lynn also told his audience about the fig tree in the middle of his aunt Grodie's chicken pen. "Them brown egg layers fertilized her fig tree."

"And another thing," Lynn said. "We always wore long sleeves to pick figs, because that fig syrup will break you out! I made a mistake and put a couple of figs in my shirt pocket the other day and I got a rash on my breast," he said, patting his chest.

I was pleased to learn that Lynn, like me, is a pragmatist when it comes to harvesting his figs. Pointing to a bowl of enormous figs on the table in front of him (a variety called pound figs, because of their size), Lynn said, "I had to pull these early, because me and a mockingbird was having a fight, and it was either I pick 'em or he'd have 'em." The pound figs were a marvel. One was large enough to cover the palm of my hand, and if it had been made of lead, it would have weighed well more than a pound.

"Pound figs was popular here," Lynn went on. "It didn't take so many to fill a pot." He estimates that some of the pound fig bushes on the island are 200 years old, but many, he said, have been cut down.

"Used to be, everybody's fish-cleaning bench was near a fig tree in their yard," he said. "People throwed cleanings from the fish to fertilize the fig tree. That's why our figs are so healthy." Lynn argued that if an Ocracoke fig tree

Lifetime Ocracoke Islander Chester Lynn sits in front of a specimen of the unusual native fig variety that he named "Blanche Howard" after an island neighbor.

quits bearing, it's usually in the yard of a newcomer who's moved into an old house but does not know how to properly fertilize a fig. It's common to see oyster shells scattered under the fig trees of Ocracoke. "Some people think the shells are the fertilizer, but they help stabilize the soil under the tree more than fertilize it," Lynn said.

⬩ ⬩ ⬩ ⬩ ⬩ ⬩ ⬩ ⬩ ⬩ ⬩ ⬩ ⬩ ⬩

The next morning, Donna and I rented an electric golf cart, small enough to navigate the narrow lanes of Ocracoke's oldest neighborhoods and quiet enough for early morning stealth. We set out in the cool breeze to see if we could find at least some of the fig varieties that Chester Lynn had covered in his talk—the pound, the blue, the brown turkey, the sugar, the white, and the Celeste. We had already seen the Blanche Howard fig, so named by Lynn in honor of a ninety-five-year-old island resident who still lives in her family cottage on Howard Street, where a very big bush also resides. At Lynn's lecture, we'd noticed a handsome Blanche bush behind him, established from the mother plant, the figs still green. As he explained, the Blanche variety is a kind of brown turkey fig, but the "fingers" of the leaves are unusually narrow: "forkèd," as he'd put it.

On our golf cart foray, we aimed to pull a leaf from each variety we saw in order to later make tea as another point of comparison. By attending to the leaves as well as the fruit, I thus discovered the variation in fragrances among fig varieties. A Celeste, which we immediately recognized in front of a rental house on Loop Road, was stunningly fragrant, even from a good distance. Later, when we found its close cousin the sugar fig growing against a south-facing wall at the Ocracoke Historical Society, we also picked up a fragrance as we approached.

We were astonished to find a blue fig growing as tall as the two-story headquarters of Ocracoke Lightship Realty on Lighthouse Road. The limbs, heavy with fruit, were conveniently draped over an ascending handicap ramp to the front porch, making them irresistibly accessible. We sampled a dark, almost black, oblong fruit—very sweet with a note of melon, ripe and deep red to the very edge of the thin skin. The leaves of the tree were huge, but I believe the powerful scent came more from the abundant and warm, ripened fruit than from the leaves.

On Howard Street, a sandy lane where the names on the houses read like a roster of Ocracoke's oldest families, almost every yard had at least two fig bushes. At a cottage recently renovated, Donna asked permission to enter the yard and discovered in the back a very mature fig bush, with a leaf unlike any other. Most fig leaves look roughly like an old-fashioned base-ball fielder's glove, with wide fingers fanning out. This leaf looked more like an eastern cottonwood or mulberry, tooth-edged and coming to a singular point at the top; no fingers. We immediately carried the leaf and one squat yellow fig to Chester Lynn's antique store for identification.

"That's the white fig," he told us. "Not many of those on the island."

Later, Donna and I would split the fruit in half. It was very sweet and unusually crunchy with seeds, larger than the Celeste but not as large as the other varieties we'd found. Inside, the red middle was surrounded with a whitish margin. Now that I've studied the leaf and compared it to photographs online, I've come to suspect that the Ocracoke white fig, as Lynn called it, is actually a Marseilles, the highly productive variety that won the heart of Thomas Jefferson.

Outside his business on Back Road, Chester Lynn showed us the pound fig he had grown from a cutting in his great-grandmother Helen Fulcher's yard. As far as I can tell from research, the name "pound" is unique to Ocracoke. This fig might actually be the variety known more broadly as the Brunswick, or magnolia, fig, with a fruit that can grow very large.

Lynn also pointed out a lemon fig—a variety he says originated in Italy.

That fig had a definite note of citrus and was sweeter than the pound fig. It had a lingering, satisfying sugar taste on the tongue. Further investigation revealed that this variety is also known as an Italian honey fig.

We asked Lynn about the fig tree we'd seen up the street in front of Zillie's, a gourmet grocery store and wine shop, where the proprietors had hung signs in the limbs warning customers "No Pickum the Figum."

"Around here, if nobody's letting 'em pick their figs and the figs go rotten, people almost consider you a communist," Lynn said, grinning. "That's a pound fig at Zillie's."

Funny, we had asked a man who was hosing down the porch at Zillie's earlier that morning what variety it was, and he'd said brown turkey. We went back in the afternoon and asked again. The young woman at the cash register said it was a "Turkish" fig. We'd also asked about the blue fig at the real-estate office, and a woman with a not-from-here accent told us it was "just your standard Ocracoke fig." Apparently, younger folks and transplants on the island are not clued into the richness of the fig varieties around them. According to Bob Polomski, at the School of Agricultural, Forestry, and Environmental Science at Clemson University, 470 varieties of figs grow in the Southeast. And according to agricultural extension agent Charlotte Glen, in Chatham County, identifying figs can be all the more confusing, because the varieties often have multiple names.

*   *   *   *   *   *   *   *   *   *   *   *

Ocracoke's celebration of figs continued on the community square, ending the first day of the festival with a square dance and a live band, which drew many locals and some tourists. On the second day, we sampled the famous Ocracoke fig cake, which has been featured in *Gourmet* magazine. The recipe was created in the 1950s, when Margaret Garrish, an Ocracoke native, substituted figs for the dates called for in a cake recipe. Such improvisations have always been a staple of island life. The grocery boat delivers only once a week to Ocracoke. You use what you have on hand.

Even before the advent of the fig festival in 2013, residents celebrated Garrish's fig cake with an annual bake-off, testing the skills of local and off-island cooks in two categories: traditional and innovative. This year's innovative entries included three fig upside-down cakes, a gluten-free cake, and an elaborate, thin-layered chocolate cake with mascarpone between the layers and topped with fresh figs. The winner was Allison O'Neal's fig cream tarts.

The judges were looking primarily for "figginess," according to the follow-up story in the *Ocracoke Observer* newspaper.

Visiting the various festival vendors, we tried delicate cream puffs topped with fig icing and washed them down with some bracing yaupon and fig tea. (Yaupon is a coastal holly from which the indigenous people made medicinal tea centuries ago.) We also brought home a jar of the satisfying peach and lemon fig preserves created just this year by photographer Trudy Austin and decoy carver John Simpson. (Like most Ocracokers, these two have multiple talents and enterprises to earn their keep on the island.)

For dinner on our first night, we ordered the fig pizza at Dajio Restaurant, which came with fresh figs, caramelized onions, blue cheese, and prosciutto. To me the blue cheese was a little too much competition for the delicate figs. I wondered if Gorgonzola, more sparingly applied, might have worked better. Dajio was also offering a fresh smoked fish platter served with fig preserves, which smelled delicious.

On the second evening, we visited the new Flying Melon Café and shared a pristine seafood platter—flounder, scallops, shrimp, and crab cake, all perfectly grilled. We finished with "Figs Foster," a dessert of ice cream topped with figs in liqueur concocted by chef Mike Schramel, who moved to Ocracoke after a lengthy stint as a caterer in New Orleans. On our last morning on the island, we waited in a long line at Ocracoke Coffee to share an order of fig cream cheese on a bagel and a fig muffin—both magnificent.

But the very best application of figs we experienced all weekend was quite unexpected. It came at lunch in a booth at the festival operated by the Ocracoke Oyster Company. Certified pitmaster George Turner smokes his barbecued meats with fig wood. "It's a sweeter wood, and it burns hot. It smokes very well," Turner's wife, Janille, explained as she dished up a pork barbecue sandwich. It was so deliciously smoky, we went to the restaurant the next day for more.

I asked our server if the Turners have to procure fig wood from the mainland. In the two years the restaurant has been operating, she said, neighbors and friends who trim their fig trees annually have brought the Turners enough wood for their smoker. Theirs was some of the best pork barbecue I have ever tasted. As my late stepfather, Ralph, used to say, "If you were to put this meat on top of your head, your tongue would beat your brains out to get to it."

Next trip, I am going for their brisket.

Back home from Ocracoke, Donna and I took our fig leaves, carefully bagged and tagged, and set about making tea. The white fig, the one with the unusual leaf without fingers, made a fine tea, sweet and simple. The taste of the Blanche Howard, however, was strong and a bit sour—something akin to asparagus. The blue fig tea was less sweet than the white but definitely drinkable.

Jim Harb had never tried fig tea until I'd told him about Alice Gerrard's instructions. He immediately picked leaves from his Kadota, brown turkey, and purple mission figs in Tennessee and made tea. He complained of a grassy, medicinal flavor. I suggested that he try making tea from each variety separately. Still, Jim said, the grassy taste persisted, though he found that the unwelcome taste seemed to dissipate as the tea cooled.

We have made iced tea from the Celeste leaves at home. It is subtle and refreshing. Adding a little sugar or honey—whether iced or hot—may help to encourage the doubtful. Taking a little sliver from the middle of the fig and dropping it in the bottom of the cup or placing the slice as a garnish on the lip of a tall glass of iced fig tea also enhances the flavor. I have read that some folks recommend boiling the leaves rather than steeping them, which might be a quicker method. You can dry the leaves gently in the oven and save them for use throughout the year, but in my experience the best flavor comes from leaves fresh-picked.

Fig tea, consumed regularly, has been shown to lower harmful triglycerides and the amount of insulin required by the body—a home remedy for diabetes. The fruit itself is high in fiber and calcium and has antioxidant properties, too.

Fig leaves can be used to wrap fish for baking in the oven or cooked on the grill, much in the way that grape leaves are used in many Mediterranean recipes. The key is to place the fish or vegetables on the shiny side of the fig leaf, not the hairy side.

It's now the last day of August—the end of my Celeste fig's production and always a day of remembrance for me. It is my father's birthday, though he's been gone for thirty-six years. He died the day after he turned sixty, on my birthday. So tomorrow I will celebrate my latest circle around the sun.

This year's crop from the Celeste is also the first that my mother has not been able to enjoy. She died in February, the month of our goat's milk tasting, well before this year's fig leaves had even begun to unfurl. She was always thrilled when the figs began coming in. We'd have them fresh off the tree for breakfast most mornings as long as the season lasted and then later in the preserves that Donna made. Mom said she never knew how much she liked figs until she moved to Carrboro.

The Celeste is towering and still full of big, healthy leaves today, though the fruit is all but gone. I know better than to walk barefoot underneath it. Yellow jackets are hovering and landing on the last scattered bits of fig that have fallen out of the beaks of birds on the topmost branches. I can see only one high, half-eaten fig warming in the summer air this morning, its red center opened to the daylight by a squirrel or crow that left it torn, midmeal. As I shield my eyes against the sun, a black swallowtail butterfly meanders around and lands on the fig. It pumps its wings and then folds them together and settles in to take an easy taste of the sugary nectar.

I tell myself I will be brave this winter and prune the Celeste more severely than I ever have, once all the leaves have dropped and the architecture of the branches is stark against the winter sky. Because the fig latex oozes out when a branch is cut, I'll wear long sleeves, as Chester Lynn instructed.

This time, however, I'll save the wood, cut it into small pieces, and let it dry. I've already done my homework. Several cooks' blogs suggest that it doesn't take much—a couple of branches or some chips on top of hot coals—to get the distinctive smoky flavor we sampled on Ocracoke Island. In Turkey, apparently, cooks make skewers out of fig wood, which, when put on the grill, flavors both meat and vegetables from the inside out.

I found that cooking with fig wood was also mentioned as a hot new trend in 2001 in a short piece in the *New York Times*. One Manhattan chef was using it to smoke lobster and pizza. Chez Panisse, in Berkeley, was using it back then to smoke poultry and fish. I'm thinking fig wood might be an interesting ingredient for smoking cheese, and I plan to propose this idea to my old friends Flo Hawley and Portia McKnight at the Chapel Hill Creamery, where their Dairyland Smoked Farmer's Cheese is already a favorite. I'll be happy to supply the wood, if they want to experiment. I'll also share a big bundle with Jim Harb.

Drying the wood is supposed to take between three and six months. Maybe by late spring next year, Jim and I will catch some North Carolina mountain trout (the easy way, at a trout farm) and stuff them with mint and pecans—a favorite recipe he introduced me to many years ago. We'll cook it over an open fire at my cabin in the Blue Ridge, as we've so often done, but never before with fig wood. I can hardly wait.

September

Scuppernongs

OF ALL THE FOODS DESCRIBED IN THESE PAGES, SCUPPERNONGS HAVE been the one item that most often creates a puzzled look on the faces of people who did not grow up in North Carolina. Many from outside the Southeast have never heard of these grapes, much less tasted them. But for those who grew up eating them, scuppernongs create profound memories of family traditions. Nothing else tastes quite like a scuppernong, a variety of muscadine grapes. But it is not just the flavor that is distinctive. The golden scuppernong and the dark blue, purple, or black muscadine (also sometimes called bulloses) are peculiar fruits because their hulls are so thick. This is not a grape you eat whole but rather one you must squeeze and bite to get at the good stuff.

In the little town of Columbia in northeastern North Carolina, home of Full Circle Crab in the soft-shell crab chapter, Donna Campbell and I watched from a distance as Butch Kirkman of Scuppernong Produce — a roadside stand next to the local Dollar General franchise — explained to a curious woman from Brooklyn, New York, how to eat a scuppernong. This is apparently a common conversation, because passersby on their way to North Carolina's Outer Banks often have their first experience of scuppernongs here, along the river that gave the grape its name; more on that story a bit later.

How to eat a scuppernong? First, search the surface of the hull for the site where the stem once fastened the grape to the vine. Point this little bull's-eye on the hull toward your tongue and grasp the grape between your upper and lower front teeth, wrap your lips halfway around it, bite down, and then squeeze the grape with your fingers. The viscous insides of the scuppernong will pop into your mouth, bathed in a luscious sweetness. The insides generally hold together and are remarkably chewy — much chewier than an ordinary table grape from the grocery.

According to its detractors, the "meat" of the scuppernong has a texture reminiscent of, shall we say, the product of a bad cough. But clear your mind of this idea. The juice is divine. The translucent, full-bodied innards of the scuppernong must be chewed for the seeds to be loosened and spit out. The seeds can be swallowed, which I often did as a child, but they are probably best removed, if digestion is a concern. Some people eat the hulls, but these are likely to be less sweet and are definitely leathery. They are, however, worth sucking on to get every last drop of the unparalleled juice before you dispose of them.

Once you've eaten a scuppernong or two, you can appreciate the labor of making jelly, which involves popping the grapes open by hand—several quarts of them, at least—and sieving the juice away from the hulls, seeds, and jelly-like innards. Juice extraction is usually done through cheesecloth or a cone strainer that comes with with a wooden pestle. I am grateful that my mother and grandmother were up to the task when I was a child. In those days before air conditioning, they would create jars of jelly in small batches over a hot stove when September's heat had hardly dissipated.

If you do plan to make jelly, here is a significant tip offered by the North Carolina Agricultural Extension Service in a circular published in 1917 titled *Canning and Preserving with 4-H Recipes*: "Scuppernong jelly made without the hulls is of a light amber color and quite flat and insipid. When the hulls are added a beautiful red color and a delicious acid flavor is obtained. . . . It is hoped that North Carolina will make a specialty of its scuppernong jelly and that the club girls will take great pains in putting out a fine product." ("Club girls" were young women trained by the state to be extension demonstration agents, and they traveled North Carolina showing their female peers how to preserve food.)

The largest commercial crops of muscadines and scuppernongs in North Carolina are produced today in and around Duplin County, where the Duplin Winery has expanded exponentially since the 1970s to become, by its own account, the largest winery in the South, with a tank capacity of more than 1.4 million gallons. Along with its satellite tasting room and re-tail shop in Myrtle Beach, South Carolina, Duplin Winery reportedly draws more than 100,000 visitors a year.

The market for muscadines and scuppernongs has also been enhanced by the discovery, as reported by the National Institutes of Health in 2007, that "an extract of the skin of muscadine grapes can inhibit growth of pros-tate cancer cells in the laboratory." These and other research findings have led to many start-up efforts (in North Carolina and elsewhere) to produce and market dietary supplements made from muscadines, promoting them as antioxidant, anti-cancer, and anti-inflammatory agents. Other companies are producing and selling organic muscadines and scuppernongs and their juices based on the promise of similar health benefits. Auman Vineyards near Fayetteville and Uncle Henry's Organics in Rose Hill are two such growers. Our research, however, took us to Columbia, where Vineyards on the Scup-pernong has been selling grapes, making wine, and racking up awards for its products for a decade.

In 2006, Jack Bishop turned fifty and retired from a successful career as a general contractor and developer. Some years before, he and his wife, Grace, had bought three farms in Tyrrell County with the idea of developing home-sites along the Scuppernong River. When the bottom fell out of the housing market, Bishop asked Marc Basnight, then president pro tem of the North Carolina Senate, what he could possibly do with his beautiful land besides building houses on it.

Basnight, by then a vocal proponent of locally sourced food, had one word for Jack Bishop: *scuppernongs*. Bishop says he then respectfully suggested to the senator that he'd been out in the sun too long.

"Scuppernongs?" Bishop asked.

"Yes," Basnight said. The senator believed the grape had a great future in the area, and after all, Bishop's land was right along the river from which the native vine gained its name.

Basnight had been in the food business for a long time. When an arsonist burned down his celebrated Lone Cedar Restaurant, on the causeway between Manteo and Nags Head, in 2007, he and his wife and daughters started over, using green building techniques for their new spacious and light-filled restaurant. They also began listing menu items that detailed the provenance of the fresh local seafood and vegetables they served. They grew their own kitchen herbs on the premises. No surprise, then, that Basnight thought Bishop should grow grapes. Not long after, the news broke about the anti-cancer properties of North Carolina's native grape.

"North Carolina has gone from having about 30 to 130 wineries," Bishop told us. "When the pharmaceutical properties of these grapes became known, the business exploded."

Raised in Nash County, Bishop was familiar with cropping tobacco — a labor-intensive, dirty, and demanding endeavor. To him, the idea of a vineyard, of making wine, sounded like a happy retirement. He might have imagined himself becoming the gentleman farmer tending his crops and spending his evenings on the veranda of the house he would build in sight of his luscious vines in one direction and the placid Scuppernong River in the other.

"What I didn't know," Bishop said, standing in the stifling September heat beside the buildings that make up his wine-making operation, "is that these grapes are just like tobacco. You have to work every plant four times in the season. This is real farming. It's hard work—quite an undertaking, as I found out. I could have made a lot more money doing other things. But it has been an adventure." He shrugged and halfway smiled.

Bishop wore flip-flops, shorts, and a T-shirt. His sunglasses were strung around his neck. Tanned, slim, and clearly a man of high energy, Bishop might have just stepped off a sailboat that afternoon, but he pointed us toward a pen full of lanky birddogs beside one of his storage buildings. "I train English setters on the side," he said. His cell phone rang for the third time since Donna and I had arrived at the vineyard.

After his phone call, Bishop explained that he'd been harvesting grapes as fast as possible over the past two weeks, some days from three in the morning to nine at night. "We've had two tropical storms blow through here during the same period with a foot of rain and winds that hit fifty miles per hour," he said, his jaw hardening. His team had been trying not to lose the crop to the wicked weather. Bishop then introduced us to his donkey, Barney, the vineyard mascot who had been watching us from behind a fence near the barn, far away from the dogs. "The first wine we ever made is called Jack Ass Red." Now Bishop grinned in earnest.

Today, Vineyards on the Scuppernong grows twelve varieties of grapes, nine of which are handpicked and shipped to the produce section at Food Lion grocery stores in North Carolina, Virginia, and South Carolina. The other varieties go into wine making, and these can be harvested by machine; it doesn't matter if the hulls of the wine grapes pop open. However, harvesting scuppernongs is tricky. As Alexia Jones Helsey explains in her detailed history of wine making in North Carolina, "Scuppernong grapes, even on the same vine, mature at different times."

Bishop had thirty people working for him that season. They had been culling fresh grapes the day we visited. The grapes are sold in quart containers, picked up from this site by the tractor-trailer load. We peeked inside a refrigerated shed where the fresh grapes are stored. Pickers gather the grapes from the vines in waffled plastic laundry baskets and then cull and wash them and place them in the containers for shipping.

Bishop said his winery operation produces 10,000 cases a year. He is particularly proud of bringing back to North Carolina the Catawba grape—a native variety that New York wineries adopted some years ago. Catawbas are used to produce the number-one selling wine in New York State, Bishop

Jack Bishop presents a sample of the morning's harvest at Vineyards on the Scuppernong in Columbia, where guests can partake in wine tastings, vineyard tours, and boat rides on the Scuppernong River.

said. His vintage is called Catawba Belle, a semisweet white that has won several awards, from the North Carolina State Fair to the Finger Lakes International Wine Competition.

When he began, Bishop hired a top wine-making expert to guide him. "I didn't even know how to make vinegar back then," he said.

Now the operation has eight steel vats; the largest holds 25,000 gallons. Bishop is clearly proud of his one-of-a-kind grape press, which was built from the engine and body of a World War I German army tank. The press sits on a concrete slab under the roof that extends from the metal building where the wines are blended in vats and bottled.

Making wine from scuppernongs is different from making wines from *Vitis vinifera*, the species of grape that is used for the majority of all wines produced in the world. *Vinifera* grapes are used in familiar wines such as chardonnay, pinot noir, and cabernet sauvignon. *Vitis labrusca* is a second species, mostly found today in the Northeast and Canada, though North Carolina's native fox grape and the Catawba grape fall under this category. Scuppernongs, however, are of the *Vitis rotundifolia* species and are very sweet.

Bishop decided to be creative with his wines, combining novel ingredients. With vinifera grape juice he produces a chardonnay, which is flavored with peaches; a dry Riesling, flavored with Granny Smith apples; and a white zinfandel, called Corolla Lite (a play on the name of the Outer Banks lighthouse), flavored with raspberries. "Tyrrell," named after the county where he is located, is a wine made from 100-percent merlot grapes, another award winner.

In the *Vitis rotundifolia* category, however, Bishop's "Black Beary" (featuring a bear on the label) is a dessert red that is made exclusively from muscadines and blackberries. The Jack Ass Red is pure muscadine and is the vineyard's top seller. "Simply Scuppernong" is precisely as labeled, and it is a very sweet white. Other seasonal bottles are flavored with cranberries and strawberries. One special dessert wine features flavors of cherries and chocolate. These are wines designed for slow sipping, not heavy consumption. They are very distinctive and—to judge from their sales volume—clearly popular.

Bishop bought and restored Columbia's historic firehouse, on Highway 64 just past the Scuppernong River bridge as you head east toward Manteo. The facility now serves as a tasting room, wine shop, gourmet grocery, coffee bar, and café called Elements. The shop is directly across the main highway from the Tyrrell County Visitor Center, a popular rest stop visited by half a million guests on their way to the coast every year. Bishop also conducts winery tours, which begin in downtown Columbia at the waterside board-walk. Visitors travel by pontoon boat up the Scuppernong River and arrive at the elaborate dock in front of Bishop's cottage, with its wraparound porches and Charleston-style shutters. The house has been featured more than once in *Southern Living* magazine for its award-winning design. Guests then travel by hay wagon through the vineyards.

Bishop's 300 acres are fastidiously manicured, with row upon row of grape vines, each numbered and labeled with a brass plate affixed to trellis posts that designate the variety of grape growing down the line. Several very old tombstones sit in the yard between his house and the vines that stretch beyond as far as the eye can see. This land once belonged to the Davenport clan, a prominent family in Tyrrell County. (J. F. Davenport owned a tavern and boardinghouse in Columbia before the Civil War.) Enormous pecan trees shade the yard, and one lone fig, recently planted, stands sentinel beside the rusty fence of the Davenport graveyard.

Bishop depends on his son, Bud, to fill in as tour guide and winery manager when he is otherwise occupied in the operation, which also includes a retail shop in Manteo. Bishop also likes to hunt and fish. He estimated that about 150 deer live on his property, but they don't bother him. "There are enough grapes out there for the deer and the bears and us," he said.

According to the Vineyards on the Scuppernong website, North Carolina can lay claim to being the first place in the nation where the settlers made wine. Of course, that's not accounting for the beverages made by Native Americans. As North Carolina's distinguished historian David Stick explained in "Indian Food and Cooking in Eastern North Carolina 400 Years Ago," the first English explorer, Arthur Barlowe, "did not record what beverages the Indians served him and his companions, but he did say that the Indians customarily drank wine *'while the grape lasteth'* and water *'sodden with Ginger in it, and blacke Sinamone, and sometimes Sassafras, and diuers other wholesome, and medicinable hearbes.'"*

By 1835, a man named Sydney Weller established the first commercial vineyard, in Halifax County, North Carolina. "Weller Halifax" was an acclaimed wine, and the vintner is also credited with naming Medoc Mountain (now a state park in the county) after the wine-growing province in the Bordeaux region of France. Weller even produced scuppernong champagne.

According to Jerry Bledsoe's book *Carolina Curiosities*, North Carolina led the nation in wine production by 1840, with 6,000 acres in vineyards.

Some thirty-three wineries were producing more than a million gallons of scuppernong and muscadine wine, Bledsoe says. Many, however, were destroyed by the Civil War.

Alexia Helsey states that a Confederate colonel took ownership of the large Tokay vineyard north of Fayetteville after the war and began producing high quality scuppernong wines that were advertised in the *Washington Post*. The Medoc winery also continued under new ownership, and another vintner established a successful winery in Weldon. A colony of French grape growers even set up shop in Ridgeway (home of the sweet cantaloupe). Though conditions in the Ridgeway area were initially compared to the Provence region of France, the operation eventually failed.

In one fictional account, a North Carolina vineyard cursed and in ruins after the Civil War is restored to some semblance of its past productivity by a white entrepreneur from the North with the help of his black neighbors. The story, "The Goophered Grapevine," appeared in the *Atlantic Monthly* in 1887, written by the pioneering African American novelist Charles Waddell Chesnutt, who grew up in Fayetteville. It was his first published short story.

Contrary to all these efforts to bring wine back to prominence in the state, North Carolina eventually imposed prohibition in 1908 — the first state in the South to ban alcohol. Except for a rogue winery in St. Helena, near Burgaw, which was run by Italian immigrants who were allowed to grow grapes as long as they sold all their wine out of state, it would be the early 1970s before the Fussell family launched its scuppernong-based winery at Rose Hill in Duplin County. A winery in Germantown, near Winston-Salem, followed in 1981, and in 1983, the Biltmore Estate established the state's third twentieth-century winery. Today, many more North Carolina wines are produced of the *Vitis vinifera* variety, especially those coming out of Yadkin County.

Back in 1957, the North Carolina legislature, which represented many "dry" counties where the sale of spirits was still rigorously prohibited, nevertheless adopted an official "state toast," which mentions the scuppernong:

> Here's to the land of the long leaf pine,
> The summer land where the sun doth shine,
> Where the weak grow strong and the strong grow great,
> Here's to "Down Home," the Old North State!
>
> Here's to the land of the cotton bloom white,
> Where the scuppernong perfumes the breeze at night,

Where the soft southern moss and jessamine mate,
'Neath the murmuring pines of the Old North State!

Here's to the land where the galax grows,
Where the rhododendron's rosette glows,
Where soars Mount Mitchell's summit great,
In the "Land of the Sky," in the Old North State!

Here's to the land where maidens are fair,
Where friends are true and cold hearts rare,
The near land, the dear land, whatever fate,
The blessed land, the best land, the Old North State!

* * * * * * * * * * * *

Not all scuppernongs are grown in North Carolina for toasting purposes, of course. Clara Brickhouse, now in her eighties, was born in Columbia at her grandparents' house. She is tall, and her dark features are chiseled. On the day we visited, she wore a black head wrap, but a few curling tendrils of gray hair escaped to flank her face. Her white cotton blouse hung comfortably over a long khaki skirt. Both were neatly pressed. Her garden shoes were rubber clogs with a leopard pattern print — the only bit of whimsy in her outfit. She had a regal bearing, and because it is the custom in eastern North Carolina to address an elder by his or her first name and add the more formal "Mister" or "Miss" to show respect, Donna and I called her Miss Clara.

"I can still see my grandaddy's big old house in my mind," Miss Clara said, sitting in the breezeway of her tidy modular home, a Bible open on the table before her. "It stood right outside of town next to a great big pine tree that was the only one along that road, so they called it Lonesome Pine." She closed her bright eyes and opened them again. "The road back then was narrow. There was no Highway 64," she said. "The road was called Scuppernong Drive coming through Columbia. The railroad came into town back then, too, but not so far out as my granddaddy's place."

Clara's grandfather was a sharecropper from coastal Hyde County. He moved inland for work several times — from Columbia to Aurora and then to Washington County, "along about where you see Mackey's Ferry Peanuts now, over there at Roper," she told us. It was on the Roper farm that Miss Clara first remembers eating scuppernongs. She was a teenager by then.

It would be many decades later, when Miss Clara set herself up to grow and sell scuppernongs as a hobby, that she chose her current residence. It sits alongside another stately pine, this time in the little community of Travis, very close to U.S. 64 and not far from the headwaters of the dark and tranquil Scuppernong River.

Though the North Carolina legislature designated the scuppernong grape as the official state fruit only in 2001, it has grown wild in these parts for centuries. The name comes from the Algonquian Indian word *askuponong*, which translates to "the place of the sweet bay tree." (The sweet bay magnolia, *Magnolia virginiana*, is tolerant of periodic flooding and thrives in the swamps here.)

North Carolina nature writer, musician, and avid waterman Bland Simpson tells us that his ancestors the Spruills, who settled in 1690 along the south side of the Albemarle Sound in what would become Tyrrell County, gave the Scuppernong River its present name, an adaptation of the Indian word that they undoubtedly heard spoken by their native neighbors.

Over the years, the word "scuppernong" has come to have many pronunciations. During our visit, Miss Clara would sometimes refer to the grapes as "scuffernongs." My mother always insisted upon calling them "scuppernines," conflating the cultivar name "scuppernong" with the larger category of muscadine grapes, which are mostly red or purple, of which the scuppernong (the bronze grape) is but one variety. Farther south, in Alabama and Florida, you may hear the name pronounced "scupnun" or "scuplin."

The indigenous people used them as a wild food source. The first English settlers in Tyrrell County did, too, calling them the white grape at first and making a simple wine from them. A local man named Isaac Alexander is generally credited with first cutting and cultivating the white grape—which he named after the Scuppernong River, where he found the grape while hunting—in 1755. However, there are also reports that the Anglican priest Charles Pettigrew "discovered" the grape later, around 1774, on property he purchased in what is now Tyrrell County. Pettigrew was a prominent figure who is still remembered in the area—Pettigrew State Park, on Phelps Lake (once called Scuppernong Lake), is named for him.

Pettigrew partnered with several neighboring plantation owners, including the Josiah Collins family, who owned Somerset Place, now a state historic site dedicated to the full interpretation of plantation life in the era. Somerset vividly depicts the hardships endured by enslaved Africans who brought their formidable agricultural and building skills to bear on the region. It was here that Pettigrew and his neighbors created the Lake Company, an enterprise that used the enslaved people to build the thirty-foot-wide, hand-dug canals, still visible and running from Lake Phelps through the broad, flat fields of Washington and Tyrrell Counties. These canals helped to drain the swamps for planting and were used to ferry rice, corn, wheat, and timber to market in the eighteenth century. Pettigrew planted cuttings from the scuppernong grapes he found along the river, and he also built a historic chapel that's still standing in Creswell, not far from Miss Clara's house.

In a column she wrote in October 1970 for the *Charlotte Observer*, the horticulturalist Elizabeth Lawrence speculated that the Isaac Alexander and Charles Pettigrew stories about the origin of the grape's name and first cultivation are probably both true. She also quoted a work from 1860, *The Shrubs and Vines of North Carolina*, written by Reverend M. A. Curtis, who contradicted the claim by some that the scuppernong was first cultivated on Roanoke Island and not by settlers along the Scuppernong River. That controversy continues to this day, however, with some arguing that the famous "Mother Vine" now on private property in Manteo is the original cultivar and is more than 400 years old.

Disputes about first cultivation aside, the unusually large, hard-hulled bronze grape definitely grew wild throughout this region and much farther south. Even before the first band of English explorers commissioned by Sir Walter Raleigh landed here, Giovanni da Verrazzano, a Florentine navigator who was exploring the region in 1524 on behalf of France, recorded in his log that he saw "many vines growing naturally" in the valley of the Cape Fear River, presumably close to what is now the city of Wilmington.

After traveling with Ralph Lane to the Outer Banks in 1585 on the second English expedition to Roanoke Island, astronomer, mathematician, and translator Thomas Hariot wrote *A Brief and True Report of the New Found Land of Virginia*, which was published in 1588. Hariot was enthusiastic about the proliferation of wild grapes he saw on the shores of what would become North Carolina, describing what was probably the smaller fox grape and then the larger scuppernong. He predicted a great future in the region for the making of wine: "There are two kinds of grapes that the soile doth yeeld naturally: the one is small and sowre of the ordinarie bignesse as ours in England: the other farre greater & of himselfe iushious sweet. When they are plãted and husbandeg as they ought, a principall commoditie of wines by them may be raised."

"I began my garden in 1975," Clara Brickhouse told us, "right here, when I became born again. It started as a hobby to keep me out of the world and to keep me from going back to the bad things I was doing!" Clara had returned home after a number of years in New York. She craved a simpler life and became deeply involved in her church but offered no details about what she might have been escaping from in New York.

"I didn't know one thing about gardening," she explained, "and I didn't have no husband. God saved me. I give God the glory. It's a gift. That's why I can't stop all this gardening. That's where my power comes from." She smiled.

Miss Clara said that getting her start as a grower wasn't easy. For three or four years, she covered her expenses by baking pies and other desserts that she sold from the back of her car. "I made pies and took them to the crab house, and the workers bought them. I didn't just want a garden. I wanted a pattern, a blueprint, something neat. I went from year to year planting, and the fruit and berries started multiplying. It got so big, and I got so old that I've had to cut back every year." She guffawed with delight. She's had no problem with predators—neither bears nor deer, she said. (Tyrrell County is famous for supposedly having more bears than humans within its boundaries.)

Miss Clara went into the kitchen to retrieve a sample of her scuppernongs. "Muscadine is the family name," she said, returning with a quart container. "There are thirty-two names in the muscadine family—Early Fry, Late Fry, Supremes, Doreen—I can't remember them all." She ordered some of her plants from a catalog company and bought a few others at farmers' markets.

She grows grapes ranging from a half-inch to nearly an inch in diameter. She also grows a late Concord—"a little on the sour side," she said, scrunching up her nose. "They all taste different. I like these little scuppernongs the best. They've got the best flavor of all the muscadines. But people want the big ones. People think they're getting more for their money with the big grapes, but they're not, because a quart is a quart!

"Wisdom comes with age," Miss Clara continued. "Nobody wants to get outside in the fresh air anymore. They don't want to work. Consider the ants—how they toil in the summertime to prepare for the wintertime. You have to prepare. Starting September and October I get my food ready. That way I don't have to go out if I don't want to. I am a loner. I don't entertain. My time is *my* time. People talk on the phone. It's a waste of time. I do volunteer work at Meals on Wheels, the food pantry, and for my church over in Plymouth."

Miss Clara still drives. Her white pickup truck with a camper top is twenty years old and in pristine condition. She was proud to say that she has no cable TV and no air conditioning. She believes that air conditioning will give you arthritis, which she does not have.

"I have eighteen grape vines out there," she said. "Some ripen early, starting in mid-August, right after the blueberries are over. The Doreens [the largest of her white grapes] start in August. Right now is the peak week in September, and some late-season ones come next month." She will take these to the Scuppernong River Festival in Columbia the second weekend in October. "Now these little ones"—she touched the carton of grapes on the table—"will hang on the vines even in a storm. But the great big ones can't hang through a heavy wind."

I asked if she ever made scuppernong jelly, as my grandmother and mother always did.

"No. That's too much work, fooling with the seeds and all," she said. "One time Mr. Jack Bishop gave me some wine, and I took that wine and some orange juice, and I made some orange wine jam." She laughed. "I carried him a jar, and he said he wanted me to put labels on it and sell it in his store, but I couldn't do that. I don't drink wine, but I can make jam out of it! I don't make anything out of my grapes, just sell them fresh."

Miss Clara prunes her vines in February or March. "Can't do it before then, cause they'll bleed to death," she explained. She fertilizes the plants three times in the growing season with 10-10-10 fertilizer—at the first of April, in May, and then once more in either June or July. She has been known to sell her crop across three counties.

"When I started at the farmers' markets at Plymouth and Edenton, I was the oldest person and the onliest woman," she said, nodding her head. "And I was the first one to come in the morning and the last one to leave at the end. You got to stay focused. I used to try to play music, but I was more interested in the gardening. My neighbor told me that if I would stay at that keyboard and play it as much as I stayed in the garden, I would be good at music." She chuckled. We presented Miss Clara with some of the preserves that Donna had made from the Celeste fig tree back home. I also told her about making fig tea and how delicious it is.

Hearing this, Miss Clara was practically bouncing in her chair. "You know, the Bible says let the fruit be for food and the leaves for medicines. Everything out there is food and healing! Get bark from any kind of fruit tree and put it in water. You got apple tea. Peach tea. That's where the healing is at — in the trees and the plants. Not in the meat — the pigs and the chickens. It's in the trees. I eat my blackberries and blueberries in the morning. I get my food and my medicine that way." We sat and contemplated this truth.

"You ready to go see the garden?" she finally asked.

We nodded and stood up. "Well, let me go get my hoe and I'll meet you out back." Miss Clara sprang up from her chair and went deep inside the house.

Donna looked at me. "Did she say hoe?" We both intuitively knew, based on experience with our grandmothers, that the tool is a precaution against snakes. Yes, there are still water moccasins in these swamplands, the descendants of the snakes that plagued the diggers of those thirty-foot canals on the plantations.

We stepped out into the bright sunshine and headed for the backyard. Miss Clara's garden was immaculate. The grass was a bright green, thick and thatched, and though the ground was wet from so much recent rain, the spongy grass seemed to keep the moisture below. Two long rows of scuppernong vines were neatly hung on trellises that flanked the house and stretched toward the rear of the yard, where blackberries were trained along the back fence. The blueberry bushes were widely spaced for easy picking, and the other fruit trees were flourishing. Though Miss Clara said she was cutting back on her plantings, she pointed to a new apple tree, recently set out. Birds called all around us. The whoosh of traffic heading to and from Manteo on Highway 64 was like an ocean in the background.

We joined Miss Clara under the lonesome pine, admiring the layout of her plot, and Donna asked about snakes. Miss Clara leaned on her hoe. "One day I was up on the deck looking down this way and asked myself how that big limb got out there under this pine tree. And then that big limb moved!" We shuddered. "I took care of it," she said, leaving us to imagine the confrontation.

She pointed out her two oldest scuppernong vines, which were planted even before her house was placed on the property, she said. After forty-one years, they are now drying up and dying, as scuppernongs tend to do at such an age. Miss Clara accepts this as part of the cycle of life and has no plans to replace them. This summer was not a good one for blackberries, either, she

Clara Brickhouse leans on her hoe and surveys the yard where she took up gardening after returning from New York to her birthplace in Tyrrell County. She grows and sells scuppernongs, Concord grapes, and blueberries.

said. "I have forty-eight blackberry plants over there, and I only got three quarts this year." Locals have reported that the same has been true of pecans this season—they didn't even ripen. They've stayed green. And the busybody squirrels that are the first to harvest them seem to be missing in action, we've heard.

"There's going to be a famine in the land," Miss Clara said abruptly. "Get ready for the floods, the earthquakes—everything, honey. It's going to be just like everywhere else overseas. It's the beginning of it. This world is coming down. But, thank God, there's going to be a new one." She threw back her regal head once more and laughed, looking into the cloudless sky.

We stood together in the sunshine in silence, contemplating the long view of the ancient land before us, cleared so long ago with backbreaking effort to create a platform for agriculture. As we were preparing to leave, Miss Clara called out. "Don't forget to put in the name of my garden," she said. "It's the Garden of Eden."

October

Apples

prolific, regionally varied in spelling and pronunciation, and not always obvious in origin. In the days of subsistence farming, when families simply ate whatever they could grow, a productive apple tree was a prized asset. Some apple varieties became heirlooms, passed along from one generation to the next, often carrying a family member's name. Others were lost or forgotten, but their stories remain, mostly hidden in old nursery catalogs.

Distinguished southern apple historian and pomologist Creighton Lee Calhoun Jr. lives in North Carolina. Though he is now in his eighties and stays close to home on his fifteen-acre farm in Chatham County, Calhoun compiled a 331-page encyclopedia, *Old Southern Apples*, with the assistance of his late wife, Edith, as his editor.

In addition to finding and preserving many "lost" varieties, Calhoun attempts to explain the complex web of names surrounding heirloom apples. For example, an apple variety called Aunt Sally (or sometimes Aunt Sallie's Everbearing) was sold by at least two nurseries in North Carolina around the turn of the twentieth century. It was likely named for Sally Caroline Ridings, a Virginian who married and moved south to Allegheny County in North Carolina in 1824. The story goes that she brought a root from the family apple tree with her and later gave all of her female descendants a root sprout so that the apples might continue ripening down the family line.

Another variety, called Aunt Rachel, produces juicy, pale-yellow fruit with thin red stripes. This apple has spread across Chatham County in the Piedmont, but the story of its namesake, Calhoun writes, has been lost to memory.

In earlier days, apples were put to many good uses, though not all varieties were fit to eat right off the tree. Some were best fried; others were baked in pies. Some were dried for ready nourishment in a hard winter. Some made good jelly or vinegar. Others were fermented to make cider or stronger brandy. Some were preferred for applesauce and apple butter, and others were consigned to the animals, particularly horses.

Heirloom apples don't look like the brightly colored, uniformly sized, and artificially shiny apples we see in supermarkets. In fact, antique apples are identified by their irregular shapes and the stripes and blemishes on their skins. Some have a greasy coat, others a rough or mottled surface. "Pretty" is not an adjective Calhoun uses much in his descriptions of southern heirloom apples.

The keeping qualities of old North Carolina apples are also widely varied. Some of the heirlooms listed in Calhoun's book are reported to last well into spring if properly stored—meaning they shouldn't touch one another and are to be set out in the cellar where the air can circulate around them, not in a barrel. As the saying goes, "One bad apple . . ."

Some apples are at their best only for a few days. Others may benefit from a cold snap to sweeten, and we tend to think that the best apples come from the North Carolina mountains in fall. But there are varieties that thrive much farther east into the Coastal Plain. Some ripen in summer.

The fabled Mattamuskeet, or Skeet, variety is said to have originated in Hyde County, near the coast where the wide and shallow waters of Lake Mattamuskeet draw thousands of migrating waterfowl each November. Legend suggests that the Mattamuskeet Indians first planted the Skeet apple from seeds they extracted from the gizzard of a goose. The Skeet is perfect for making apple butter, says Calhoun, and is often harvested as late as November. The flavor of this apple actually improves the longer it's stored, he adds.

Sadly, many of the early apple varieties that once grew in family orchards all over the South are now extinct. More than half of Calhoun's pages are devoted to lost apples. As Edward Behr puts it in *The Artful Eater*, "Now that we have a selection of fresh fruits year-round, we eat many fewer apples than we once did."

However, antique apple hunters, like classic car enthusiasts or collectors of old sterling and china, are keeping the history alive. They rummage through old journals and seed catalogs, looking for descriptions of a particular apple from centuries past. They cross-reference reports of size, shape, color, flavor, skin texture, degree of acidity, and the month of their ripening, all in an attempt to determine if an old apple tree—left abandoned in a field or sprouting on the edge of an old homeplace—might be a known or missing heirloom. Their hunting is made more complicated by the various names that may have been ascribed to a single variety. Calhoun tells of a variety listed as Yellow June, which, he explains, is sometimes also called White Juneating and Hoover June. His description goes on: "A southern apple of unknown origin that ripens at the same time as Carolina Red June. It should not be confused with Yellow Sweet June, which is a synonym for Hightop Sweet. Yellow June is probably identical to White Juneating. Many apples called Yellow June are actually Early Harvest, which has the synonym of Yellow June."

Confused? Me, too. Antique apple identification—keeping up with all the *noms des pommes*—is probably best left to the experts. Still, every apple has a story, and these narratives are a valuable part of our culinary history. Apples have always been important in the diets of North Carolinians, from the mountains to the coast.

For our purposes here, we'll taste five varieties of North Carolina apples and explore their origin stories. All are fresh-eating apples, and all have their peak harvest in October. You can still find them yourself from at least a few growers who are committed to preserving this distinctive bit of Tar Heel heritage.

Ron and Suzanne Joyner live on a farm that's so remote they urged Donna Campbell and me to meet them at the Ashe County Farmers Market, in West Jefferson, for our first visit. At this friendly, shoulder-to-shoulder market on Back Street, the Joyners sell a range of heirloom apples to eat and young apple trees to plant. Their Big Horse Creek Farm is twenty-two miles northwest of West Jefferson and fifty miles from Boone. It's two miles from their house just to reach a paved road.

As Ron put it, "We are in the coolest corner of the coolest corner." The corner he is referring to is the one created by the boundaries of Virginia to the north and Tennessee to the west, an area of North Carolina once known as the "Lost Province." Ashe County has recently been promoting itself to visitors as "the coolest corner of the state," and the Joyners are wedged way up into the crook of that elbow, where cool is quite literally correct. Their farm occasionally gets lake-effect snow that comes roaring down from Lake Michigan, Suzanne told us. As weather spotters, the Joyners keep diligent records of such storms. "We got more than eighteen inches of snow over one weekend a few years ago," Ron said.

Their farm has a 270-degree view and is within sight of Mount Rogers and White Top Mountain to the north, but their orchards enjoy a southern exposure. "Our closest neighbor is a half mile away," Suzanne said. "And we only see two electric lights at night." Taking advantage of such true dark, Ron built an observatory on the property, and he photographs objects in deep space with an astronomical camera.

Until this year, the Joyners always had plenty of water for their apple trees. "Our mountain normally weeps with water," Ron said, but in the summer of 2016 the orchards suffered from an unprecedented drought. Their household water supply comes from twin springs, which, in thirty years, never quit running for more than forty-eight hours. But when we met at the Farmers Market, in September, Ron and Suzanne had been without running water in their home for six weeks and counting.

Big Horse Creek Farm is planted to its edges with heritage apples, and the Joyners offer more than 350 varieties that they graft themselves onto one of three varieties of semidwarf rootstock. Most years they ship some 2,000 plants nationwide. This year they celebrated their first order from North Dakota. They can finally say that they have customers in every state except Hawaii.

Each year, customers submit their requests by March, and the Joyners graft plants to order and keep them growing until it's time to ship nearly a year later. For most of this summer, they have had to haul water up the mountain to ensure that their young plants survive. They transfer creek water to large containers, which they truck uphill from the lower part of the property. They hand-water every plant. It has been a grueling season, probably the worst since they left their research jobs in Raleigh and moved here, thirty years ago.

The Joyners, who are now in their sixties, occasionally hire help for the massive task of pruning their mature trees. This year, two women — sustainable agriculture students from Appalachian State University in Boone — helped out. "The trees just get bigger as we get older," Suzanne said.

One thing that has gotten easier over the years, however, is reaching customers from their isolated location. Before the days of the internet, the Joyners had to take out magazine ads and otherwise depend on word of mouth for business. Now their extensive website details the traits of each heirloom apple they sell along with a bit of its history. Big Horse Creek Farm is one of a few businesses in the country with such an extensive stock. Sometimes the farm receives referrals from giant, mainstream nurseries, such as Stark Brothers, a company that dates back to the early 1800s and was the first to license and market both Red Delicious and Golden Delicious apples. Stark customers who contact the Joyners are usually looking for a rare heirloom.

Contrary to popular belief, planting apple seeds does not produce trees that match the apple from which the seeds came. As Edward Behr explains in *The Artful Eater*, "Without the techniques of grafting (or of rooting a branch), each tree in the world would constitute its own variety, distinct from every other." The Joyners reproduce their heirloom trees by a process known as dormant spring grafting. As they explain on the website, "A shoot or twig (known as a scion or scionwood) is collected in January or February and stored under refrigeration until grafting season. The process of grafting itself is quite simple. A selected piece of scionwood is inserted into the root-stock of a young apple tree where, over time, it will heal and fuse together to produce a new tree. We carefully nurture this young tree over the summer so that by the fall planting period we will have a strong, healthy one-year-old tree ready for you to put into the ground." The Joyners will also graft trees from scion wood provided by customers or from collectors who have found a specimen they would like to add to their collection.

In addition to the trees they place in two-gallon containers to sell at farmers' markets and other venues during the fall and the grafted plants they ship around the country, the Joyners also sell scion wood — ten- to twelve-inch new growth branches from their apple varieties that can be used by other growers. "A good grafter can get four or five plants out of one twelve-inch stick," Ron explained.

Because the Joyners have no more room in their orchards for new trees, they will graft a variety they want to collect onto a mature tree. "These trees produce several kinds of fruit, which is very eye-catching," Ron said. One tree near their house has eight varieties of apples that ripen over time on various limbs.

The Joyners are contributing to the preservation of heirloom apples from across North Carolina and well beyond. Ron worries that with global warming, many cold-climate apples will simply fade away, making the south-ern varieties that can survive warmer weather essential. Though their pri-mary work is propagation, the Joyners also sell bushels of apples to the pub-lic. They see this activity as part of their educational mission. "More than any other fruit, humans have a connection to apples," Suzanne said. "There is no other fruit with the diversity of flavor, color, and uses."

"And we need to show people what is happening to our food sources and the value of these heirlooms," Ron went on. "Another part of our mission is to be independent, self-sustaining, and self-reliant." The Joyners freeze and can vegetables from their garden to last year-round, and they enjoy fresh venison in hunting season. They buy milk and coffee from the grocery, and yes, they eat out once in a while, Suzanne added.

The Joyners have built long-distance relationships with many cus-tomers, which are a big part of their compensation for a vocation that allows them to escape for only a week or two in December and another week or two in June, when they head to the eastern shore for bird watching. As with most people in agriculture, their business has its ups and downs. They've had

Suzanne and Ron Joyner offer their harvest to neighbors at the Ashe County Farmers Market. They graft and preserve more than 350 varieties of heirloom apples at Big Horse Creek Farm in the remote northwestern corner of North Carolina.

problems with potting soil, fertilizer, and occasionally with rootstock. In a good year, however, the Joyners will harvest two to three tons of apples. They also do their part for the local economy; they are the biggest customer at the tiny post office in Lansing, where they ship out all their products.

Ron grew up in an itinerant military family that finally settled in eastern North Carolina on the Tar River in Nash County. He earned a degree in wildlife biology from North Carolina State University and then conducted lab research on the effects of air pollution on plants. Suzanne, who is from upstate New York, started out at North Carolina State's design school in architecture but eventually turned to biology, with an emphasis on biochemistry. She worked for the pharmaceutical giant Burroughs Wellcome, in Research Triangle Park, for many years. After two decades in Raleigh, however, the Joyners moved to their mountain farm in Ashe County.

Suzanne proclaimed that even after all these years of growing apples, she can still happily eat applesauce every day. For Ron, cider is the standby, and he is fond of the year-old Molly Chomper Cidery that neighbors established in the old Lansing School, down the road from the farm. Last year, the Joyners sold forty bushels of apples to be made into cider there. It was labeled Big Horse Creek, after their farm. They agreed that the best cider and the best applesauce are made from a blend of apples, not from any single variety.

Lee Calhoun, the author of the southern apple encyclopedia, was the Joyners' teacher and mentor, whom they met when they still lived in Raleigh. "I had always been interested in heirloom vegetables, and one day I invited myself to the Calhouns' house, in Chatham County," Ron explained. It was from Lee and his wife, Edith, that the Joyners became fascinated with the mystery and variety of old apples. Though he doesn't hunt for lost apples so much anymore, Ron is still hoping to track down an old Cherokee variety called Kittageskee that dates back to the 1850s. He says it's a yellow apple — small and adaptable. Every nursery in the Deep South was growing Kittageskees at one time, he told us. It was also imported from Georgia to France, but Ron has yet to find anyone with a memory of this tree and its fruit.

* * *

At our second meeting, in October, at Boondock's, a popular brewpub and restaurant in downtown West Jefferson, Ron and Suzanne brought samples of five apples that had ripened since our first visit. Ron wore his trademark brown fedora, and Suzanne, as usual, had her thick hair pulled back and braided down her spine. Both were dressed in jeans and flannel shirts. Donna and I sat down with them for an afternoon meal, and they told us about the history of each apple variety they had brought us in separate, labeled bags. They still had no running water in the house—now more than two months without.

As to flavor and favorites, Ron was quick to say that everyone's palate is different, and he would never share his preference for any particular apple. He also was adamant that apples should be kept at room temperature. The best way to sample them, he said, is to take a big bite and notice "the explosion of flavor, aroma, texture, and crispness." For her part, Suzanne likes to peel an apple first. Both agreed that it would be good to have crackers available to clear the palate between tastes when we sat down to sample the fruit they brought us.

"We have been brainwashed to eat apples that are bred for shipping," Ron said. "And people always want the big apples, but that does not make them the best." He said he often fantasizes about what it would be like to visit the part of China where apples originated. "They have whole forests of apple trees there," he said dreamily. "Can you imagine a forest where every tree is a different apple? Just the fragrance! Think of it."

Back at the cabin in Little Switzerland, in front of a blazing fire, Donna and I put out a tray of our sample apples, uncut and labeled by name, for visual comparison. On another platter, we prepared half-inch slices of each variety, ready for tasting. (Despite Ron's advice, we couldn't all bite into whole apples—we didn't have that many.) We put out a small basket of plain crackers and a cup of water for each taster.

My neighbors Alvis Smith, originally from New Hill in western Wake County, and Dennis Williams, from Clement in Sampson County down east, joined us that night. Both men are retired and both were North Carolina farm boys raised in the 4-H Club and Future Farmers of America. Though they attended college to prepare for careers away from the farm, they have never veered from a deep appreciation of their rural roots—the beekeeping, cow milking, and hog killing that marked the seasons of their parents and grandparents. Jim Harb, our consultant in the earlier chapter on figs, was also with us from Knoxville. We began sampling our "flight" of apples with the Junaluska, an heirloom with a Native American name.

The Junaluska is a rather clumsy-looking greenish apple, much wider than tall, with blotches of rust and dots of gray all over the skin. Jim had the first bite and taught us a new word: malic, an acid in fruit that delivers a pleasantly sour taste. The Junaluska had some malic, all right, and it had a tough skin, too, "like a winesap," Jim suggested. We all agreed it was a firm apple, with a "pretty nice texture," as Dennis noted, but not overly juicy, which may have been a result of the drought conditions this year. Jim pointed out that while the Junaluska was tasty, the apple did not have a very long finish. In other words, the flavor disappeared quickly, which made me want another bite and then another. Pretty satisfying apple overall.

Tom Brown is a heritage apple expert who has found and identified more than a thousand old varieties, including the Junaluska. He works out of his home in Clemmons, North Carolina, near Winston-Salem. As Brown explained in a story for BlueRidgeNow.com, he sees his work as a race against time as old apple trees are cut down or die and as elders who remember the bygone names and flavors are also leaving us.

Brown's passionate hunt for the Junaluska led him to a mountaintop home in Macon County, where he met a ninety-three-year-old woman who had two apple trees that she called John Berry Keepers. The description of the apples resembled that of the Junaluska. The trees were growing about eight miles from what had been Silas McDowell's orchard in the mid-1800s. Silas McDowell—whom I first learned about while writing the *Literary Trails* guidebook series on North Carolina authors—was a botanist, apple grower, and writer. He published in *Harper's Weekly* and a number of regional publications and also served as the local clerk of court in Franklin, the Macon County seat. A lively raconteur and student of local history, McDowell collected specimen plants for the Harvard botanist Asa Gray. He was also the first to theorize and write about "thermal belts," those microclimates on the sides of mountains where frosts and freezes tend to occur less frequently than on ridgetops or in the bottoms. Fruit growing is especially favorable at such middle altitudes, where rapidly moving cold air from above tends to hold down warmer air and keep it from rising higher, even as the air below the thermal belt in the bottoms can grow colder at night.

Of the Junaluskee apple, as he spelled it, McDowell wrote in a letter to a friend, "The original tree was owned by a Cherokee Chief of the above name, residing in Macon or Cherokee County, N.C., I do not now recollect which. When the state purchased of the Indians this portion of their territory, Chief Junaluskee refused to part with his lot on which grew his favorite tree. To induce him to part with it, the Commissioners agreed to allow him $50 for his apple tree."

Junaluska, who fought alongside Andrew Jackson and reportedly saved the military leader's life, later unsuccessfully lobbied President Jackson in Washington to halt the plan for Cherokee removal from the region. Following the tribe's forced march to Oklahoma in 1838 on what came to be known as the "Trail of Tears," Junaluska eventually returned to North Carolina, where he farmed until his death in 1868. He is buried on the Snowbird Indian Council grounds in Robbinsville.

In the 1800s, various versions of the name—Junaluskee, Junaliska, and Journalaskia—appeared in nursery catalogs and magazines, according to Tom Brown. It was described by A. J. Downing (*The Fruits and Fruit Trees of America*, 1854) and W. H. Ragan (*Nomenclature of the Apple*, 1905) as medium-large, roundish oblate, and yellow with some russet, as having a short stem and flesh that was yellowish and rich, and as ripening late. Brown's research continued, including a published call in the local newspaper for memories from elders about the apple. Eventually, three different old-timers in the region sampled ripe apples that Brown believed were possibly the Junaluska. All of them independently agreed they were the very apples they remembered from their youth.

Brown shared scion wood from the Macon County Junaluska trees with a number of growers who also sell heritage apple trees. He grafted Junaluska trees for donation to members of the Eastern Band of Cherokee Indians. Three of these young trees were planted at the Junaluska Memorial and Gravesite, where Chief Junaluska is buried. Brown also supplied Junaluska apple trees to the Methodists' Junaluska Assembly near Waynesville and to the Western Band of the Cherokee in Oklahoma.

It was amazing to reflect on this story and our communion with history that night through the taste of a Junaluska apple.

* * * * * * * * * * * *

Our second apple, the King Luscious, was Donna's favorite. It was juicy and sweet, with a flavor akin to grape. It was not as firm as the Junaluska—"not hard on the teeth," as Donna put it—and we all agreed the flavor lingered longer.

Our King Luscious sample was a third bigger than the Junaluska and the largest of our five apples. It was red with yellow striping and quite lopsided when sitting on its bottom. The stem was off-center, and the cavity where the stem connected was deep.

Strictly speaking, King Luscious is not an antique apple, Ron Joyner had told us. According to Calhoun's book, King Luscious keeps well and "was found in 1935 growing as a chance seedling near Hendersonville, North Carolina." Notably, the village of Fruitland, in Henderson County, was the site where European settlers first planted apple trees in the state, and the county is part of North Carolina's most productive apple-growing region, distinguished by the prevalence of Silas McDowell's "thermal belts." Today, Henderson and Polk Counties account for nearly 70 percent of the state's commercial apple crop, according to the state Department of Agriculture.

Of the five apples we tried that night, readers are more likely to find King Luscious in some of the smaller commercial orchards in the state than any of the others. One of the prime destinations in the state for heritage apples is Southern Heritage Apple Orchard, at the nineteenth-century Horne Creek Farm in Pinnacle, North Carolina. Pomologist Tom Brown donated a hundred different varieties of heritage apples that he discovered after they had been "lost," and they are now in the farm's collection, which numbers around 400 varieties. Visitors there can find the Junaluska, the King Luscious, and the next apple we tasted, the Magnum Bonum.

* * * * * * * * * * * * *

The Magnum Bonum (also called Maggie Bowman, Magna Bonum, Red Bonum, and Bona) was the third and smallest apple in our taste test. It got very high marks from historian Lee Calhoun, who suggests that it would be on "everybody's list of the top ten southern apples," with the ability to grow "from the mountains to the sea." He notes, however, that it should be picked quickly once ripe. John Kinny (also known as "Squire" Kinney), of Davidson County, North Carolina, is credited with first growing this apple, from the seed of a Hall apple, in 1828.

The Joyners' Magnum Bonum snapped when we cut into it and was intensely aromatic. This apple was Dennis's favorite. Jim found it too soft. To me, it tasted a lot like a good, store-bought apple juice and was very refreshing. As Dennis said, it was "very apple-y." Once again, we all wondered about the stress of drought on all of these apples. Ron had warned that the textures might not be as crisp as usual. He noted that many of his apples had thicker skins this season as a protective measure against the lack of rain. "When you see trees trying to bloom at the wrong time of year, as we have, that's another sign of extreme stress," he said.

● ● ● ● ● ● ● ● ● ● ● ● ●

I'd asked the Joyners to bring us one of the apples they'd discovered and named themselves. What they call the Husk Sweet was a wild seedling that was growing in the woods on their property in 1985. The Joyners named it for the tiny village of Husk, near their farm. Ron had declared it "the child's version of an apple: white, crisp, and all sugar."

Usually apples given the name "sweet" or the older term "sweeting" don't really have unusually high sugar content but rather an absence of acid. Ron had already warned us that he could tell by simply looking at this year's Husk Sweet crop that they would not live up to the name. The Husk was indeed the most water-starved and heat-stressed apple in the lot. Alvis took a bite and called it "washed out."

We agreed on that analysis and turned our attention to the Coffey Seedling, another big apple with a very deep cavity. It was mostly red, with some yellow/green blotches. It was not an apple I had requested from the Joyners, but Ron wanted us to try it, and I immediately understood why. It was different. The flavor reminded me of a gewürztraminer wine. Alvis, Jim, and I agreed it was our favorite of the lot, even if the apple smelled "a bit like wet straw," as Alvis put it.

Calhoun documented the Coffey Seedling as having appeared in an 1890 catalog published by the Catawba County Nursery in Newton, North Carolina (near Hickory). It is a member of the expansive Limbertwig family of apples and was reported to have produced huge apples — up to twenty-four ounces in weight.

Calhoun goes on to say that another nursery catalog placed this apple's origin in Caldwell County, in the foothills due north of Catawba. Years ago, Calhoun found an apple called a Coffey Seedling, but he says the apple was identical to the Dula's Beauty. Dula is a common surname in Caldwell County—the most notorious member of the family being Tom Dula, the legendary pretty boy who supposedly murdered his sweetheart, Laura Foster, in Happy Valley, just outside of the town of Lenoir. Dula is buried in this beautiful valley. (The song "Tom Dooley," recorded by the Kingston Trio, tells his story, as does Sharyn McCrumb in her novel *The Ballad of Tom Dooley*.)

This provenance comes with an asterisk. Ron Joyner was told that the Coffey Seedling might have originated in Watauga County, as Nancy Moretz, who is a descendent of the Coffey family there, claimed. Ron nevertheless lists the apple in his farm's inventory as "identical to the Dula Beauty, planted by J. A. Dula of Lenoir."

The next night Donna made a pie from all of the Joyners' apples that we had left after our tasting, and it was spectacular. The blend of fruits was subtle, and Donna's scratch crust was masterly. And yes, ice cream was involved.

Our evening apple sampling confirmed the view of Edward Behr in *The Artful Eater*. "In sampling different varieties from one orchard to another," Behr wrote, "one comes to understand that an essential apple virtue is its unexpected variety of flavor, its surprises from apple to apple, tree to tree, and especially from year to year — produced largely by those imperfectly understood influences of soil, cultural practices, climate, and weather."

The inconsistency in taste, size, appearance, and sweetness that we experienced in our test suggests a valuable lesson about the ephemeral nature of our lives. This idea, as well as the simple value of mixing apple varieties to make a pie, is not something that the contemporary produce section in the supermarket conveys so readily.

The next afternoon we set out to meet Bill Carson, the proprietor of the Orchard at Altapass, on the Blue Ridge Parkway. Located at Milepost 328.3, between Mount Mitchell and Linville Falls, this orchard was originally planted by the Clinchfield Railroad in the early 1900s, after the company had built a precipitous series of eighteen tunnels that allowed the railroad to ferry coal, mostly from Kentucky, over the Continental Divide here and down to the town of Marion and on to Spartanburg and points east and south. The orchard sits in a thermal belt on the side of the mountain, where the Toe River flows to the west and the Catawba River flows to the east. With the railroad in place, a resort town named Altapass sprang up at the turn of the century. Its two hotels and golf course boomed until the railroad discontinued passenger service up the mountain. Then the Blue Ridge Parkway was built in the 1930s, bisecting the orchard. Upkeep of the apple trees would be checkered in the years that followed.

Finally, in 1994, the orchard went up for sale, and a developer drew up elaborate plans to install scores of houses above the parkway. With uncanny timing, Bill Carson's sister, Kit Truby, came to town and saw an ad in the weekly newspaper for the orchard. After a two-hour walk around the property, Truby had a strong impulse to buy the 288-acre orchard. In the same day, she managed to secure a contract ahead of several others who had already made offers on the owner's answering machine. But when Truby called, she got through to the owner, and they quickly signed a contract. The ambitious developer persisted, however, now offering Truby more and more money for the parcel on the upper side of the parkway. Truby decided to save the entire viewshed for future generations and instead sold the land above the parkway to the Conservation Trust for North Carolina. On the lower acreage, the family developed a nonprofit center to honor mountain culture and history and to continue growing and selling apples from the old orchard.

Truby's brother, Bill Carson, and his wife, Judy, agreed to help run the project. Bill had already retired from IBM, where he had been vice president of the Federal Systems Division, working as an aerospace engineer on several major initiatives. He led the software development for the Saturn rocket used in the Apollo moon mission, the Patriot Missile System, and the first Global Positioning System (GPS). Carson likes to say that, thanks to his sister's purchase of the orchard, he "went from IBM to apple overnight." He also told us he had learned the hard way that "it's easier to put a man on the moon than it is to grow apples in the Blue Ridge."

Carson, now in his mid-seventies, is a local hero. The orchard, while still dependent on philanthropy, has become an important draw for visitors and a center of local community activity — flatfoot dancing, old-time music, and hayrides on weekends from May to the end of October.

"It's a huge accomplishment," said Houck Medford, Carson's best friend and the former director of the Blue Ridge Parkway Foundation. "Bill is one of the most genuine people I've ever met in my life."

A consummate storyteller, Carson makes countless visits to public school classrooms in the region to ensure that students know their local history — how the native peoples used the land where the orchard sits as a passage through the mountains and how a friend found a 10,000-year-old spearpoint nearby. He tells tales of the orchard's first full-time resident, Charlie

McKinney, whose surname is shared by many in Mitchell County. In his life-time, McKinney had four wives and forty-eight children.

Carson also dons a Revolutionary-era patriot's uniform to present the story of the Overmountain Men, who marched through Altapass all the way down to King's Mountain beyond present-day Charlotte to take on the British in October 1780. Only after Carson started the orchard project did he learn that it had been his fifth great-grandfather Robert Young who was the sixty-two-year-old patriot credited with killing Major Patrick Ferguson, the leader of the British troops at King's Mountain. Young used a rifle he called "Sweet Lips," which always draws a laugh from Carson's audiences. When his aunt first told him of the family connection to this historic battle, Carson knew in his bones that caring for the orchard was his proper destiny.

Among the 2,000 apple trees that local workers manage to prune in stages every other year, there are thirty-some varieties of apples at the Orchard at Altapass. Carson planted several of the Magnum Bonums himself. "Those apples go fast, because people love them," he said. He plans to propagate more of these heirlooms with the help of Doug Hundley, another veteran North Carolina pomologist who lives up the road in Newland.

King Luscious also grows in several areas through the orchard. "They are not good pollinators," Carson said. "They are late to bloom and were hit hard with fire blight that killed the tops of the trees this year, so they are easy to spot." Still, Carson said, the King Luscious is a popular apple and sells quickly because of its large size.

In Carson's pick-your-own scheme, orchard visitors are simply issued a bag and invited to roam the orchard. He tells his guests as they head out on the terraced mountainside, "Pick any apple you see, polish it on your shirt, and take a bite. Spit it out, toss it, or eat all you want of it, but if you like it, put it — or what's left of it — in the bag." Patrons bring their harvest back to the big red orchard building and pay by the pound.

By far the most popular apple with local folks, Carson said, is the Virginia Beauty, which was favored by the late bluegrass legend Doc Watson, who came down from Deep Gap to Altapass every year to get his supply.

"I tried to get Doc to play at least three chords just one time, so I could say he'd been on our stage here, but he never did," Carson explained. Watson would, however, call ahead to make sure his order of Virginia Beauties would be ready for him. "Every time he came, I had a whole list of people who had asked me to call them so they could come and 'accidentally' meet Doc Watson." Carson grinned.

Bill Carson, a storyteller, historian, apple grower, and conservationist, relaxes in costume at the orchard house where apple pickers meet local guitar and banjo pickers for entertainment at the Orchard at Altapass on the Blue Ridge Parkway between Mount Mitchell and Linville Falls.

Part of the Virginia Beauty's popularity, he said, comes from the local tradition of wrapping them individually in newspaper, stowing them in the pantry, and then taking them out at Christmas. "By then, you can scoop them out and eat them with a spoon," he said. Ron Joyner had likewise reported the popularity of the Virginia Beauty with his customers. The variety originated about an hour north of the Joyners' farm.

The Orchard at Altapass also grows more familiar varieties—Golden Delicious, Grimes Golden, Stayman Winesap, and Yates. It sells cider, fudge, jams, jellies, apple cider doughnuts, honey, and ice cream. The lunch pavilion serves locally sourced meats and vegetables, including pinto beans and corn bread. This down-to-earth center celebrating mountain culture—"saving the good stuff," as Carson describes it—is especially popular with children and families and is usually humming with visitors, even on weekdays when local musicians are not performing.

It was a relatively quiet weekday afternoon when we sat with Bill Carson, after he had come in from a full day of storytelling to middle schoolers up in Avery County. He was still dressed in his Overmountain militia outfit, looking quite dapper. As we talked, customers streamed in from the windy bluster outside, interrupting Carson to give him a hug or a wave. He called most by name.

Recently, Carson's sister, Kit, signed over the entire orchard to the nonprofit Altapass Foundation the family had established and agreed to a permanent conservation easement with the Conservation Trust. Carson proudly showed us a map of how many other landowners in the area had done the same—a patchwork of tracts that adds up to more than 2,000 acres preserved from further development.

When we finished our interview, Carson took us out back to the deck attached to the orchard headquarters that overlooks the mountains we'd just fingered on the map. Though the air was cold and a rain shower loomed to the west, directly in front of us a half rainbow arched straight down from a sun-caught cloud and into the valley. The air stung my cheeks and my eyes welled. We stood in silence for a while, admiring the colors. I hugged Bill, grateful to his family for preserving this land, where heirloom apples grow and where children can still hunt for them and test their sweetness.

November

Persimmons

THE SECOND HARD FROST OF THE SEASON DESCENDED ON THE Piedmont two days before Thanksgiving. A predawn temperature of twenty-eight degrees finally took out the pots of nasturtiums and geraniums that flanked my front door. Nearby, a cabbage-leaf coneflower — seven feet tall with a single yellow bloom at the top — was bent over like a freshman walk-on after one too many sprints down the Carolina basketball court.

The day before, the leafless persimmon trees at Carrboro Elementary School were still in full fruit, orbs suspended high like tiny burnished lanterns, dusky red as if a cloud of smoke had come by and clung to them in patches. Those persimmons would serve as backup for the pudding requested for our Thanksgiving table — we had shaken down fruit from these trees in years past — but on this day I hoped to score some fruit from the persimmon experts whom Donna Campbell and I planned to visit in Chatham, Montgomery, and Guilford Counties.

American persimmons (*Dyospyros virginiana*) are a prime example of a food that requires us to confront our human place in the bigger scheme of ecology. You can't plant a grove of American persimmon trees and expect to reap a reliable crop in a decade. The trees spread easily from seed, but individual plants are either male or female, and both are required to make fruit. Unfortunately, it's difficult to determine the gender of an immature plant for several years unless you have a trained eye. Moreover, once a tree is producing fruit, the persimmons ripen and drop on their own accord, depending on the vicissitudes of weather, bagworms, and wind — not necessarily when people are ready to eat them.

As the eastern North Carolina forager and writer Janet Lembke explained in her essay collection *Shake Them 'Simmons Down*, "Patience is the key to success in eating any variety of common persimmon in its fresh state. If they offer the slightest firmness when touched, they are not ready. But when the skins seem filled with an almost liquid mush, rejoice and bite in, catching the sugar-sweet juice as it runs down your chin."

Shaking the tree is the best way to harvest the ripe fruits. Of course, a ready persimmon will often be bruised and leaking once it has taken a fall from the tree. It is not, therefore, a product to gather mechanically, warehouse, and ship later. For all these reasons, American persimmons have never been a commercially viable fruit. They just don't keep. At the time of their ripening, the best thing to do is to eat them immediately or make a special treat, such as bread, pudding, or jam.

To prepare a batch of persimmons, you must first extract the seeds — a labor-intensive process that usually involves a cone-shaped sieve and wooden pestle. You can use the pulp immediately, turn it into jam, or freeze it for baking later. Persimmons come with an abundance of pectin built right into the fruit. (Pectin is a polysaccharide that, when heated together with sugar, is a natural thickener.) To become a successful jam or jelly, many other fruits require the addition of commercial pectin, but not persimmons, though some jam makers add pectin anyway.

Persimmon pulp can also be dried, as the Algonquins did centuries ago, creating something like what we now call a fruit roll-up or fruit leather. Three Algonquian dialects had similar words for dried fruit: *putchamin, pasiminian,* and *pessamin* — hence the name English colonists eventually adopted for the American persimmon.

Watching the indigenous people prepare persimmons was of great interest to the first English explorers who came to what is now coastal North Carolina. The naturalist and navigator Thomas Hariot wrote about the fruit in his account of the year he spent on Roanoke Island with John White, beginning in April 1585. Sir Walter Raleigh sent Hariot on the second expedition to the New World because Hariot had begun to master the Algonquian language with the help of Manteo and Wanchese — the Indians who returned to England with a reconnaissance party after the first expedition the queen sent to the New World in 1584. *A Brief and True Report of the New Found Land of Virginia,* also mentioned in chapter 9, provides Hariot's written inventory of the native foods he encountered and contains the first description of the persimmon in the English language. Hariot compared the fruit to the European medlar: "Medlars: a kind of verie good fruit, so called by us chieflie for these respectes: first in that they are not good untill they be rotten: then in that they open at the head as our medlars, and are about the same bignesse: otherwise in taste and colour they are farre different: for they are as red as cheries and very sweet: but whereas the cherie is sharpe sweet, they are lushious sweet."

Hariot's comparison of the American persimmon to the medlar was apt. Medlars (*Mesipilus germanica*) are the fruit of a small flowering tree belonging to the rose family. Originating in the Middle East, medlars were cultivated by the Romans and popularized by Charlemagne, who insisted that they be planted along the path of his conquests. The medlar is one of few

European fruits that become edible in winter, and like persimmons, they are high in bitter tannins. Because they are not edible until they are "bletted" (or not quite rotten, as Hariot says), the mushy brown pulp of the medlar was often made into jelly or combined with sugar, cinnamon, ginger, and eggs to make a custard that might fill a pastry tart. This list of ingredients for a medlar tart appears in a cookbook published in 1665, *The Accomplisht Cook; or, The Art and Mystery of Cookery*, by Robert May. May's formula is strikingly similar to the African American and European American recipes for persimmon pudding that still grace many a Thanksgiving table today.

American persimmons (not the large, bright orange varieties from Asia seen in grocery stores) are native to all 100 counties in North Carolina, but it seems this fruit has never been universally popular, probably because biting into a persimmon before it has ripened is a torture to the tongue. The bitter flavor is obnoxious, but the immediate texture the fruit creates between the cheeks is worse and has been compared to eating cotton or having a mouthful of talcum powder.

Naturalist John McPhee once tried to swallow a large spoonful of slightly unripe persimmons that the wild food guru Euell Gibbons had just stewed up for him with maple syrup over a campfire: "Each mouthful tasted fine on entry," McPhee writes, "but quickly turned into something like a glut of blotting paper, requiring a half dozen swallows to squeeze it down." Stories and practical jokes involving unsuspecting persimmon eaters coaxed into an untimely taste of the developing fruit are the stuff of family legend in North Carolina and beyond.

The U.S. Department of Agriculture's *Farmers' Bulletin* #685, first published in 1915 and updated several times up to a final 1942 edition, made an extraordinary assessment of the persimmon's place among American fruit trees in the early twentieth century:

> The persimmon tree has received more criticism, both adverse and favorable, than almost any other known species. Those who have discussed the food value of the fruit, from the earliest chroniclers to recent writers, have prophesied that the tree would soon be accorded a place in our gardens and orchards. Those people, on the other hand, who have been acquainted only with the immature fruit or with the young sprouts in cultivated fields had nothing to say in its favor and have bent their energies toward its destruction rather than its propagation and cultivation.

I called Jeff Michael, a longtime persimmon pudding aficionado raised in Stanly County, to ask about this historically mixed review of persimmons. Michael is director of the Urban Institute at the University of North Carolina at Charlotte, a think tank that addresses the social, economic, and environmental challenges facing the region. His kin are dotted all around Morrow Mountain and the Uwharrie National Forest, where Jeff, his wife, Autumn, and their four energetic children escape to a little farmstead on weekends. He immediately warmed to the topic, telling me that he has come to believe that North Carolina has what he calls a "persimmon pudding belt" that runs diagonally through the Piedmont more or less along the corridor of Interstate 85, beginning above the Triad and stopping just short of Charlotte.

"I have been talking about this forever," Michael said. "As a rural boy, there were certain foodways you just assumed you shared with other people from rural North Carolina—like eating collards and black-eyed peas for New Year's and loving ham biscuits. When I went to college in Chapel Hill in the 1980s, these familiar foods gave me an instant connection with a lot of my Tar Heel classmates. But I also noticed that when I mentioned the persimmon pudding that I grew up eating around Thanksgiving time, the response was not uniform. Going home with friends on weekends to eastern North Carolina, I remember families being taken aback at the mention of eating persimmons. 'That is what the pigs eat,' they said."

The USDA bulletin from 1915 confirms Michael's report: "Probably the most common use of the fruit is feed for hogs. As a rule, the hogs are merely turned loose in lots where persimmon trees have come up naturally . . . furnishing forage for hogs from the last of August until early winter."

Though Jeff Michael traffics in empirical research at the university's Urban Institute, he confessed that he has not yet taken a statistically significant sample of contemporary North Carolina persimmon eaters to compare with those who are averse to the fruit. He could then geo-code the responses, he said, to confirm his theory, but he was pretty certain of the general boundaries of the persimmon pudding belt.

Donna and I thus set out to conduct further unscientific research to test Jeff Michael's thesis. The informal experts we visited had plenty to say about the trees themselves, the lore surrounding them, and the best recipes for this beleaguered native fruit.

We left on our persimmon expedition at half past seven in the morning and headed south from Carrboro on Mount Carmel Church Road toward Chatham County. Squinting at the fields where pumpkins had ripened a month before, we could almost believe the grass was snow-covered. The frost was thick and glittering. The pleasant scent of wood smoke from a farmhouse leaked into the car as we sailed by.

It takes a while to cross Jordan Lake — so wide along this stretch. A lone boat occupied by two hardy fishermen was perfectly reflected in still water, but we did not envy them in such cold. Once beyond the shoreline, we came to Highway 64, which runs east and west between Raleigh and Pittsboro. The daily rush of commuters was knotted up at a traffic light. We crossed over 64 into another world, an older time.

Pines and more pines, a thick understory, and then suddenly there was historic Ebenezer United Methodist Church like an island in the forest — a striking Gothic Revival–style building from the 1890s, moved to this spot when both the sanctuary and its members were displaced by the flooding that created Jordan Lake nearly a century later, in 1981. "Sanctuary" is still the operative word. Though subdivisions are encroaching farther and farther south of the metro area of Raleigh-Durham-Chapel Hill, great swaths of undeveloped land and working farms persist in these parts.

Our first stop was the spread owned by Charles W. Holland, a second-generation farmer and retired logger, now the proprietor of a sawmill and a collector and purveyor of fine woods.

Mr. Holland's youngest son, Peyton, had recently married and built a house alongside his dad's property. (Peyton was also our source for his mother's Juneberry pie recipe, shared in chapter 6.) We had arranged to meet at Peyton's house. He and his wife, Kara, have so far raised three brown and white ducks — Elvis, Priscilla (who turned out to be a drake), and MoMo, so named for her Mohawk headdress. They are agreeable birds that come when called, and we tarried with them beside the pond before going inside to inspect the persimmon wood that Peyton and his father applied luxuriously throughout the new house.

Persimmon trees belong to the ebony family, Peyton said. The wood is very hard, so hard that he optimistically installed it in the form of tongue-and-groove flooring in the upstairs area that he and Kara have planned as a

Persimmons

playroom for the children they hope to raise someday. Persimmon paneling also covered several walls and doors in the house, along with an interesting array of maple, cypress, black walnut, cherry, yellow pine, cedar, willow, and poplar. Such are the advantages of belonging to a family in the wood business. But persimmon, our host said, is the least common wood to be put to such use. It was strikingly beautiful with its bold streaks of black and a fine, tight grain that swirled with subtle color gradations.

"Somebody called my dad and said he had two tractor-trailer loads of persimmon wood that came from clear-cutting a forest," Peyton explained. "I knew right then that I wanted it. The kitchen nook in the house where I grew up had persimmon paneling, and my imagination was always stoked by the patterns in that wood when I sat down for breakfast. I guess Daddy handled every board in this house at least thirty times. He milled it and then helped me put it up." Though Peyton is still boyish in appearance, his voice is as deep as the luster on his paneling.

"When persimmon is fresh-milled," he added, "the wood is almost purplish with reddish brown streaks. As it ages, it changes."

Guests are invited to remove their shoes when they enter the house, but Peyton and Kara have reconciled themselves to the likelihood of sanding and resurfacing the floors more than once after their offspring have their way with the place.

After our tour, we put our shoes back on and headed down the gravel road a quarter-mile to meet Peyton's father. We found him in the sawmill yard, supervising Wade, a young helper, who was chopping at a thick piece of fatwood with a hatchet. Fatwood, rich in resin, usually comes from the stump or taproot of the longleaf pine, the state tree of North Carolina. Wade was quickly filling a galvanized bucket with fragrant six-inch shards to be used as fire starter over the coming winter.

Nearby, a rusty oil drum had been outfitted with a lid and stovepipe. The drum was radiating welcome heat. Smoke swirled over our heads. The sun had finally peeked over the tree line and the frost was going liquid, running in quick rivulets off the tin roofs of all the outbuildings around us.

Seventy-three-year-old Charles Holland, clad in a Chatham Lumber Company cap, a plaid shirt, dusty brown work boots, a pair of soft Pointer overalls, and a navy blue jacket, invited us to sit down under the lean-to by the makeshift stove to visit. The melting frost dripped through a hole in the tin over our heads and pattered on the bench between us as he began to talk.

"When you saw fresh persimmon into boards," he said matter-of-factly, "it's so ugly people don't even like it. So what you do—see, I've got a pile of the wood right there." He pointed. "Me and the good Lord will age it. You put it up on a couple of logs and you let it sit." He paused. "But what I've learned over time is that you can't go too long. A good rule of thumb is about four months. If you go beyond that—now some of Peyton's wood, the majority of his, was perfect—but some I had to pull out before we carried it over to the house. The reason being, it was too long before we got around to sawing it." Mr. Holland looked off in the direction of the conveyor belt, an enormous saw blade, and a tall pile of sawdust beyond.

Pointing to the woodpile, Mr. Holland said, "What that persimmon does, it puts off all these different colors when it spalts." (Spalting occurs when dormant spores of various fungi begin to grow in air-dried wood.) "That's how all the colors come about."

He continued: "Some of that stuff like we used in Peyton's door casings come from a young tree. If you get a young tree, it'll have the imprint of how the tree grows, and there's a certain way you saw it to get that look. You have to quarter-saw it. In other words, you go straight across, just like you was sawing straight through that barrel." He pointed to the rusted barrel where the fire was crackling. "And that's how you would get the picture—the design—of that tree to come out on the boards. But persimmons—most people don't know nothing about 'em. You don't really know what the wood's going to look like until you sand it."

Mr. Holland went on to explain that woodyards reject persimmon because, like walnut, it tends to darken the pulp when mixed with other woods. Because pulpwood is primarily used for paper production, discoloration is undesirable. Persimmon was favored, however, in the early years of North Carolina textile manufacture. Its uniform hardness and capacity to stay smooth under continued wear made it ideal for the creation of the shuttles that were used in mechanical looms around the beginning of the last century. The wood was also popular in the making of gunstocks, handles for small tools, heads of golf drivers, and pool cues.

"When I was small," Mr. Holland said, "my daddy would cut a small persimmon tree and make wedges out of it, and that's what we'd throw trees with. Persimmon wood is so hard you can use it for a wedge to make the tree lean and fall where you want. We kept some of them wedges with us all the time. But the biggest use of persimmon for me is to make siding out of it. I just love it for the character and the colors you get. Anything unique—that's what I like to fool with."

Persimmons

Charles Holland, an expert on persimmons, holds one of the many wooden bowls he's turned on a handmade lathe at his sawmill in New Hill.

Mr. Holland broke into a smile and stood, smoothing down his overalls. It was time for a tour of the woodyard and the shed where he turns thick slabs of wood into bowls on a rig he invented. We set off with our hands in our pockets against the chill.

Giant boards of walnut sawed and stacked for tabletops and bar tops rested beside a rack of rough-hewn magnolia planks. Cedar had been cut and piled for closet linings. Elsewhere, Mr. Holland pointed out neat stacks of maple, oak, and enormous poplar planks that were ready to fill the orders of builders and decorators in several counties.

"You know that Lantern Restaurant in Chapel Hill?" Mr. Holland asked. We nodded. "That's my wood there."

Andrea Reusing, winner of the James Beard Award for best chef in the Southeast, recently asked Mr. Holland to come dine for free on one of his tabletops. He demurred, but the invitation clearly pleased him. "One year I give her a whole bucket of my persimmons, too," he said.

He stepped toward a tall, tarp-covered block and pulled back the cover to reveal a rack of persimmon wood. The extra-thick lumber had been squared off at the ends for mantelpieces.

"It's not that much persimmon around anymore," Mr. Holland said ruefully, "and the sad part of it is, a persimmon tree works great. When I was a boy, we used to have a bird dog, and when the persimmons would start getting ripe, every morning you could hear that dog. He'd be barking down by the trees. Mama would say, 'He's got a possum down there.' And I'd go out, and sure enough that dog would stay right there at that tree and bark, and that possum would be up there eating persimmons, the little ole bitty ones. Possum would just keep on eating till he was full."

Historically, such predictable animal behavior pleased hunters, particularly in the North Carolina mountains. Opossums (the only marsupial native to the North American continent) can reliably be found among the ripening fruit, which makes them easy quarry, and if they have already been stuffing themselves with persimmons for a few days, they are so much the better to eat.

The old expression "For every possum there is a persimmon tree" is not unlike the saying that for every pot there's a lid, though in the case of possums and persimmons, the comment today may generally be understood as pejorative, for both possum and persimmon are more likely to be seen as nuisances, not delicacies.

Times have indeed changed since Smoky Mountain writer and camp cookery master Horace Kephart declared possum to be a fine dish to be prepared only after freezing weather has set in and only in the company of sweet potatoes, preferably stuffed around the possum in a Dutch oven and cooked over coals. "Serve hot, *without* gravy," Kephart urges in his *Camp Cookery*, first published in 1910. "Bourbon whiskey is the only orthodox accompaniment."

"The sad part about it," Mr. Holland continued, "is the possums are not going to have many persimmon trees left. Nobody knows them nowadays. They ought to leave the hickory trees and the persimmons a little more just for seed, and then they'd come up and the animals would have them to eat. Everything eats them—squirrels, raccoons, bear, deer. Of course the deer durn near eat about anything." He laughed. "They come up here in my sawdust pile and play. They play like young'uns."

Hunters in North Carolina are wise to a deer's attraction to persimmons and often set their stands in proximity to the trees. Old-time musician Scott Manring told a Greensboro writer that he often sees deer raise themselves up on their two hind legs to pick persimmons off his trees in Pleasant Garden, south of Greensboro.

"And another thing," said Mr. Holland. "My daddy always told me you're not going to find persimmons on every tree, because there's a male and a female tree, and that's true. It takes probably fifteen years for one of the females to make fruit. And I am sure you know that if you get them before they're ripe, they'll turn your mouth wrong-side-out-ways. It'll roll your lip right up! But if you let the frost get on them like this morning, they'll get so sweet. When they get mushy, that's when they're good. I got a sister that makes persimmon bread. Now that's something good. That is tip-top there."

As we prepared to leave, I asked Mr. Holland if he had ever tried persimmon beer like they make in Durham at the Full Steam Brewery, whose owners recently invited customers to bring in their persimmons and share in the creation of a beer called "First Frost." Mr. Holland shook his head and smiled. "Shoot," he said. "You can make beer out of anything. You can make beer out of manure." He laughed.

We thanked him for his time and the chance to learn more about the persimmon, both wood and fruit.

Though Charles Holland fears a diminished appreciation for persimmons among coming generations, our second appointment of the day offered some hope. I had found Melissa "Mel" Bunker on *The Farmer's Almanac* website. There she is referred to as the "Persimmon Lady of North Carolina." The *Almanac* editors had recently begun consulting with her annually for help with their winter weather predictions, based on her study of local persimmon seeds.

Bunker lives in Star, the geographic center of North Carolina, on the edge of the ancient Uwharrie National Forest, a little more than an hour southwest of the Holland farm and even closer to Jeff Michael's persimmon-pudding-eating relatives. Not only is Bunker conversant in traditional persimmon lore, but she's also an ordained minister, a Chihuahua breeder, a volunteer firefighter, a writer, and — with her husband, Leon — the co-proprietor of a new business dealing in armored vehicles, personal protective gear, paintball supplies, ammunition, and body armor. She is thirty-five years old.

Bunker and her teenage daughter, Kiara, were wearing matching camouflage outfits and heavy rubber boots when they greeted us at the door of their sprawling ranch house. Kiara raced away to corral a half-dozen yapping Chihuahuas and move them into a different part of the house as Bunker led us into the sunken den. Mother and daughter had been out hunting deer this morning, she explained, but they managed to lure only a few wild turkeys to their deer stand. Bunker is an expert turkey caller and showed us a video of their morning adventures to prove it. The big birds were not yet in season, so mother and daughter did not take aim, except with a smart phone.

The Farmer's Almanac discovered Mel Bunker after she'd posted some information on Facebook about how to prepare for winter. She explained to us that her grandfather Thomas Henry Little Jr., nicknamed Possum, taught her what she knows of weather prediction using persimmons.

"He taught me a lot of things," she said, leaning back into the couch. "He had persimmon trees in his yard in Spout Springs over in Harnett County. He was a farmer and a moonshiner, born and raised in Mobile, Alabama. My grandmother married him when she was thirteen. He served as a combat engineer in the army and then worked as a telephone lineman, which took him all over North Carolina. Every fall, I'd play around his trees and get ripe persimmons stuck to the bottoms of my shoes. It was gross."

Little took his granddaughter down to the basement to clean her shoes one day and showed her a thing or two about persimmon seeds. She still has the snips he always used to cut into the seeds.

The seeds of the persimmon are flat, dark, and rock-hard, about the same size and thickness as seeds from a large watermelon. Because of their near-indestructibility, Confederate soldiers sometimes used them for buttons. They also roasted and ground them up as a coffee substitute during the hardships of the Civil War.

John Lawson, one of the founders of the eastern North Carolina town of New Bern, reported in his 1709 travelogue, *A New Voyage to Carolina*, that a group of Native Americans he met were playing a game with the seeds that Lawson dubbed "Indian dice." He described the activity: "The Kernels or Stones of Persimmons" are thrown and "Winning or Losing depend on which side appears uppermost, and how they happen to fall together."

For predicting weather (another game of chance), Bunker said the persimmon seed must be skillfully halved on the narrow side and opened like a locket. Inside, a white membrane will reveal a ghostly image of a knife, fork, or spoon. The utensil appears like a photographic negative, white on the seed's dark background.

Bunker said a spoon means we'll be digging snow. A knife predicts "a winter so cold it will cut you," as her grandfather put it. The fork predicts a mild winter "and good eats," she added. Based on the seeds she'd collected this fall, Bunker was predicting a mild start for the winter of 2016: "Then the bottom will drop out, and we'll have lots of precipitation, including ice, well into March."

It sounded unusually harsh for North Carolina, but Bunker will be prepared. She hunts meat and forages for wild berries. She grows her own food and cans most of it the old-fashioned way—in pressure-sealed jars, wasting nothing. She invited us into the upstairs kitchen, where her cupboard was stocked floor-to-ceiling with quart jars of ready-made chicken noodle soup, sweet potato slices, corn, tomatoes, asparagus, green beans, white potatoes, and more. The jars glowed with promise. Then she opened one freezer after another to show off her icy larder of wild turkey, venison, and blackberries.

Bunker has trained as a survivalist, and among her self-published books is a guide called *The Modern Caveman*, offering instructions on how to get by in case of a nationwide power disruption. She argues that since U.S. citizens have become totally dependent on all things electric and electronic, most

Melissa Bunker, an avid forager, home canner, and survivalist known to readers of *The Farmer's Almanac* as the "Persimmon Lady," holds a persimmon seed that she's just cracked open and that predicts a rough winter ahead. She lives in Star, near the Uwharrie National Forest.

folks won't have a clue what to do, and after a few days, chaos will overtake the country. Only those prepared will survive.

She kindly insisted on loading us up with quarts of food — all we could carry — when Kiara walked back into the kitchen. "Giving away food again, Mom?" Her mother smiled.

We headed back outside, arms full of jars. The sky was now deep blue. Not a cloud anywhere. Holly berries hung heavy on the shrubs at the corner of the house — another sign of a hard winter coming? Mother and daughter confessed that they were headed back to the woods to spend the afternoon in the deer stand.

As we were about to depart, Bunker used her teeth to pry open a persimmon seed so that we could see it in the bright sunshine. An image in the membrane looked like a knife, the promise of colder temperatures to come.

● ● ● ● ● ● ● ● ● ● ● ●

It was time for lunch. In my experience, not too many North Carolina restaurateurs prepare dishes made with persimmons, even in season. But we happened to be in striking distance of Lucky 32 Southern Kitchen, a Greensboro establishment that has been known to offer roasted turkey with persimmon gravy. On occasion they've also mixed up their own teriyaki-style barbecue sauce with persimmons as a foundational ingredient. They sometimes make a persimmon hard sauce that's laced with Southern Comfort and a persimmon pudding that's doused with a splash of local scuppernong wine. We set the map app for the restaurant's address.

Last year, at a Sunday brunch at Lucky 32's twin restaurant in Cary, I was wowed by a simple but luscious persimmon jam, served on the side with the kitchen's signature buttermilk biscuits. I inquired about the jam maker and soon went to meet "Jammin' George" at the Piedmont Triad Farmers Market, on the west side of Greensboro. I bought two dozen jars of his persimmon jam to give as holiday presents and sampled a few other flavors on site.

George Daher, retired from a life of international travel in the defense industry, launched into his jam-making business by gathering locally available fruits. He likes to throw in unexpected ingredients that make for some novel combinations — peach and hot pepper, raspberry and dark chocolate, and cherry and Cheerwine (a soft drink made in Salisbury). He works out of a shed in his backyard.

"After I retired, having me home all the time was something new for my wife," George explained to me. "She wanted her kitchen back, so I built my own."

Though Jammin' George has now given up his stand at the farmers' market, a neighboring booth belonging to Woodmill Winery still carries most of his forty-some flavors of jam.

George buys his persimmons from local growers, including Gene Stafford, who in 2008 launched what he believes is the only persimmon festival on the East Coast. The event is usually held in the fall just a few miles from the farmers' market.

After our lunch of greens, beans, and flounder at Lucky 32 (unfortunately, no persimmon treats on the menu that day), we were on our way to meet Stafford and his dog, Ansel, at the festival site, which was once a part of a working farm.

●　●　●　●　●　●　●　●　●　●　●　●

In 1889, Gene Stafford's great-grandfather Edward L. Stafford acquired 1,000 acres in Guilford County. By the 1930s, he still had 550 acres between Beaver Creek to the north and Reedy Fork to the south; they were divided at his death among his seven sons, one of whom was Gene Stafford's grandfather. Gene's mother and grandparents raised him on this rolling farmland that is roughly equidistant from the villages of Oak Ridge and Colfax. Coming down Stafford Mill Road from Highway 68 toward the small portion of the land that Gene maintains, we see a surprising number of old buildings — toolsheds, hay barns, chicken houses — left standing (or leaning) right in the middle of high-end subdivisions. Several of these developments bear the family name, in combination with a developer's unimaginative add-on — Stafford Estates, Stafford Glen, Stafford Oaks.

An imposing, rock-faced Tudor mansion with a complicated roofline was set unusually close to the road, but we could study it only for an instant as we passed. A shambling barn squatted like a big red hen on the immaculate front lawn and obscured a full view of the house behind.

This odd mix of contemporary and historic dwellings was both marvelous and haunting. It seemed as if any moment we might see a mansion dweller drive in and unload his golf clubs from a BMW, while a woman in a feed-sack apron could just as easily step out of a nearby shed hauling full pails from a milking session. Gene Stafford's spread, however, was 100 percent in the past.

We pulled up in the yard. Stafford was outside working. He was wearing a festival T-shirt with a blazing red persimmon on his chest. His curly white hair was mostly hidden under a black ball cap also festooned with an embroidered persimmon — another piece of festival merchandise. Stafford's glasses and beard, also white, gave him a look that was at once professorial and grizzled. He was tending to pots of young persimmon trees. The emergent twigs were no more than a foot tall and had been set in half-gallon buckets lined up along the south side of a woodshed. We parked beside the well house where several half-bushel baskets of black walnuts had recently been gathered.

"There are eight walnut trees within sight of the front porch of this house," Stafford said, after we made quick introductions and admired the surrounding view. The white two-story farmhouse in the middle of this clutch of buildings was constructed around 1780 with a kitchen and dining room added in 1930. Stafford said his grandfather often told him stories about how the oldest part of the house and a separate kitchen building (now moved) once served as the Old Red Hotel, built with hand-hewn and pegged timbers that are still visible in the attic. The hotel served as a stagecoach stop in the eighteenth century. Discernible tracks from the old roadbed still run through the property behind the house and curve out of sight into the woods. Stafford told us that British general Charles Cornwallis likely made his way down the old stagecoach road along here to Guilford Courthouse. Cornwallis lost the battle that ensued in March 1781—a setback that would lead to his surrender to General George Washington in Yorktown, Virginia, in October of the same year.

Behind the residence a garage housed a rusty red 1968 Chevy pickup. Stafford said he also has a 1950 Chevy panel truck that he's been restoring with persimmon paneling on the inside and an exterior painted the color of dark persimmons to advertise the Colfax Persimmon Festival.

After our orientation to the premises, I couldn't wait any longer and blurted out a burning question: "So you of all people must know for sure, having picked a certain date for your festival: What ripens persimmons? Is it really the first frost like so many people say?"

Stafford took a deep breath. "God," he said and shook his head. It was not an exclamation but an answer. "God ripens them. Frost almost ruined them this year. It seems like the one thing people *think* they know about persimmons is that it takes a frost to ripen them. It's just not so. We usually finish harvesting before the first frost. We start picking them up off the ground in late September. People for miles around here let me harvest their trees for the festival. Three of us do the harvesting—my cousin Bobby Ray; my best friend, Dennis Manness; and me. Two others help with the pulping. I have ten or fifteen trees at my house not far from here, and I guess we work with about forty or fifty trees total. We put in six to seven hours a day, three days a week, over four to five weeks to get them ready to freeze. We lay out tarps under the trees that have started dropping fruit. We check the tarps every other day, gathering up what's fallen."

Stafford pointed to a collection of slender six-foot trees a few yards away. "Those trees have been there about five years. There's no way to tell the sex of persimmon trees until they bear or do not bear fruit, which is usually five to seven years or more. So you need at least one male tree with the females and years of patience!"

"Did you plant them?" I asked.

"The deer planted them," he said. "They plant them all over. I guess we've cut down hundreds of persimmon start-ups in this field over the years. We leave the trees that come up at the edges. They like the light at the edge of the woods."

Deer ingest persimmons—pulp, seeds, and all. Passing through the deer's digestive system, the seeds are scarified or roughed up by enzymes that help them germinate in soil. Likewise, a seed taken from the fruit for planting must be sanded or otherwise abraded by hand so that moisture can permeate the hard coat.

"Another thing everybody seems to know about persimmons," Stafford said, "is that they taste terrible if they're not ripe. So people who've had that experience never want to taste another one." He winced. "And those who've never tried them are afraid of them, because they've heard that. So I guess that accounts for pretty much everybody in the world as it relates to persimmons." We laughed.

Stafford smiled wryly and then admitted that he was still tired from this year's festival, held three weeks before, when it rained buckets. The folks who came out anyway complained about the weather. Stafford lost money from the reduced attendance, though he still had persimmon pilgrims who came from as far away as Canada, Florida, South Carolina, and the closer urban centers of Charlotte and Asheville. Every year the folks who come and where they come from surprise him.

The activities and the vendors whom Stafford engages for the festival highlight the history of the farm. Civil War and Revolutionary War reenactors set up camp in one area and give cooking demonstrations. Old-time musicians perform on a rough-hewn stage he added onto the storage barn near the road. Blacksmithing, woodworking, flint napping, and molasses making are among the most popular craft demonstrations. Food vendors offer up pinto beans and corn bread, fried apple pies, barbecue, chicken stew, and sometimes a selection of locally made wines and beers. Persimmon fudge and persimmon ice cream are popular, too.

Stafford sells his persimmon pulp on site, and a Winston-Salem vintner recently used it as the prime ingredient in a wine that won best in show for amateur wines across a five-state region. A distillery east of Raleigh also bought Stafford's pulp with the seeds intact for the creation of a new brandy.

Stafford's frozen pulp comes in two-cup plastic bags—the perfect amount for making bread or pudding, he said. He showed us the freezers, still stocked with the bright orange blocks, which he'll continue to ship nationwide in dry ice until they're all gone, far ahead of next season's gathering.

Stafford, a photographer and former art teacher at Guilford Tech, started the Colfax Persimmon Festival in 2008, the year his mother, Frances, died. Filling the farm with people, music, and food was, and still is, an antidote to the loss of the only parent he knew. It's also a way to pay ongoing tribute to his grandparents Charlie Eugene Stafford and Lelur (pronounced *Lil-yer*) Pitts Stafford. Proceeds from the festival help cover taxes and maintenance of the historic property, he explained.

Stafford led us down steep rock steps that dropped into a root cellar under the granary. The cellar is likely on the site of what was the original homestead cabin (pre-1781) on the property, which was later replaced by a grain storage building. Twenty-year-old preserves that Stafford's mother and grandmother put up were still there, vivid with their original color. It was a bittersweet moment. Stafford said the root cellar probably stored the old hotel's perishables and its precious stash of brandy back in the day.

Twelve buildings still stand on this property—tobacco barns, a chicken house, a packhouse, and the blacksmithing shop that Gene's grandfather built in 1919—all of which help him tell the story of his family's farm and illustrate the folkways of an earlier time, including North Carolina's heritage of making persimmon treats once a year.

The hardships of farm life are not lost on Stafford, who was born here in 1942. As a child he lived in the farmhouse with his mother, her parents, and, for a time, his grandmother's parents. On winter evenings, young Gene would carry a glass of water upstairs to his bedside table. On many mornings when he woke up, the water in the glass would be frozen solid. Only two of the seven rooms in the house had wood stove–generated heat. Electric lines reached the house in the 1940s. The first indoor bathroom was installed in 1955.

"I learned back then that we don't need all the things we have today," he said wistfully.

From early on, Stafford was interested in visual art. He was the first in his family to go beyond high school—initially to Danville Tech, where he learned drafting, which wasn't particularly satisfying. Then he landed a Spencer Love Fine Art Scholarship to go to the University of North Carolina at Greensboro, where he took up photography. Stafford still exhibits and sells his work across the region. His fine-tuned visual sense enhances his appreciation of the farm, which he never tires of photographing.

With friends, neighbors, relatives, and hired hands, Stafford has restored or improved all of the buildings. The last helpers—a two-man team from Surry County—said they would help him rebuild the garage after it was destroyed by a fallen walnut tree only if Stafford would allow them to bring their dog Herbie to the work site, drink a beer on their breaks, and get paid on Fridays. "They did a great job," he said. The garage and new porch on the side were built from reclaimed lumber.

The blacksmith shop, still chockablock with his grandfather's tools, is especially important to Stafford. He relished showing off the bellows and anvil and the odd assortment of wrenches and wagon-wheel parts that his grandfather had accumulated.

Hiking back toward the main house, Stafford pointed out the Flemish bond pattern on the chimney. "These bricks," he said, "are 235 years old. Some have a dark, glass-like finish. That's from using oak in the kiln. It could raise the temperature so high that it actually glazed some of the brick."

Ansel Nikon, Stafford's black-and-white Catahoula hound/shepherd mix, had been following us around the farm. All at once, the dog took off in the direction of the woods and the grassy bottom beyond. Ansel must have sensed that we were headed that way. Stafford had cleared a trail through the woods to the base of a giant poplar tree, which he said we must see. He offers this little hike as a part of the persimmon festivities, too. Ansel, with his herding instincts, turned and doubled back toward us, running at top speed with all of his teeth showing. The effect was not menacing but playful. We egged him on.

Delicate green clusters of ground cedar flanked the path and stood out against the brown leaf rot. The trees cut the late afternoon light into yellow shards that highlighted the path. We finally reached the poplar, amputated more than once by lightning. Despite the damage, it was still imposing, with a circumference that would take at least half a dozen people holding hands to circle it. As we were looking up into the colossal, leafless branches, I asked Stafford his opinion of the accuracy of persimmons in weather prediction.

"It's got to be true, no question," he said, straight-faced. "I mean, who made up all that stuff about woolly worms? Who would believe a woolly worm? Around here, for the last five years, all I've had in my seeds are spoons. Spoons mean snow to shovel, right? It snowed in Colorado and Wisconsin every one of those years. So the seeds are accurate; they just don't predict *where* the snow will be." Stafford cautioned that it takes a professional to cut the seeds, lest a spoon be accidentally nicked and appear to be a knife. One must be wary. He recommended needle-nose pliers and a box cutter to open

Gene Stafford—handling a wheelwright's tool in the blacksmithing shop where his grandfather stored farm equipment—is the host of the annual Colfax Persimmon Festival, held on the Guilford County land that has been in his family since 1889.

the seeds for inspection. I was beginning to fully appreciate his wry sense of humor.

After our short walk in the woods, an afternoon chill descended and we came back to Stafford's "persimmon store" in the garage, where we stocked up on pulp sufficient to make three puddings. I asked about recipes. Stafford said someone told him recently that his pudding is darker than some others. This, too, he pretended, was a vexation to him. "Older people like me make them with a hand-cranked eggbeater. Younger people use a whisk, or an electric beater. Could that be the difference? I don't know. I do know that I was born old." He looked down.

Like the sawyer Charles Holland, Gene Stafford believes that old customs are at risk with regard to persimmons. "It seems to me that traditions tend to skip a generation," he said. Most of what Stafford learned about persimmons came from his grandparents, and he knows the persimmon festival is something of a quixotic venture on his part. He was married once but has no children to leave the farm to, and he's not sure how much longer he can keep the event going. Then, in the next minute, he was talking about the idea of building a new meeting center across the field near the tobacco barns, to make the farm more of a year-round community venue for weddings and other gatherings. Realtors, he said, have hounded him to put the property on the market for development.

"I guess I could be driving a Porsche." Stafford shook his head and sighed. "But I told the last realtor who called that I wanted five million for the farm. No one has bothered me since." He grinned.

It seemed that only in his photography has Gene Stafford fully adapted to the twenty-first century. He shoots and prints with digital equipment without guilt or regret. "Some people tell me with their noses in the air that they still shoot with *film* because it's more *true*. And in the next breath they'll admit to printing their photos digitally. That's as bogus as believing frost turns a persimmon."

◦ ◦ ◦ ◦ ◦ ◦ ◦ ◦ ◦ ◦ ◦ ◦

The next day Peyton Holland sent along his great-aunt Annie's persimmon bread recipe. Donna and I used the pulp we bought from Gene Stafford and followed the recipe precisely, or so we thought, including its suggestion to add pecans. The result was pure ambrosia, but it wasn't a bread at all. The loaf did not pop out of the pan to be sliced. The texture turned out more like bread pudding. Served warm, however, it was much sweeter and more satis-fying than any persimmon pudding I'd ever tasted before. Here's the recipe:

....

VERY OLD PERSIMMON BREAD RECIPE
from Annie Flinchum

2 cups persimmon pulp	3 eggs
1 stick melted margarine	1 3/4 cups self-rising flour
1 1/2 cups sugar	1 tsp. cinnamon
2 cups milk	1 tsp. vanilla

Can add raisins or nuts or both if desired.
Beat eggs, sugar, melted butter, cinnamon and vanilla.
Then add persimmon pulp.
Stir in flour and milk.
Pour in a well-buttered, 9 × 13 pan and bake at 325 degrees for
45 minutes to an hour until firm, but don't dry it out.

....

Pondering our experience with this recipe, I called Jeff Michael again. He told me that he and Autumn had recently copied a dozen old family recipes that they wanted to preserve. Jeff's mother, Phyllis Huneycutt, was downsiz-ing and moving to a new house. The persimmon pudding recipe, passed to Huneycutt by her mother-in-law, Della Kirk Michael, was one of the most prized in the collection. Another recipe was for persimmon cake, also from Grandma Michael. I told Jeff about our recipe from Annie Flinchum and the confusing result.

"I know there are lots of variations on persimmon pudding," Michael said. "My mom makes hers in square pans and pours the batter no thicker than a brownie — about an inch deep."

It dawned on me then that we had used three small loaf pans, pouring the batter far deeper than an inch in each. If we'd used the 9 × 13 pan specified in Annie Flinchum's recipe, the bread would have been much firmer, hence the warning at the end of her recipe not to let it dry out. Ah-hah!

"Yes, that might be the answer," Michael said. "Autumn's father, who's from Rowan County, made us what he called a pudding one year. It was almost cakey, not like my mother's recipe at all. I guess there's a whole spec-trum. Mom told me the other day that my grandmother always cut the flour down by half. That made her persimmon pudding more like custard, and the mixture would caramelize around the edges of the Pyrex dish. We thought that was the best texture ever."

I checked a few other recipes. Chapel Hill's maven of down-home cooking, Mildred Council, aka Mama Dip, grew up in the Baldwin Township of Chatham County, where notably the three main thoroughfares are Tobacco Road, Tar Heel Road, and Persimmon Hill Road. Her pudding recipe, also based on two cups of persimmon pulp, calls for ingredients similar to Annie Flinchum's, though Mrs. Council recommends one cup of white sugar and one cup of brown sugar, and by her lights, raisins and nuts are mandatory. She uses a 9 × 12 pan.

Burlington (North Carolina)–born Nancie MacDermott, in her book *Southern Pies: A Gracious Plenty of Pie Recipes, from Lemon Chess to Chocolate Pecan*, uses only two tablespoons of flour to which she adds one cup of sugar, three-quarters of a cup of evaporated milk, two tablespoons of melted butter, and two eggs (along with the usual spices). She whisks these ingredients together (sugar last), then adds one and a half cups of persimmon pulp and pours the whole mixture into a pie crust! So her version is essentially a custard pie, not unlike the aforementioned medlar tart recipe from 1665.

In *North Carolina and Old Salem Cookery*, the late Beth Tartan offers a recipe that adds cornmeal and sweet potato to the pudding. Tartan notes that too much spice can kill the flavor of the persimmons, though she suggests that coconut may be added to good effect. She also recommends pouring the mixture no thicker than an inch deep in the pan.

Photographer Jan G. Hensley of Greensboro sent me his mother's recipe for persimmon pudding, and it also calls for a cup of grated sweet potatoes. The recipe is quite old, he said. It came from his mother's mother, whose first husband was a Confederate soldier. Hensley fondly remembers taking his mother to one of Greensboro's many parks and setting up a ladder under a large persimmon tree so that he might shake the limbs while his mother gathered the persimmons that fell below, sometimes pelting her on the shoulder or head. Jan said whether the pudding is served hot or cold, a dollop of fresh whipped cream on top is nonnegotiable.

After studying all these recipes, I realized that the cooks in this random sample of North Carolina all happen to come from the Piedmont. I could add others, such as Bill Smith of Crook's Corner restaurant, in Chapel Hill, and that restaurant's cofounder (with Gene Hamer), the late Bill Neal. Both Bills confessed in print to pilfering persimmons for pudding, as I have, from the Carrboro Elementary School trees.

So maybe Jeff Michael is right. Perhaps persimmon pudding making, if not persimmon eating in general, is more concentrated in a narrow swath in the middle of the state. Why? I can only speculate. Is it that persimmon trees were better appreciated in the Piedmont than elsewhere because textile workers admired the enduring quality of the wooden shuttles made of persimmon wood—a durability much like their own as they labored long hours under harsh conditions and without adequate appreciation?

Of course, it is simplistic to divide the world into two camps—those who appreciate persimmons and those who don't—but let's go back for a moment to the medlar. The bad rap on persimmons might well have originated with the deep stigma that was already cast on medlars by the brightest literary lights of England. Because of the medlar's peculiar, open-ended crown and its oozing, mushy brown middle, Chaucer crudely referred to the fruit in his poetry as an "open arse." Later, in four different plays, including *Romeo and Juliet*, Shakespeare used the medlar as a metaphor for defiled and decadent characters who rotted before ripening.

We might therefore infer that explorer Thomas Hariot's comparison of the persimmon's qualities to the medlar's took unfortunate root among our forebears. Persimmon—bark and/or fruit—was further promoted in the eighteenth and nineteenth centuries for its medicinal properties as an oral or topical treatment for such ailments as hemorrhoids, external ulcers, gonorrhea, syphilis, thrush, dropsy, diarrhea, and dysentery. This advertisement probably did not add to the fruit's cachet as a prime ingredient in holiday desserts.

Furthermore, the unfortunate durability of the low joke—feeding the unripe to the unsuspecting—has created an additional public wariness of persimmons. Then there's the modern shame attached to eating possum—that is, roadkill. Ironically, the opossum, forever linked to persimmons in our rural mythology, was also given its English name by another North American explorer, Captain John Smith, who co-opted the Algonquian word *apasum*, which meant "white animal" or "bright beast." Smith wrote in his notes from Jamestown, Virginia, in 1608, "An Opassom hath an head like a Swine, and a taile like a Rat, and is of the bignes of a Cat. Under her belly she hath a bagge, wherein shee lodgeth, carrieth, and sucketh her young." Not exactly the most flattering description of the persimmon-loving marsupial. Yet, because of Smith's declamations the opossum "rapidly became the symbol of the natural wonders held by the American colonies and was dissected and discussed at length by Europe's leading scientists . . . and played an important role during the transition from medieval to enlightenment in science," according to William J. Krause, professor of anatomy at the University of Missouri and a leading authority on the opossum.

I would further speculate that our citizens' capacity to enjoy eating possum did not precipitously decline until North Carolina became the "Good Roads State" and we began to deride possums for their inability to cross a road safely, even as we began barreling through their territory at night in four-wheeled, two-ton hunks of metal with our bright lights shining into their eyes. And no, possums are not blind.

Those of us, along with the possum, who still appreciate persimmons and have had many happy occasions in their company at the Thanksgiving table must understand this history to help others overcome it. It falls to us, literally, to gather the ripe fruit and share it more broadly. Let us adopt the model of Charles Holland, Mel Bunker, Jammin' George Daher, Jeff Michael, Gene Stafford, Jan Hensley, and all those faithful professional and home cooks who know what sweet surprise still grows in our woods and parklands, beside the elementary school playgrounds, and at the edges of the fields, propagated by deer and possum, and best cultivated by lack of human interference.

December

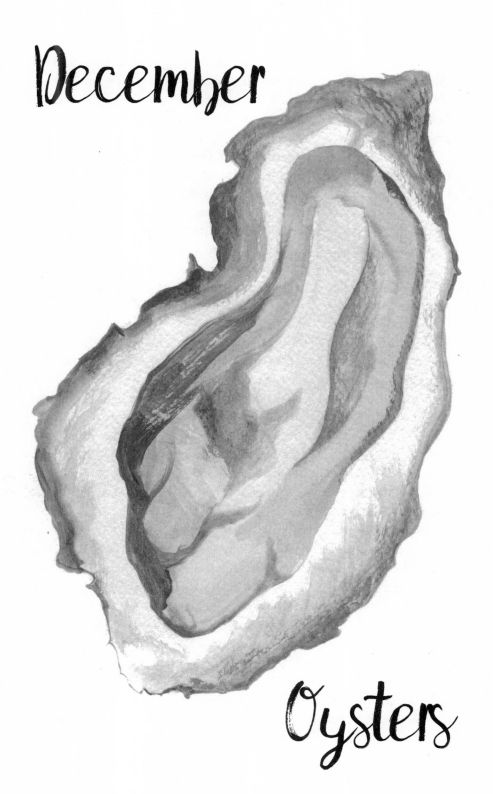

Oysters

I DON'T REMEMBER EATING OYSTERS AS A CHILD. THEY WERE ADULT party food, except for that one Christmas when my uncle Lamar subjected the whole Eubanks family to his oyster dressing—a dark, damp mash-up of corn bread and crackers with occasional gray, gelatinous lumps that seemed to pull everything toward a taste too fishy for Christmas, according to my grade-school palate.

Then, in college, everything changed. One night, I made my way with friends from dark-blue Durham over to the light-blue Carolina camp in Chapel Hill. There, Brady's Restaurant, on the site of today's chic Siena Hotel on East Franklin Street, served up hot, plump, and explosively juicy fried oysters nestled on waxed paper in a plastic basket alongside crinkle-cut fries and a little dish of chilled slaw. I was hooked.

Nearly four decades later, I've come to prefer the naked, just-shucked oyster. No matter how much I love horseradish, hot chilies, lemon, and butter, the measure of a great oyster to me is in a brisk and briny flavor that requires no adornment.

So let's begin with the critical facts. First, forget the notion that eastern oysters (*Crassostrea virginica*) are suitable to eat only in those months spelled with an *r*. Modern refrigeration has made oysters available year-round. Even so, North Carolina watermen say that our oysters are at their best when the temperature in Tar Heel estuaries has dropped and held steady at around 45 degrees for a good stretch of days and nights. This condition is most likely to begin in the month of December and can last through March, though not always. Yes, traditional oyster roasts in the state's coastal villages have been going on for many years in October and November, but I am trying to steer you to the very best experience possible.

Second, you must know that North Carolina oysters have had their share of detractors over the years. In the 1905 *Report of the Bureau of Shell Fisheries*, issued by the state of New Jersey, an oyster packer named C. H. Lighthiser declared the Chesapeake Bay oyster far superior to any other from states farther south. Of our bivalves, he said, "They are not of the same class and will always be put on the market to meet the demands of entirely different classes of consumers. North Carolina oysters are notably inferior to those caught in the local waters."

Of course, this propaganda was being published even as overharvesting and poor stewardship had gravely depleted the famed oyster beds of the Chesapeake. Because of these conditions, oystermen from New Jersey, Maryland, and Virginia had begun invading North Carolina waters as early as the 1890s, poaching our local oysters and bringing them back to their packhouses to seal them in tins and fraudulently label them as coming from the Chesapeake.

Competitive voices from the Gulf of Mexico also rise up from time to time. In 1993, the food writer Calvin Trillin told a friend from Louisiana about a new warning issued by the University of North Carolina Sea Grant Program to avoid consuming raw oysters for fear of a particular bacterium. The Louisiana man responded, "I don't blame someone in North Carolina for avoiding oysters. I'd avoid them too if I had to live there. North Carolina oysters taste like marshmallows that have been fished out of the pool at the YMCA." Ouch.

Third, you need to know that in the relentless rush to culinary convenience, a new technique has been devised to make the preparation and presentation of oysters on the half shell utterly expedient for restaurateurs and home party hosts. One packinghouse described the benefits of IQF (Instant Quick Freeze) oysters: "A resourceful new process makes these oysters on the half shell quick and convenient as never before. Just thaw and serve. Water glazing preserves taste, texture and prevents freezer burn. Perfect size for appetizers. Conveniently Packaged. 12 oysters per layer/144 count box. Ready to serve. No shucking, No waste."

Icesters? Shuck and jive, I say. So to be clear, we are in pursuit of *native* North Carolina oysters, which may offer to us, as near as possible, the experience of our forebears. We are looking for the bivalves that come from North Carolina waters and are brought to our mouths within days or even hours of their being lifted from the brine. As it turns out, this experience is no longer so easily accomplished. I had no idea.

●　●　●　●　●　●　●　●　●　●　●　●

On the way to the coast to begin our research, Donna Campbell and I stopped at Reynolds Seafood Market in Kinston. Johnny Reynolds greeted us at the counter. An affable man in his early sixties, he was wearing a burgundy apron. Reynolds, along with his younger brother, Chuck, have been sharing recipes and helping Kinstonians pick the right fish and shellfish for their dinner tables for decades. Downtown and a stone's throw from the Neuse River, the market carries the usual accoutrements of an eastern North Carolina fish market—wide coolers of iced-down fish overlapping in neat rows. On this morning, croaker, red snapper, sheepshead, and mounds of fresh shrimp were at the ready. Behind the coolers, a line of veteran fish dressers occupied a counter with deep stainless steel sinks, where they scaled, rinsed, filleted, weighed, and wrapped up orders. Above their heads hung enticing color photos of grilled scallop kabobs, seared tuna, Alaskan crab legs, and butter-flied shrimp. "May the World Be Your Oyster" was the message on a plaque below these photos. Shelves of hush puppy mix, seafood breading, cocktail sauce, and Cajun rice mix and a rack of shrimp deveiners, oyster knives, and scalers filled the walls on either side of the main event. A drift of Styrofoam coolers lounged atop a soft drink box waiting for customers who forgot to bring their own.

I asked Mr. Reynolds where we might find the best North Carolina oysters.

"I've had them everywhere," he said, hedging, knowing he had an eaves-dropping audience of curious shoppers, "from Rose Bay down at Swan Quarter, from over at Topsail Island, all around. They're all good. But with the rain we've had lately — eight inches four days before Thanksgiving — the oysters have suffered. They have to open up constantly to filter the storm water runoff that's pouring into the creeks and rivers. That's not good. One week the local oysters are perfect, and the next week they're not. The state closes down the beds when it rains like that."

Reynolds said he didn't know whether North Carolina has water regu-lations more stringent than those of our neighbors to the north in Virginia, where the oysters he's selling today have come from. "I do know we have a lot of hog waste around here. That's for sure," he said darkly.

Reynolds admitted that he's come to rely on a particular packinghouse in Kinsale, Virginia, for the shucked oysters he will sell by the gallon or half gallon for stews and frying. "They pack them well, and I trust the product," he said.

We thanked Mr. Reynolds for his candor and hit the road again.

* * * * * * * * * * * *

Another thirty-six miles down Highway 70, we decided to stop for lunch at a waterfront restaurant in New Bern that shall go nameless. The place is contemporary and pleasant with windows looking out on the confluence of the Neuse and Trent Rivers. As soon as we sat down, a cheery server came over to ask if we'd eaten there before. We had not, so she launched into an enthusiastic description of the chef's penchant for locally sourced seafood, meats, and farm-to-table vegetables. "Ninety percent of everything we have comes from within fifty miles of here," she concluded and asked for our drink orders.

Donna was tempted by the oyster po'boy and asked where the oysters were from. The server said she'd have to ask.

As we waited, we heard the same pitch from another server behind us, touting the virtues of local. Outside, the day was chilly and bright. An impetuous wind stirred up a regatta of little Sunfish sailboats circling on the far side of the bay. They looked like tightly wound toys suddenly set loose. Our iced teas arrived. Eventually, our server returned, a bit sheepish. "The oysters are from Louisiana," she said and went on to explain that it took a while to find out because the kitchen "did not like to be questioned." I ordered a Cuban sandwich; Donna the crab cake. Strike two for North Carolina oysters that day.

● ● ● ● ● ● ● ● ● ● ● ●

When we reached Morehead City in the afternoon, we headed straight for Blue Ocean, a seafood market recommended by friends at the North Carolina Coastal Federation. The federation recently procured local oysters there for the annual Low Country boil and oyster roast it hosts for members and friends at its headquarters in nearby Newport.

Clayton Rusich manages Blue Ocean. He asked us what we were after. His story was the same as Johnny Reynolds's.

"We could have sold a hundred bushels of oysters at Thanksgiving," Rusich said, "but the runoff from that big rain was not good."

We soon learned that Rusich is a California native and an actor. He earned a culinary degree and worked as a chef for several years before happily settling into his current role as fishmonger. Without hesitation, he said that the best oysters he's had in North Carolina were from Mill Creek, on the northern bank of the Newport River. This carried some extra weight, coming from a former chef who presumably has eaten a good many oysters from different waters. North Carolina historian David Cecelski would be pleased with Rusich's opinion of Mill Creek oysters because he, too, extols the virtues of Newport River oysters in his studies, calling them "some of the saltiest and most delectable oysters harvested in America." Cecelski grew up about five miles from Mill Creek.

Rusich said he also likes the oysters from Core Sound, just a bit farther up the coast. Core Sound takes its name from the Coree Indians, the original inhabitants of the area around Harkers Island. Wanchese—the Indian who was taken back to England by the first English explorers, along with the Algonquin Indian named Manteo—was believed to be a member of the Coree tribe. The indigenous people of this area loved oysters, amassing huge mounds of shells as sacred totems on the east end of Harkers Island and on Shackleford Banks, long before the European settlers came. This region is one area that gives cause for optimism about the future of oysters. It is now home to a successful demonstration project led by the North Carolina Coastal Federation with funding from the North Carolina Clean Water Management Trust Fund. The North River Wetlands Restoration Project has revitalized nearly 5,000 acres in the headwaters of the North River, returning farmland back to its natural state, which in turn helps to control runoff and bacteria. Through new plantings of native species, the salt marsh restoration improves shellfish growing waters.

"The ersters hev arroived," is how people say it on Harkers Island, where the local dialect, still in use, is a combination of old English pronunciations, anachronistic vocabulary, and original words developed by the Core Bankers.

"Really, it doesn't get any better," Rusich continued. "Our local oysters have a nice flavor—salty and meaty, with a good mouthfeel. They get better when it's been cold for a while. By January and February, they are really pristine."

Rusich said he sells 90 percent of the unshucked local oysters he acquires to upscale restaurants and oyster bars such as the Ruddy Duck, on the Morehead City waterfront. But on that December day, both the shucked oysters in plastic cartons and the unshucked oysters on ice were from out of state. A pattern was beginning to emerge.

* * * * * * * * * * * *

A causeway at the mouth of the White Oak River runs from Bogue Banks to the village of Swansboro, originally the site of yet another ancient Algonquin Indian settlement long ago displaced. The colonists who took over were primarily shipbuilders and seamen. They incorporated Swansboro in 1783. They later turned to shipping timber, tar, and turpentine from eastern North Carolina forests. When the Depression hit in the 1920s, fishing and shrimping became the primary enterprise. Today, Swansboro is a destination for people who love architecture, history, and antiques shopping and for eco-tourists with kayaks who are drawn to the marshland mazes of Hammocks Beach State Park.

Jimmy Phillips has been running a seafood market, which bears his father's name, Clyde Phillips, on the causeway since 1954. His trawler, *Captain Phillips*, was docked beside the store. A lone pelican floated idly by while the leading edge of a cloudbank was heading out toward the Atlantic. The market's white board beside the front door listed the day's offerings: flounder, sea bass, speckled trout, and red drum. The words "shell oysters" had been rubbed out, a faint ghost of a promise.

The building's exterior was hurricane-worn. Inside were concrete floors, bright-green doorframes, and dingy walls covered with sun-faded pictures of boats. A single framed poster featured satellite images of Hurricanes Floyd and Dennis with the only caption needed: "1999"—a year of unforgettable disaster for eastern North Carolina.

Hurricane Dennis had set the stage early that September, lingering over the coast and dropping six inches of rain. Floyd soon followed, adding fifteen to twenty more inches in twelve hours and leaving great swaths of the region under water. Fertilizers, pesticides, sediments, topsoil, human and animal waste, and animal carcasses all flowed into coastal estuaries within a week, yet the massive fish kills that were predicted did not happen. Apparently Dennis had signaled the fish to head out to sea before Hurricane Floyd literally flushed the entire Tar, Neuse, Albemarle, and Pamlico river system. The fish and shrimp catches in the season that followed were large, but only for those who had boats big enough to work out in the open ocean, not in the rivers. Those operations were able to avoid financial disaster.

After my quick survey of the offerings on ice in the market's cooler, the guys at the counter directed me to the office off to the side. Mr. Phillips was tucked behind a desk. On the office wall beside him were welding tank valves with dangling hoses. A watch cap and camo outfit sat on top of a box, and a windowsill was filled with green soda bottles laced with elaborate cobwebs. Mr. Phillips rose slowly and edged me back out to the black vinyl chairs in the retail area. He sat, too, crossing his arms over his puff vest and blue work shirt. The propane gas heater near us was cranked up and felt good. I asked Phillips what he thought were the best oysters in the state. His eyes closed behind his glasses.

"It depends what you mean by best," he said quietly. "There's best yield, best quality, best size, best flavor."

I felt foolish. "Best flavor," I said.

Jimmy Phillips then became the third person in the day to endorse the bivalves from Newport River. In second place, he said, were the oysters from the New River around Sneads Ferry and in Stump Sound, on the backside of Topsail Island. "Pollution has closed all the beds up this river," he said, meaning the White Oak, visible from the market's front window. "There's lots of oysters up there, but we can't get them. The demand is still there, but they closed us down."

"They" are the North Carolina Division of Marine Fisheries. Water testing has shown that the lower White Oak River is impaired by bacterial contamination created by storm water runoff. In 2015, the Environmental Protection Agency made a grant to the North Carolina Coastal Federation and East Carolina University to begin working with homeowners in neighborhoods around the town of Cedar Point to distribute a simple device to redirect gutter downspouts away from impermeable driveways and into rain gardens or onto lawns. Redirecting and retaining storm water on land instead of letting it flow into our rivers and estuaries has been shown to reduce contamination by half, and sometimes up to 90 percent. However, implementing this solution has meant sending project volunteers door to door to enlist the participation of private property owners. It's a slow haul.

Someday the cleanup may be sufficient, but until then, Mr. Phillips said, he's had to sell oysters from Maryland, which pains him. "There was not a lot of salt in those," he said, his face wan and expressionless. He also sells oysters from the Pamlico Sound. "That's a big area. They dredge them up there," he explained. "But those coon oysters, or clusters—to me they don't have the flavor either."

So named for their resemblance to the paws of a raccoon, an animal also known to fish out oysters and eat them greedily, coon oysters are small, grow close to shore in shallow water, and form in clusters. As the food writer André Gallant explains, "Their still-forming shells are sharp enough to slice skin or even a rubber boot." This assessment is true: I have a long scar on my right heel from jumping off a low dock onto a pile of sand at Topsail Island many years ago. The oyster shell was hiding like a knife in that sand, and recovery from the slice required several stitches and a fair amount of Jack Daniel's. But I digress.

Dredging wild oysters mechanically brings a higher yield than the old-fashioned practice of tonging them by hand—a labor-intensive process that involves a single person wielding a long pole with a basket at the end. The tongs are dipped in the water and scissored over the oyster beds to bring up individual shells and clusters.

Of mechanical dredging, the Division of Marine Fisheries warns, "Studies have shown that excessive use of these harvest methods can damage oyster beds. The state only allows mechanical harvest in specific deepwater areas where hand harvest is impractical, and monitors the harvesting to protect the oyster beds."

It was, in fact, the practice of such dredging that first overwhelmed North Carolina's once-prodigious wild oyster population just before the turn of the twentieth century, and the state has been trying to recover from the damage ever since. The "Oyster War" of 1891 pitted out-of-state dredgers against the local tongers and resulted in a legislative ban on oyster harvest by nonresidents (the aforementioned pirates from the Chesapeake). By 1889, a new spate of state laws prohibited unshucked oysters from being shipped out of state, so Baltimore-based companies came in and set up canneries across eastern North Carolina. Fishing crews and people who'd never been involved in the oyster business jumped in to take part in this economic boom.

North Carolina watermen continued to harvest wild oysters well into the twentieth century in an unsustainable fashion. With intensifying coastal development over the years, our oysters have been in danger for a long time now. Hog waste, it turns out, is not the culprit so much as hydrologic alterations that come from the local landscape, which we have increasingly ditched, drained, and paved.

North Carolina's coast began to be discovered in the 1960s, and according to Coastal Federation director Todd Miller, growth and development over the years has come from a variety of factors, including tax policies and the popularity of second homes.

My personal theory is that the implementation of laws legalizing the sale of mixed drinks in North Carolina restaurants and bars in 1980 also seemed to accelerate coastal development. Multistory hotels, upscale restaurants and bars (instead of humble fish camps), and second-home condos and houses bought by inland families and out-of-staters began to fill in our sounds and shorelines. Formerly modest North Carolina coastal towns started to look more like the high-rise cities just across our state lines: Virginia Beach to the north and Myrtle Beach to the south. In those states, hard liquor had already been flowing with fewer restrictions for many years, and our neighbors' coastal development showed it.

In 1987, an epizootic infection called Dermo (*Perkinsus marinus*) —

a pathogen that causes the degradation of oyster tissue — overtook our oyster beds and shifted the focus away from encouraging commercial production to rescuing our rapidly compromised oyster stock. Conditions have improved now, but Dermo and another disease known as MSX remain a threat. These diseases thrive on stressed oysters that have been compromised by bad water quality.

Jimmy Phillips remembered when even the smallest seafood sellers shucked and packed oysters for their customers, as he once did in the 1950s and 1960s. "But now if we can get North Carolina oysters," he said, "they sell so good in the shell, we make more if we don't have to shuck them. Of course, there's still tractor-trailer loads of oysters coming in here from Texas and Louisiana all the time."

The bottom line, according to figures quoted by the Coastal Federation on a web page dedicated to oysters, is that "oyster populations are on the decline in North Carolina. Some estimates indicate the population is at 10 percent of historic levels due to disease, poor water quality, overfishing, and natural disaster."

I thanked Mr. Phillips for the history lesson and asked about the best way to drive to Sneads Ferry, where we planned to eat dinner at a historic restaurant. On the map, it looked like the most direct route from Swansboro was a road that skirts Camp Lejeune, but Mr. Phillips explained that access along there is limited to vehicles with military permits. We'd have to drive northwest to Jacksonville and go all the way around Camp Lejeune and the U.S. Marine Corps Special Operations Command to reach Sneads Ferry and Topsail Island.

* * * * * * * * * * * *

Since 1946, the Riverview Café has been serving seafood brought in from the New River, which is right out the restaurant's back door. I was certain we were going to get authentic local oysters at last! If the restaurant's glass pie case, filled with mile-high meringues, was any indication, we were in for the real deal from start to finish. Not only did the restaurant's white board list oysters, grilled fantail shrimp, backfin crabmeat, catfish, and flounder, but the sides du jour were fried squash, fried okra, fried mushrooms, and mac and cheese.

Donna asked our server about oyster stew. Riverview offered two varieties, she said — one made with milk and another made with water and cornmeal. The latter was novel to both of us—perhaps a poor man's stew? But we decided instead to order "Local Steamed Oysters" along with some fried scallops.

Oyster stew has always been a Campbell family favorite. Donna's father, John Pierce Campbell, made it every Christmas Eve. He would bring home fresh oysters from his regular December fishing trip to Hatteras Island. John began his recipe with finely chopped onions sautéed in a generous amount of butter. (As mentioned earlier, in the Campbell family, the only way to involve butter is with a heavy hand.) Then he would add milk and heat the broth to scalding, never boiling. He'd drop in the succulent oysters, followed by freshly ground pepper and a dash of salt, and it was ready to serve.

Earlier that day while I was driving, Donna had looked up on her tablet the origin of oyster stew and its connection to Christmas. According to the History Channel website, the American tradition of oyster stew originated with Irish Catholic immigrants, who abstained from eating meat on Christmas Eve. In Ireland, they had always made a broth with butter, salt, and milk. Then they added the main ingredient: a dried fish called ling, which was cured with salt and rather chewy, though the milk apparently helped to tenderize it. Finding no ling in North America, the Irish substituted the reliable oyster.

Based on the carbon dating of ancient canoes pulled out of Phelps Lake, North Carolina's second largest freshwater lake, located in Washington and Tyrrell Counties, Native Americans had been working both fresh and salt waters, harvesting oysters for many thousands of years before their English conquerors quickly adopted them as a first-rate source of protein. Collected by hand in shallow waters, the oysters eaten by the indigenous people might have also been used as an ingredient in stews, but they were likely first thrown on a cook fire until the lips of the stony shells began to part and then eaten on the half shell.

                           ▪ ● ◉ ◖ ✦ ◀ ● ◀ ◗ ◆ ◗ ◆

Our first course finally arrived at the Riverview Café. There was onion in the hush puppies, and they were not too sweet—a very good sign by my lights. The blue cheese dressing for our tossed salads was delivered in an unmarked bottle—house-made! Then the scallops arrived, barely dusted with seasoning and flour. They were golden and extra sweet. It had been a long day of waiting for this feast. We were smiling after every bite.

Next the server arrived wearing oven mitts and carrying an old splatter-paint Dutch oven. When she set the vessel down, Donna gingerly removed the lid to reveal a dozen steamed oysters, round and rock-like. Each one was a heavy handful. We dived in, shucking them ourselves. They were magnificent, in no need of the drawn butter that came with them. I poured the butter instead on my baked potato.

Of course, we would finish the meal by splitting a piece of old-fashioned chocolate pie. The crust was buttery, the chocolate was real boiled pudding, and the airy meringue lifted the whole dish to the heavens.

When the young woman who brought us all of these celestial gifts eventually returned with the check, I complimented the oysters and asked if they came right out of the New River today, where the sun was now setting dramatically out the window beside our booth.

"Those oysters you had are from the *North* River," she said, "down near Beaufort and Morehead City."

I gave her a puzzled look. She said, "It's a little tidal river about eighteen miles long."

So yes, we had eaten oysters from the general area described by our interview subjects as the best. The Newport and North Rivers both run into the Back Sound, which connects to the Core Sound. But why were we not eating oysters from right out the back door? The shell game continued.

The next morning we paid a visit to Mitchell Seafood, a Sneads Ferry operation that has changed names fairly recently but has been at this site, less than a mile from the Riverview Café, for more than forty years. Randy Millis runs the place, as did his grandfather, uncle, and father, by turns, before him. The Mitchell name is from Randy's best friend, Charles Mitchell, who bought the operation a few years ago but insisted that Millis, who is forty-four, keep running it. Their slogan is "Always Fresh. Always Local."

"This place is all I remember as a boy," Millis said. "I followed my granddaddy around here, went out with him on these boats. Nowadays, it's about an eighty-hour-a-week job."

Millis was sitting in the company office surrounded by files and phone books, a thermos, take-out coffee cups, and a nearly empty bag of potato chips. Over by the microwave, several cans of powdered creamer sat beside a dusty bottle of Crown Royal whiskey, a roll of paper towels, and half a loaf

Randy Millis contemplates the current economics of the fishing industry
in his office at Mitchell Seafood. Since he was a child, Millis has spent his days
on the boats and docks of this Sneads Ferry enterprise that was run in
succession by his grandfather, uncle, and father.

of white bread. The walls were handsome yellow pine — beaded board that
had been shellacked to a shiny patina. A painting of a trawler with "Edith M"
inscribed on the bow took up most of one wall.

"That was my grandmother's name," Millis said. Locals and Topsail
Beach regulars knew Edith Millis as the "Shrimp Lady." For many years,
she ran a reliable seafood stand on the Surf City causeway to Topsail Island.
Millis still owns that business. His brother, Michael, runs it now, and they
still call it the Shrimp Lady.

Millis has an Opie Taylor look — red hair, prominent ears, blue eyes,
ruddy skin, and a sweet smile — though he seemed to be carrying the yoke
of too many working hours. We strolled out to the docks behind the office
where hundreds of waxed boxes were already assembled, stacked, and ready
to fill with shrimp and other seafood. Two young men in hoodies and bright
orange waders told Millis they were heading out to tong some oysters.
Donna followed them down the dock with her camera.

"They're allowed to bring back two bushels apiece on the weekends,"
Millis said. "Five bushels a day is the maximum we can bring in during the
week." The inboard skiff the young men were loading up was small and sat

low in the water. With tongs and buckets and coolers, the boat was crowded. Around here, Millis explained, the retail price on a bushel of oysters was about sixty-five dollars, with not much profit for a day's work, given the strict limits on the harvest.

I told him about the North River oysters we'd eaten the night before at Riverview Café and asked why we hadn't eaten his oysters. "You had those pretty little rock oysters, I bet," he said. "Ours are not so uniform in size. The restaurant folks like oysters that fit in their steamers with the right count."

I didn't understand. Donna explained later that in a Dutch oven, you want all the oysters to require the same amount of steaming time, which means they need to be similar in size.

"We only sell the oysters we get from right out here in this water," Millis continued. "We sell right out the door. People call and order a few bushels at a time for roasting. We have people come down from Chinquapin, Clinton, and all up that way. In the other direction, Wilmington" — *Wimminton*, as he says it — "is as far as I have to go with my oysters before I'm sold out." He added that no oyster generally stays around his place for more than two or three days. "We move it out to keep it fresh." Refrigerated, oysters can stay alive for up to two weeks in the shell, he said.

"Selling such small quantities of oysters doesn't contribute to the bottom line very much, then," I said. One of Millis's assistants, who had been silently following us around the docks, suddenly jumped into the conversation and began a passionate harangue about fishing regulations. "They hold us to catching seven drum at a time," he said, balling his fists at his sides. "They say there are not many drum left out there. Well, we see drum all the time. There's plenty still out there. Those college students they send down here to count fish either don't know how to count or don't know a red drum when they see one."

Randy Millis was more measured in his critique. "I know the regulators are trying to help us," he said earnestly, "but what's happening is that the fishing permits are so limited — only seven or eight people in this area have permits to catch sea bass, for example. That's how they're doing away with the small operations. They're putting us out of business with these limits. My granddaddy sat me down a long time ago and told me the deal. He said that federal regulations mean you can't keep enough of what you catch to make a living anymore. And he was right. I wouldn't recommend this business to anyone nowadays. I told my twenty-one-year-old son not to come to work with me here. Instead, he's in the construction business. He called me the other day and said he wished he was back on the water, though." Millis looked away and shook his head.

According to census data, new construction in Sneads Ferry has surged since 2000, creating an 80 percent increase in the local human population. The growth has primarily come from the expanding military presence and the resulting demand for new housing on the Sneads Ferry side of Camp Lejeune. Several colossal apartment complexes have sprung up on Highways 172 and 210, where additional gates into the base have been cut through the scrub. One such complex, under construction, was named Oyster Landing. The name is ironic, because C. M. Mitchell Construction — another Mitchell family business, in addition to this seafood operation — has benefited from the very same building boom that threatens the edibility of oysters and other sea creatures in the vicinity.

I asked Millis about an effort to promote the recycling of oyster shells. This project, launched by the North Carolina Department of Environmental and Natural Resources, encourages restaurants and individual consumers to save their shells so that they can be dumped back in the water to build up old and new oyster reefs where young spat (baby oysters) can affix themselves and grow.

"We grew up putting oyster shells in our potholes." Millis grinned. "But you've got to put them back in the water nowadays if you want to keep the oysters coming. We recommend to our customers that they recycle the shells."

The Division of Marine Fisheries has reported that North Carolina has one of the most active shellfish restoration programs in the country. Yet the tax breaks provided to restaurants for participating in shell recycling was defunded by the legislature in July 2013. The recycling continues, but not at the same pace. It has dropped from about 20,000 bushels of shells per year over the ten years of the tax break to approximately 3,000 to 6,000 recycled bushels per year after the repeal, according to the Coastal Federation. Clearly the tax break was an important incentive to restaurants. At least oyster shells are still banned at North Carolina landfills.

Randy Millis said that the guys around his place would be cooking up some seafood later in the day if we'd be interested in hanging around. A large stainless steel grill stood at the ready nearby. "We eat a lot of seafood around here," he said wistfully.

With more than 12,000 miles of estuarine shoreline, the second-largest system in the country, North Carolina has spawned plenty of little seafood markets suitable for the roving oyster disciple to explore. However, after talking to Randy Millis, we were discouraged. Heading toward Topsail Island for a look around, we pulled into a retail seafood outlet on the causeway, where huge flats of Maryland oysters had just been unloaded from a truck. We turned back and decided to drive north toward the Pamlico Sound, hoping to see firsthand one of the relatively new oyster farming operations in the state that we'd read about. We were beginning to get the picture. In addition to salt marsh restoration to benefit historic wild oyster beds, cultivation has become another way to bring more local oysters back on the market.

A state law that dates back to 1858 first authorized the building and seeding of oyster beds for harvest, but only recently has the practice caught on again, partly due to the demonstrated success of bold new cultivation techniques now being pursued in Virginia and farther up the Eastern Seaboard.

If Randy Millis represents the past, then perhaps the oyster farmer Chris Matteo represents the future. Matteo's Chadwick Creek oyster farm, in Pamlico County, has received a fair amount of publicity. Pamlico is one of North Carolina's poorest counties. Its great, flat swaths of farmland and forests, marshland and water stretch as far as the eye can see. The county is home to several game preserves. Fewer than 14,000 residents are scattered over Pamlico's 218,000 acres of land interspersed with 151,000 acres of water.

In sailing circles, Pamlico is best known for the quaint village of Oriental, a boaters' haven that caters to travelers on the Intracoastal Waterway who often end up buying houses there. The county is also familiar to many a privileged Tar Heel kid who went to summer camp in these parts. As we rolled into the village of Grantsboro, a single sign listed the familiar names and their ascending distance from the intersection of Highways 55 and 306 — Camp Vandermere 14, Camp Seafarer 15, Camp Sea Gull 17, Camp Don Lee 18, Camp Caroline 19.

From Grantsboro, we continued on Highway 55 to Bayboro, where Mayo's Seafood Restaurant had recently opened adjacent to the brand new bridge that spans the Bay River and where small trawlers can easily bring in fresh seafood for the restaurant's constantly changing menu. Mayo's offers daily seafood specials (often a platter involving shrimp, trout, flounder, or even New England lobster) and at least one enticing landlubber's dish that can range from a bowl of great northern beans to brown sugar–glazed pork chops to country-fried chicken.

From Bayboro, we picked up Highway 304 leading toward Chris Matteo's 110 acres, which include 8 acres of deeded creek bottom. Here, the former New York hedge fund manager started growing his oysters in the spring of 2013. Matteo must pay taxes on his underwater land, but he is also grandfathered into a permanent shellfish franchise sanctioned by the state. Nowadays, the Division of Marine Fisheries issues such permits only on a five-year basis. Matteo's deeded water bottom dates back to the early 1900s and was originally owned by a member of the Mayo family — clearly a common surname in Pamlico.

The 6,000-acre Jones Island Hunt Club surrounds Matteo's home and oyster operation. The house of his nearest neighbor is half a mile away. It's a pretty lonesome drive along the pristine but sparsely populated Highway 304. When we reached the entrance to the hunt club, we found a formidable wrought iron gate. It was locked. We were not totally sure if we were on the right road into Matteo's operation, and there was no whisper of a cell phone signal out there, so we drove another three miles directly into the middle of Goose Creek Game Land, where N.C. 304 abruptly ended and an upward spiraling ramp connected it with a new road, N.C. 33. We stopped to get our bearings and strategize when Donna noticed a small piece of plywood, no bigger than a real estate agent's sign, painted white with a bright red arrow pointing down a dirt road to the right. There was only one word on the sign: "Oysters." We cheered.

The short road dead-ended at water, and we soon learned that we were in Hobucken, North Carolina, where the R. E. Mayo Seafood Market backs up like a big white hen onto the edge of the Intracoastal Waterway. The establishment has been in business since the 1950s, said Kaitlyn Hanna, who was minding the supply store, where anchors, rope, fishing gear, motor oil, and an extravagant selection of T-shirts and ball caps were offered for sale. Her coworker in the marina, Mark Jones, came out from the seafood processing area in rubber knee boots and heavy gloves, which he quickly removed. He'd been unloading shrimp from a trawler that had just docked. When I asked, Hanna said that she was not familiar with the Chadwick Creek oysters of Chris Matteo but that they had some oysters that "just came out of the Bay River right here."

Jones, a trim and tall African American man who looked to be in his forties or early fifties, stepped behind the counter to fiddle with a microwave. He told us over his shoulder that wild-caught oysters these days sell for $50 to $85 a bushel. "It depends on what they can get away with and where," he said. "I think they get upwards of $100 a bushel up in Raleigh."

I was flipping through a rack of T-shirts when the microwave beeped, and before we knew what had happened, Jones had shucked a half a dozen oysters that he had steamed *in the microwave*. He offered us toothpicks and a Styrofoam bowl brimming with the gray islands swimming in their own juices.

"You need sauce, saltines?" he asked.

"Wait!" Donna was agog. "How do you know how long to cook them?"

"Until they open a little," Jones said, as if that were as obvious as the ding of the microwave.

The oysters were perfect — salty, not too chewy, and pleasantly warm and juicy. Donna and I polished off the whole bowl in short order with great enthusiasm. She picked out a T-shirt and I got a cap with Hobucken embroidered on the front — a souvenir to remember this new destination in my North Carolina portfolio. We were still shaking our heads at the surprise when we got back in the car.

* * * * * * * * * * * * *

The shadows were lengthening. We agreed to give up our hunt for Chadwick Creek today. We hadn't made an appointment with Chris Matteo anyway. We headed up Highway 33 toward Chocowinity, where we picked up Highway 17 to Williamston. We had reservations to spend the night there. We planned to end this research trip with a celebratory dinner in one of North Carolina's longest-running oyster bars, the Sunny Side, in business in Martin County since 1935. Open only in the *r* months, the restaurant was in danger of closing in 1991 but was saved by a group of investors fiercely loyal to the simple but memorable menu.

The Sunny Side once served only steamed oysters, shrimp, scallops, and clams. The new owners, however, have added Alaskan king crab legs, perhaps to draw in tourists skeptical of the local fare. "All you can eat with crab legs" has become a frequent dinner special advertised on the signs of coastal restaurants in North Carolina. The odd syntax always makes me laugh, suggesting the image of greedy diners trying to hoist as many scallops and shrimp to

Former athlete turned seafood salesman Mark Jones
microwaves fresh oysters in the shell for visitors to sample at
R. E. Mayo Seafood Market on the Intracoastal Waterway in Hobucken.

their mouths as possible using crab claws instead of forks — the kind of stunt you'd see on a humiliating game show.

Once we settled into the hotel, Donna called ahead to learn where the oysters came from for the night's feast at the Sunny Side.

"The mouth of the James River," said the host on the other end of the line. Not Virginia again! We opted to stay in for the night and to let the warm, microwaved oysters from the Bay River linger in memory.

● ● ● ● ● ● ● ● ● ● ● ●

Back home the next afternoon, I managed to catch up with Rowan Jacobsen, a distinguished food writer who lives in Vermont but who has spent much of his life eating and learning about oysters on the East and West Coasts of North America. His first book on bivalves, *A Geography of Oysters*, barely gave a nod to oysters from anywhere south of the Chesapeake Bay. Recently, Jacobsen has made up for his sins of omission by studying the growth of oyster cultivation in the Southeast, documented in his 2016 book, *The Essential Oyster*.

Jacobsen was the keynote speaker at North Carolina's 2015 Oyster Summit in Raleigh, where state legislators mingled with oyster farmers and environmental advocates to consider the future of North Carolina shellfish. The attendees were reminded that a single oyster can clean fifty gallons of water in a day, removing impurities in our estuaries and helping to balance the biologically available nutrients for all plants and sea creatures. Reducing impurities in the water also allows more sunlight to reach the bottom of the sounds and rivers, where submerged aquatic vegetation provides critical habitat for commercial fish and other species.

Jacobsen declared in his summit talk that North Carolina has the potential to become "the Napa Valley of oysters," a phrase that has been touted more than once in print since the meeting. I asked Jacobsen to explain his thesis.

"When you farm oysters," he wrote me, "you look for well-protected estuaries where you can stick cages of oysters that won't get smashed by the ocean or poisoned by urban runoff. North Carolina's filigreed coastline is ideal. You also have a nice range of salinities, depending on how close the waters are to the open sea, so you can appeal to all tastes. And the relatively warm water and long growing season means you can produce market-sized oysters much faster than the Northeast and crush them on price."

Cutting-edge oyster cultivation techniques are now beginning to be applied in North Carolina waters, Jacobsen noted. He has trained his palate in the finer points of what he calls *merroir*—the estuarine equivalent of terroir—and he favorably endorses the North Carolina oysters he's tried.

"I've had Bodie [pronounced *body*] Islands and Crab Sloughs (pronounced *slews*) from the Outer Banks and Chadwick Creeks from farther inland. All very good. I'm looking forward to tasting Atlantic Emeralds this month, and I'm eager to try Stump Sounds and Cedar Islands, too. Quality seems quite high across the board," he told me.

As Jacobsen's reference to particular appellations suggests, cultivated and wild oysters, like fine wine, now have brand names that speak to their provenance, which is the way Jacobsen manages to distinguish among the hundreds of oysters he has sampled in the United States and Canada. Many of these brand-name oysters are cultivated from spat grown in an oyster hatchery. Then the spat are nurtured in trays to the juvenile stage, before being moved to an estuary. There they are "planted," either in mesh bags that rest inside large cages that are dropped to the bay bottom or in floating cages that are carefully protected by netting from predators, such as rays, black drum, oyster drills, crabs, worms, and birds.

"I've visited operations on the Outer Banks, and I've talked with some of the growers," Jacobsen said. "It seems like most people [in North Carolina] are using similar cultivation methods right now, and that's something that might benefit from some diversity farther down the road. Off-bottom cages often result in oysters with weak shells, so I'd like to see more tumbled oysters or (in the few places where it's possible) bottom-planted."

Oysters can be tumbled in their cages, a labor-intensive process that helps avoid the weak shells that Jacobsen mentioned. Strong shells generally mean bigger oysters. Bottom-planted oysters can be successful only where tides and water movement are rather sluggish and shallow, as in our estuarine creeks. All of these methods, of course, present a steep learning curve to oystermen who are used to harvesting what nature has created without their assistance.

● ● ● ● ● ● ● ● ● ● ● ●

When we finally connect by phone, oyster farmer Chris Matteo of Chadwick Creek, in Pamlico County, reported that he'd already heard I was looking for him at Mayo's Seafood in Hobucken. That's rural North Carolina for you. Word travels fast. He also told me that Mark Jones, the man who served us the microwaved oysters, was one of Pamlico County's most outstanding high school athletes back in the day. Jones, still a local celebrity, has now put several of his children through college by working at Mayo's. Matteo told me that he'd never heard of microwaving oysters until I shared the story of our Hobucken sampling.

Matteo was born in New Paltz, New York, a college town in the Hudson Valley, where farm-to-table dining has been the norm for decades. He attended Phillips Exeter Academy, where he, like Mark Jones, was a high school sports standout. He was captain of his wrestling team, a New England champion, and a prep school All-American. He studied international relations at the University of Pennsylvania, where he also wrestled and played football. After graduation and a couple of years as a trader at Union Bank of Switzerland in Manhattan, he founded an internet startup company and served as its CEO. Matteo then spent five years as a trader at a hedge fund in Connecticut before moving to Chapel Hill to work as an analyst and trader for another hedge fund. His wife, Kelly, is a native of Whitsett, North Carolina, near Burlington. She attended Meredith College and Appalachian State and has long been a proponent of the local food movement.

After driving to the coast from Chapel Hill nearly every weekend of their married lives, the couple decided they wanted to find a way to live and work at the coast. Several years earlier, they bought the waterfront acreage in Pamlico County. After touring several oyster farms from North Carolina to Massachusetts, they decided to build an oyster farm with the help of Kelly's father, Duane Creech. They opted to use what Matteo calls "intensive, sustainable oyster mariculture grow-out methods," which make for very strenuous work.

They use double-stack bottom cages that measure three feet by four feet by one foot. "Submerged cages are great when a big storm comes along," Matteo said. "If you have floating cages it's a fire drill every day to protect them from the weather." He noted that submerged cages are also a theft deterrent, since they weigh several hundred pounds each. Oyster pilfering is apparently a long tradition in North Carolina waters, which led to the war with Virginia fishermen in the late 1800s.

"We probably have four to five million oysters out there now," Matteo told me, "and our annual harvest is around 200,000 per year and growing as our crops mature." Matteo sources his spat from Jimmy Morris in Atlantic,

North Carolina, the only private oyster hatchery selling spat in the state, and he supplements those with seed from several nurseries in Virginia.

Matteo is all about making up the current statewide deficit in home-grown North Carolina oysters. He confirmed that the majority of oysters consumed in North Carolina are imported from Virginia and the Gulf of Mexico. "Wild local oysters are at 5 percent of North Carolina's historic levels," he said, "and the oyster farming industry in Virginia and Maryland is probably twenty years ahead of us. Right now, there are only three or four farms up to scale in North Carolina. We have a small research-oriented oyster hatchery at UNC–Wilmington, but the hatcheries in Virginia, who get support from the Virginia Institute of Marine Science, are many generations ahead of us."

The demand for North Carolina oysters is undeniable, Matteo said. "I think people these days have a desire to eat things that are nuanced and reflect the area where they come from. We can't grow them fast enough," he said, even though, as Rowan Jacobsen explained, cultivated oysters can be grown much faster than wild oysters.

"The cages have multiple racks where the oysters sit," Jacobsen writes, "a foot or two from the mud and hoi polloi on the bottom, enjoying the best food the water column has to offer. It's a cushy life; all they have to do is eat and look good doing it."

As Matteo explained, after harvesting, the oysters are bagged and tagged, but rather than pricing them by the bushel, as is done with wild ones, he sells the cultivated oysters unshucked by the count (usually 100 per bag). They can bring three times the price of a wild oyster. Farmed oysters are thus almost always served on the half shell for the higher price point, and—at least in the urban restaurants in the middle of the state, where I have now sampled them—they are often tarted up with fancy adornments, such as caviar, puffed rice, pineapple, or chorizo.

Seafood aggregators travel up and down the coast buying fish and shellfish, but do they mix in the Chadwick Creek product with oysters from other farmers? I asked Matteo.

"Never," he said. "By law, a distributor can't repackage our products once we pack and tag them."

Matteo works with three distributors. One is Locals Seafood, which supplies Chadwick Creeks directly to middle- and high-end restaurants in Raleigh, Durham, Chapel Hill, and elsewhere in the state. "Locals Seafood is a smaller player—young, hungry, and flexible. I like the idea of keeping it with young people who are on their way up," Matteo said.

He also works with Simply Fresh, another small firm, and Inland Seafood, the largest distributor in the Southeast. However, Matteo is adamant that he wants to keep most of his product in state for now and will look to send his oysters south rather than north in the future. Right now, Atlanta is as far as his oysters travel.

"South Carolina is as underserved as we are here," he said, though he admitted that he can envision a time coming when Chadwick Creeks are just as well known in Charleston, Savannah, and Miami. His oysters have already been featured in *Southern Living* magazine.

I asked Matteo which is the very best month for his oysters. "December. No question about it. They are really buttery and sweet and plumped-up then. They stop feeding after it gets real cold, and then they start losing weight. So later in the season they weaken and are just not as good."

Matteo was circumspect. He knows how fortunate he is to have the resources to launch his startup. "A lot of people can't afford to get into a new business like this and not see a return for a few years," he said. "And in producing oysters, there are lots of things that can go wrong."

Matteo recounted the story of a young farmer in New Jersey whose oyster beds happened to be where Hurricane Sandy made landfall. "It takes even longer to grow an oyster up there." Matteo paused. "That guy was wiped out."

It also takes a lot of time, effort, and stamina to build such a labor-intensive business. "You have to invest heavily up front and then scale it," Matteo said. "You can't do this with only a few hundred thousand oysters in the water." He's building his operation as fast as he can.

Chris Matteo is forty-two years old and not quite ready for reading glasses. He has relished the physicality of the oyster work after sitting behind a computer for so many years in the financial industry. "And you have to learn how to be creative in developing the tools and machinery to do this work safely and efficiently," he said. "We are really inventing as we go along."

Days later, at a New Year's party, I sampled two kinds of oysters—a batch from Harkers Island, North Carolina, that were saltier and larger than the Beausoleils from New Brunswick, Nova Scotia. The caterer for the party, an old friend whom I hadn't seen in years, told me that North Carolina oysters are getting harder for caterers to come by because New York seafood houses are coming down here and paying a high price (more than a hundred dollars per hundred count) for them.

A few weeks after this conversation, I met Chris Matteo face-to-face and had the chance to taste his cultivated oysters from Chadwick Creek. He was shucking them as fast as he could at a special chefs' dinner, called "Bubbles and Pearls," at the historic Carolina Inn, on the University of North Carolina campus in Chapel Hill. The night was cold and the wind brisk, much like Matteo's raw oysters, which were the first appetizers offered, along with three kinds of sparkling wine. The next round of Chadwick Creeks were lightly battered and fried, and a third round were baked with spinach in puff pastry.

Matteo's oysters did not have the salinity of the Harkers Islanders from the New Year's party, but they were pleasantly chewy and never stringy enough to catch in the teeth. Chadwick Creeks left a mineral finish at the back of the palate, evocative of the beach. Very refreshing. Before the evening was over, it seemed as if every diner had eaten a bushel apiece.

After appetizers, we were brought oysters in a stew, a cocktail, a pie, and—finally—a sausage casserole. Samplings of champagnes paired with each dish made it all go down easily. Only a couple of women down the table had any complaint that I heard. They had driven in from Columbia, South Carolina, for this feast and found the oysters not salty enough to suit. I was surprised when they asked for a saltshaker and proceeded to dress every dish to their own tastes. Fortunately they were out of the line of sight of Matteo and the Carolina Inn's chef, who took turns describing their recipes alongside the third celebrity host, John Martin Tyler, a South Carolina Low Country chef and author known as Hoppin' John, who lays claim to having invented the most ergonomic oyster knife ever made. It was on sale that night, along with his cookbook.

Can North Carolina really become the Napa Valley of oysters? Coastal Federation founder and executive director Todd Miller suggests that it will take considerable political will and a significant investment at the state level in the decades ahead.

Meanwhile, through the UNC–Chapel Hill Institute for the Environment's Outer Banks Field Site, select groups of students have been spending a semester in Manteo since 2001. Through the Coastal Studies Institute on Roanoke Island, student research teams focus on issues of concern to coastal residents. For the past several years, oysters were the subject of the students' capstone research. One by one, these young people are gaining expertise in oyster farming: its challenges and its potential impact on the coastal economy.

The students worked with Joey Daniels, an oysterman who is growing his own brand, Bodie Island Oysters, for the Wanchese Fish Company — one of the largest commercial fishing outfits in the state. Going out on boats with Daniels and others from the Coastal Studies Institute, the students studied the impact of oyster cultivation on water quality and the health of the fish population. They also learned from Daniels — who is constantly innovating — about growing and harvesting techniques.

Daniels is a third-generation fisherman in his forties. He is every bit the seasoned seaman, with his red beard, strong, freckled arms, and "hoi toide" accent. On the day we visited Wanchese, he came out of his warehouse wearing a NASCAR cap and a light jacket. The wind was up and the Oregon Inlet was churning.

Before we found the building where Joey was constructing his own floating oyster hatchery, we had stumbled into his father's office. It was Saturday, and the senior Mr. Daniels was there, dressed in a crisply pressed shirt and talking on the telephone. Beside his desk on another table, several modems with winking lights and a tangle of Ethernet cables snaked toward a computer. Just above the electronic gear, an old-fashioned pencil sharpener was mounted on the wall.

"I can tell you that he has no idea about that computer stuff," Joey told us later, smiling, "but he knows how to sharpen a pencil."

The Daniels family had recently sold Wanchese Fish Company to an international conglomerate, but father and son stayed on for a while to help make it all work. I asked Joey why he was still doing his oyster cultivation project now that the company had been sold and presumably he could be doing something else — most anything else his heart desired.

Daniels looked across the worn docks that fan out from the village of Wanchese into the sound. We were standing on the south end of Roanoke Island, the site of the first English settlement in the United States. "I come from a commercial fishing background," he said, "and for years I've been watching my town die. Fishing is overregulated. These watermen here need something they can do. Oysters could save them. They're skeptical of cultivation, of course. They need to see it work. And you can't get your investment back fast. They say, 'Daddy didn't do it that way. Granddaddy didn't do it that way,' so they don't want to do it. But they *know* this water, the tides, the weather, the storms. We need to show them how to do something new that will work."

Daniels has named his brand of oysters after Bodie Island, which is the peninsula that forms the northernmost portion of the Outer Banks, extending from the tip of Oregon Inlet all the way north to Virginia Beach. It was once a true island, but human intervention closed the inlet at Nags Head that separated Bodie Island from the Currituck Banks to the north. Bodie is still home to one of North Carolina's storied lighthouses, which we could see in the distance across the sound from where we were standing. "So besides convincing the fishermen to give this a try, what is your biggest barrier to success?" I asked.

"Water quality is paramount," Daniels said, without a second's thought. "It goes back to the New Deal, when they started pushing up the sand dunes to close up these inlets. There used to be five inlets between here and the Chesapeake Bay. It used to be that the ocean water could wash in at Duck and Corolla and flush out the sound. But whenever a natural inlet opens up between the ocean and the sound now, the government closes it up by dredging sand and trying to stop the ocean from doing what it needs to do. Last time I checked, if you use the toilet and don't flush, it smells."

Crossing the lofty causeway later from Roanoke Island to Nags Head, you can see what Daniels was talking about. Huge infill has created a promontory for multistory condos and marinas full of colossal yachts docked along the sound.

"We've allowed all these sound-side marinas to be built, and people come down here and wash their boats off with bleach. The easiest thing is to blame the guy with the big net for overfishing, but water quality is the real problem," Daniels said. "Your oyster is going to taste like the last thing it drank."

Daniels believes that the government broke it, and the government ought to fix it. "What would it take to put in giant culvert pipes running from the ocean to the sound to let the water flow in and out?" he asks. "Stagnant water is killing us."

Brady Blackburn was in the group of ten students who completed a field study with Joey Daniels in December 2015. Blackburn characterized himself as "the grandson of foodies who are all about oysters." Though he was raised in Asheville, he has eaten more than his share of oysters, he said. His classmate Cinnamon Moore, who grew up in China Grove just outside Charlotte, had eaten oysters only one time before she began the research project in Wanchese. She declared herself to be a big fan now.

Both students completed their work toward an environmental studies major by engaging with faculty and fishermen to research and write a report called *Investigation on the Half Shell: The Social Ecological Role of Oyster Aquaculture in North Carolina*. In the science-based part of their research across three sites in the Roanoke Sound, the students compared the filtration rates of farmed and wild oysters and discovered that farming oysters does not inhibit the growth of underwater vegetation important to the fish population—a concern that has led to some regulatory roadblocks.

Within a social science framework, they also interviewed local citizens about their perceptions of oyster aquaculture. While they found that farming oysters is publicly seen as a potential economic boost for the eastern edge of North Carolina, they also encountered concerns among coastal residents about how these farms might interrupt other commercial and recreational uses of the sounds and rivers.

Blackburn and Moore are enrolled in a five-year program that combines three years of environmental studies with the completion of a master's degree in journalism in their last two years at UNC–Chapel Hill, and they are both keen to launch careers that will allow them to help better inform the public about the science behind these kinds of environmental issues.

"The social science part of our study helped me see how many different sides to a story there can be," Moore said. "There are a lot of different interests at play around oyster farming, and I learned just how hard it is to make a living on the coast year-round."

For Blackburn, getting acquainted with the regulatory restrictions on North Carolina aquaculture was a revelation. "While these regulations were created with good intentions," he said, "I think it makes it very hard for start-up operations to get permits and to make an aquaculture business work over time."

"And the regulations have been changed so much over the years," Moore added. "That fluctuation has made people skeptical of government intervention or support. We interviewed a lot of people who are just against regulations, period."

The student research team also reported that unlike other forms of aquaculture where finfish like tilapia or salmon are raised, you don't need hormones or to add fish food to the water or end up with concentrations of fish waste. In short, cultivating oysters is much easier on the environment.

The students noted that, while Virginia, Maryland, and Louisiana have established infrastructure and regulatory frameworks that support oyster farming, North Carolina lags far behind. Virginia sold 40 million oysters in 2015 compared to North Carolina's harvest of 3 to 4 million.

Andy Keeler, an economics professor at East Carolina University, is head of public policy and coastal sustainability at the Coastal Studies Institute and supervises the student research. "The students' work has made a lot of people, including me, really excited about oyster aquaculture in North Carolina," he said. "Oysters seem to be a topic that both ends of the political spectrum can agree on in this state, which almost never happens."

Keeler believes that oyster cultivation could be the way back to economic prosperity for the eastern part of the state and its watermen. "We're not talking about the heritage wild oysters of the past, or how people gathered them. But running an oyster aquaculture operation requires the same traditional skills we have in abundance here. You have to know about motors, water, and weather. It doesn't take an engineering degree. Bringing oysters back could bring livelihoods back in a depressed area where commercial fishing has not been great for a long time.

"I may be overselling this idea," Keeler continued, "but foods do tend to bring people together. The oyster industry seems to have the potential to heal some of the wounds from past environmental controversies." Keeler was referring to perennial conflicts between nonprofit environmental groups and local citizens around such issues as saving turtle habitats versus the freedom to drive trucks on the beaches.

"Oysters have already changed some attitudes toward the importance of stewardship of our natural resources. Nonprofit environmental groups, legislators, and local residents are on the same side when it comes to oysters," Keeler said.

It has been a full year since Donna and I began our oyster pilgrimage across the eastern part of the state. We have come back on the third day of December 2016, and we happen to be in the neighborhood of Sunny Side Oyster Bar in Williamston. Fortunately the restaurant is open until ten in the evening on this Friday. We did not call ahead to ask about the provenance of tonight's oysters. We are hungry, and it's late.

The crowd of patrons at the Sunny Side sits close, hip to hip, at a U-shaped counter topped with zinc. The deft shuckers stand inside the U, working through buckets of oysters, while others race back and forth bringing heaps of steamed shrimp, scallops, smaller buckets of clams, and faux wooden bowls of Sunny Side's signature simmering cocktail sauce. The only other accoutrements are oyster forks, big napkins, packs of soda crackers, extra horseradish, and lemons. The only side dish on the menu is steamed broccoli drizzled with a pale orange cheese sauce, also delivered in well-worn bowls. This sprawling building where the venerable ritual takes place has been listed on the National Register of Historic Places.

As we wait to order, we find our server's portrait among those of a dozen of his peers on the paper placemats in front of us. "Johnny" is clearly a veteran of the establishment, with Popeye arms and legs. Unlike some of the other aproned shuckers, he is dressed in shorts, tennis shoes, and a T-shirt damp from his many trips running to the kitchen and back. No apron.

"Where are your oysters from tonight?" I ask with some trepidation.

"Engelhard area," he says.

"Stumpy Point?" I ask hopefully.

"They don't always tell us exactly."

Still, this is thrilling. A friend had reported eating delicious oysters from Stumpy Point in Dare County only a week ago. Engelhard is a bit farther down the coastline in Hyde County and not as celebrated for their oysters. Still, we are about to eat wild North Carolina oysters. All is not lost!

Johnny asks how much steam we want—light, medium, or done. We go for light. Donna and I are practically levitating on the stools, elbowing each other with joy.

Johnny brings a bowl for the cocktail sauce, which is always poured at the bar, steaming hot from a stainless pitcher. Rumor has it that the current owners of Sunny Side paid almost as much for the cocktail sauce recipe with its top-secret ingredients as they did for the restaurant itself when they saved it from closing in 1991.

Johnny then brings the melted butter, also served from a metal pitcher. We sample the cocktail sauce. "I could drink that from the bowl," Donna says. It is very warm with just the right burn from the horseradish.

"Lots of people say that," Johnny tells us. "We had one fellow who used to come in here and order a tall glass of it to drink before he started on his oysters — to prepare his insides, he said, to get 'em all warm and ready." Johnny rubs his belly.

I explain to him about our disappointment this time last year when we had called and found that Sunny Side was serving oysters from Virginia.

He understands and shakes his head. "It can be hard to get them from here."

I ask if they ever serve cultivated oysters. He grimaces and says they had resorted to selling them once or twice when nothing else was available. "But you have to hope people order some other kind of seafood to go with them because they are so expensive we can't charge enough to make anything on them."

Soon Johnny is back with our half peck of Engelhards. They are gorgeous, plump, and saucer shaped. "It's a good shell," Johnny says, opening one. He points with his oyster knife. "See how the oyster comes right to the edge of the shell, all around? Now that's a good oyster." Indeed, they are so large, they hang over the edges of our saltines — more than a mouthful.

We dip some in butter, some in cocktail sauce, and some in both. It is a feast we cannot finish, the oysters are so generous. I am thankful for the experience: the Sunny Side is one of a kind.

The next day we go back to Wanchese to see Joey Daniels and learn how his oyster nursery, or "upweller" as it is called, is coming along since we saw him last. His daughter, Emma, who is now fourteen and his only child, has agreed to take a break from decorating the Christmas tree at home with her mother, and she comes with her dad to his shop on the docks. Emma helped him build the new floating oyster hatchery, with its twenty-four colandered bins, each holding some 30,000 oysters, now about the size of dimes. The hatchery

Oysterman and innovator Joey Daniels and his daughter, Emma, inspect samples from the floating oyster hatchery that they built together in Wanchese.

is floating beside the dock, next to Daniels's shop. A paddle wheel turns at one end, forcing water through the baskets of oysters. "Force-feeding them," as Joey puts it.

His more mature oysters are out in the sound in cages, about a ten-minute boat ride from this dock. Joey tells us that since we were last here, Hurricane Matthew, which spun through the area in October causing catastrophic floods and damaging winds, hurt him badly. "We had too much fresh water in the inlet." He shrugs. "Farming oysters is just like being a dirt farmer. You can't control the weather," Daniels says. The salinity of the water in Oregon Inlet dropped precipitously, to four parts per thousand. Normally the salinity is up at eighteen to twenty-four parts per thousand, he explains.

"It stayed that way for three weeks and stressed all the animals in the water," he continues. "It goes back to the lack of inlets I was telling you about when you were here before. We need that salt water infusion from the ocean, and when the inlets are closed up, there's no flush."

I ask Emma, a soccer player who is also fond of science in school, if she might take up the oyster business from her dad. Like her father she is redheaded and fair-skinned and shy but firm when she does speak. "I don't know," she says. "It's too soon to tell." Nevertheless, Emma is clearly at home around the shop with her father.

* * *

The future of North Carolina's oysters is threatened, a crisis made even more significant in our minds after our final lunch on this oyster tour. From Wanchese, we drive out toward Nags Head, past the enormous yachts moored at the docks along the causeway. I will never again drive by here without thinking of Joey Daniels talking about the bleach that boaters use to keep their hulls so very white. We pass the Basnight family's visionary Lone Cedar Restaurant, where the provenance of every local ingredient is explained on the menu.

To the south, the low winter sun makes the brown marsh grasses glow orange. Colorful whirligigs, flags, and sails flap wildly among the clutter of storefronts, motels, and restaurants trying to capture beachgoers' attentions, though in December the traffic is sparse.

Just before we reach Whalebone Junction, we pull into the Sugar Shack Fish Market, where seafood is sold raw or cooked to order. The sign outside advertises Crab Sloughs, one of the favored oysters that Rowan Jacobsen had mentioned to me a year ago. After inspecting a menu at the cash register, we order a basket of them fried. They are far and away the best of all the oysters we have sampled anywhere on this journey. They remind me of the long-ago fried oysters I'd first had in college at Brady's in Chapel Hill. So very fresh and complex in taste. The breading is light, and the shape of each is crenellated around the edges—something that can be achieved only by cooking them at just the right temperature, I have learned.

These wild oysters had just come in from Oregon Inlet near Wanchese. As Rowan Jacobsen explains in his blog, *The Oyster Guide*, "The lively currents produced by that geography make for a level of wild oyster you rarely see. The action knocks the oysters around and forces them to cup up as if they were prime farmed oysters . . . a joy to shuck, and a joy to eat—firm, a lovely balance between sweet and salty, with a buttery sweetcorn and asparagus finish (including the asparagus's astringent notes). There are some nice clammy tannins. . . . All in all, an oyster worthy of any raw bar. But you won't find them there."

Jacobsen goes on to call Crab Sloughs a "locally guarded treasure." I ask Eric, the Sugar Shack cook, how long they would be available here.

"Not long," he says. "They get fished out quick." Eric brings out a platter of unshucked oysters to show us the big, heavy shells that had been tossed in the currents. He also tells us that almost every one of the oysters in this harvest so far had pea-sized crabs inside the shell, which is the origin of their unusual name. The small crabs take up residence in these particular oysters for protection, and they never grow any larger. Many people eating the oysters raw or steamed consider the little spidery crab an extra delicacy to pop in their mouths, kind of like the surprise toy in a box of Cracker Jack.

As we sit savoring every last oyster in the basket, a slender man in docksiders, jeans, and a freshly pressed shirt comes in to pick up a half bushel of Crab Sloughs to take home. He tells us he'd be eating them "raw, roasted, in stew, and for Christmas stuffing." He almost drops the big waxed box on his way out the door, they are so heavy.

What a privilege to taste these oysters! I think of the rough, cleansing salt currents that Joey Daniels longs for, bursting into the inlets and sounds, and how they help create these sweet, buttery creatures. These were the wild native oysters we'd been hunting for more than a year.

I picture in my mind all those spots along the Outer Banks on Highway 12 toward Hatteras that have been constantly breached by storms. How the dunes are moved by wind and waves and pile up on that narrow band of asphalt, creating a constant chore for road crews moving and dumping sand back nearer to the ocean so that traffic can once again pass through.

I think of our state's unofficial Cassandras—the prophetic scientists Orrin Pilkey from Duke and Stan Riggs from East Carolina University who have cautioned us for decades against further shoreline development. Riggs has said that this effort to maintain roads on such slender barrier islands is "a lost cause that will bankrupt the state." Such warnings are validated year after year by hurricanes.

Mother Nature will win this one, I believe, and like the oysters, we humans will only be as good as the last water we are able to drink.

Epilogue

THIS SINGLE YEAR IN THE STUDY OF TWELVE NORTH CAROLINA native foods brought hurricanes, forest fires, drought, and floods. Before the New Year began, I checked in again with some of the folks we met along the way to see how they had fared.

Only two weeks after we met in late September, Jack Bishop of Vineyards on the Scuppernong woke up after the pounding rains and vicious winds of Hurricane Matthew to see by daylight that a large number of the sturdy posts in the middle of his vineyards had "snapped like the mast of a sailboat in high winds," as he put it. Many vines, still draped in grapes, were now on the ground, so heavy that four men could not lift one of them, Bishop said. It took heavy equipment to raise the vines, save what fruit they could, and reset the posts in concrete. FEMA, the Federal Emergency Management Agency, offered him three dollars for every plant that came down. Bishop scoffed at the offer and declined. He is building a new house in Manteo for his second retirement and praised his son Bud's steady hand. "He'll take over the business," Bishop said.

Jasper Evans, of Rocky Hock, reported that the same intense heat that overripened some of his cantaloupes at the end of July had also hurt his peanuts and cotton. Then the deluge from the hurricane made matters worse. He realized only half of the usual yield of peanuts and simply turned under his cotton crop. His insurance covered about half of the expenses of planting that cotton, he said. He remained serene, accepting the ups and downs of farming.

Apple growers Ron and Suzanne Joyner emailed to report that this year's Thanksgiving at Big Horse Creek Farm was a true celebration. "We were VERY thankful over that week because a lot of good things happened," Suzanne wrote. "We had two Thanksgiving dinners with special friends. We replaced our big batteries and our wind generator, so now we have a re- newed, renewable energy system! We planted our garlic crop and, most importantly, we got some great rains. So now we are real 'modern' folks — with actual running water in our house."

The drought that affected the Joyners also amplified the impact of a number of wildfires that raged across western North Carolina, north Georgia, and eastern Tennessee in November, some of which were set by arsonists. Extension agent David Cozzo reported that he didn't know whether the fires in that region had affected the ramp patches around Cherokee. Sara Jackson, at Bat Cave Botanicals, however, told me that the road into their forest farm, where the wild ginseng and ramps grow, became the fire break line for the Party Rock fire that began on 5 November in Chimney Rock Park near Lake Lure and covered more than 7,000 acres before it was over. A controlled burn actually stopped the fire short of their house and land, and Sara was impressed by the expertise of the firefighters.

A son, Griffin Euliss Thaller, was born in the middle of it all, on 10 November, in an emergency Caesarian section at the hospital. Sara came home with their newborn with the fire still moving toward them. "We kept the house sealed up, but the smoke was unbelievable," she said. "We came pretty close to having to evacuate, but we did not panic, and we stayed the course. As scary as it was, it will be good for the forest. Of course, that was not true for Gatlinburg. That destruction was unbelievable," she said with a catch in her voice. On the winter solstice, a few days before our conversation, Sara and Martin had carried the baby on a long walk in the forest. "He loved it!" she said.

Chester Lynn got in touch just before Christmas to report on the aftermath of Hurricane Matthew on Ocracoke Island. "Well, never in all my years have I called a local person a dingbatter," he said. ("Dingbatter" is a Down East term for visitor — someone who is not from there and may be in a state of confusion, to put it kindly.) "This fellow, a native, went and chopped down the fig bushes in his mama's yard. Cut them right slam to the ground thinking they was dead," Lynn explained. "But the figs can survive. They will come back, but maybe not some others. It was the first time in my life I've seen plants that a hurricane hurt so bad. The gardenia coming up my steps was beautiful. Now there's not a leaf on it. The Cape jasmine and Korean boxwoods is gone too," he said, "even some of the bay trees got hurt. The tide came in deep. Another six or eight inches, and it would have come in my house."

As the year drains away, I am left pondering the paradox: the fragility of the durable and the durability of the fragile.

Early this frigid December morning, rounding the corner of my house, walking under the now leafless fig tree, the scent rises from the frostbitten fig leaves below—the ripe sweetness is still there, unleashed underfoot. It calls to mind the August night that Donna and I set the alarm to rise before dawn in Beaufort to witness the reliable and always thrilling Perseid meteor shower before we caught the first ferry of the day to Ocracoke. We were staying in a cottage that belongs to dog-loving friends from Virginia. Since the yard was fenced, we let Nebo go out with us. Donna and I arranged ourselves on the still-warm brick walkway, flat on our backs, eyes adjusting to the night sky. Nebo was puzzled and came over to see if we were in trouble. Seeing that we were not, she went back to sniffing in the grass. The meteor shower, as predicted, was under way in all its fleeting randomness. We tried to monitor all corners of the sky at once. Every few minutes a burning bit of thousand-year-old dust would streak overhead, trailing light like the ephemeral wake of a passing boat. I closed my eyes, and for an instant I could still see the radiance.

Acknowledgments

WHEN I TURNED FORTY, MY GARDENING GENE — AN HONEST INHERI-
tance from the farmers on both sides of my family — kicked in and has driven
me to the dirt every spring since. Some days, nothing seems nearly so important as tending to the plants I have set out over the years, both in my
tiny Piedmont yard in Carrboro and in the more expansive gardens within
sight of the Black Mountain Range at my cabin in Little Switzerland. When
Mark Simpson-Vos, the editorial director of the University of North Carolina Press, encouraged me to follow up the *Literary Trails of North Carolina*
guidebook series with another project based on the state's history and culture, I started pondering agricultural possibilities.

On a long drive through the lower Piedmont one day, as I listened to a
recording of *Animal, Vegetable, Mineral* by Barbara Kingsolver, I realized I
wanted to write about food and its impact on North Carolina's identity as a
state. As my book proposal took shape, UNC Press's executive editor, Elaine
Maisner, suggested, among other things, that I would need to emphasize
my past food writing. With the exception of editing, along with three close
friends, a collection of recipe columns by the late Helen Whiting, an extraordinary cook who also happened to run the Regulator Bookshop in Durham,
my food writing experience was limited. But, as I told Elaine, my eating experience was broad and deep. So, first, thanks go to UNC Press for giving me
this opportunity to study a topic about which I am passionate but, shall we
say, mostly homeschooled.

As with *Literary Trails*, photographer Donna Campbell and I have had
the great pleasure of exploring North Carolina on a mission, this time to eat
our way across the state, which we did with gusto. Donna, an exceptional
farm-trained cook, was raised in Mecklenburg and Iredell Counties, where
she was known for a time as "Catfish Donna" for her weekly fishing report
on a local radio station — a job that preceded her founding of *Lake Norman
Magazine* in the 1980s. To Catfish Donna I owe more than gratitude, because

she was always riding shotgun on this culinary expedition and applying her wisdom, humor, and curiosity to the task. Plus, with two at the table I could always order more dishes to sample.

Artist Carol Misner created the delicate illustrations expressly to head each chapter of this book. The thinned paint she applies to archival paper looks more like watercolor than the acrylic she actually uses. Carol's exquisite, sepia-toned botanical works are offered by Williams Sonoma nationally and in galleries in Highlands, North Carolina, and Birmingham, Alabama—two towns where she has spent significant time. Carol agreed to this assignment—she had never painted a goat or a crab or a shad!—because of our friendship, dating back to the time when she was my high school geometry teacher. That our connection remains sturdy enough to warrant such a gift from her is a marvel to me. Thanks are wholly inadequate.

Debbie McGill, an editor of impeccable credentials who also worked on *Literary Trails*, once again agreed to police my commas and word choices as each chapter evolved, and she is my most trusted reader. If Debbie and I can manage this partnership long enough, perhaps some of her lessons will take.

Ben Edwards, a longtime friend and colleague, was game to read the entire manuscript in its first draft. Ben gave me, as he always has, the fresh view of someone who asks the right clarifying questions.

Of course, I am grateful to all those folks who were willing to meet Donna and me and be interviewed at length about their knowledge and experience in the fields and on the waters of North Carolina. Their permission to follow them up and down the crop rows; in the vineyards, boathouses, and orchards; in their kitchens; and at their tables was a courtesy beyond measure. I can only hope that readers enjoy their stories as much as I did and will appreciate their roles in preserving our state's foodways.

Many other old and new friends helped us uncover information and identify sources. Special thanks go to way-finders Susan Larson in Mitchell and Yancey Counties, Feather Phillips in Tyrrell County, and Jane Lonon, Evalynn Halsey, Ed and Ellie Perzel, and all the regulars at the On the Same Page Literary Festival in Ashe County who listened to me talk about this project at length and provided many fine meals and accommodations.

Annelle and Doug Williams, serious foodies who divide their time between Martinsville, Virginia, and Beaufort, North Carolina, lent us their home at the coast for our fig foray. The Old Buncombe County Genealogical Society helped me brainstorm food ideas after I gave a talk on *Literary Trails* at its annual conference in Asheville. On oysters, I got advice from the seafood monger Willy Phillips and the caterer Lora Booker. Todd Miller, the founding director of the North Carolina Coastal Federation, and his staff were also generous with their knowledge of oysters; we are all in their debt for their work to protect our coastal waters.

Alan Muskat, an expert forager, led me to many sources in western North Carolina for guidance on ramps, serviceberries, persimmons, and goat's milk. I am particularly grateful to the North Carolina Cooperative Extension Service of North Carolina State University for the many experts in every county whose job it is to answer questions about flora and fungi. I thank June S. Jolley, at the North Carolina Arboretum in Asheville, and the extension specialist Charlotte Glen and the pomologist Lee Calhoun, both of Chatham County, for their dedication.

Special thanks are due Roxanne Henderson and Michael Brown for reading the chapter on shad and approving the story I told there about Roxanne's uncle and aunt. Thanks, too, go to Jim and Dawn Shamp and to Alvis Smith and Dennis Williams for taste-testings with me. I am grateful to my stepsister, Susan Dempsey, my brother, G. Ray Eubanks, Virginia Crank, Kathy Caine, and Nancy Hardin for caring for my mother on occasions when I was doing field research. My go-to gardener, Jim Harb, and I began our friendship in a kitchen, and I'm sure we'll keep cooking together as long as at least one of us can lift an iron skillet.

Thanks go to the photographers Jan G. Hensley, Liza Plaster, William Early, and Ali Morrow (assisted by Salem Morrow), who supplied certain images we could not have gotten otherwise. Kudos to Richard Paschal, a wizard at photo retouching, who made everyone look his or her best.

I am indebted to so many hands at UNC Press: editorial assistant Becki Reibman; copy editor Julie Bush; project editor Jay Mazzocchi; designers Kim Bryant and Jamison Cockerham; editorial readers Andrea Weigl, Vicky Jarrett, and Bland Simpson; and Dino Battista, Ivis Bohlen, Ellen Bush, Gina Mahalek, Catherine Cheney, Michael Donatelli, and Susan Garrett in marketing. My deepest gratitude goes to Elaine Maisner, whose steady eye and good advice are always welcome.

To every cook who prepared the dishes described herein, here's to the years of their ripening as residents of the Old North State.

Bibliography

GENERAL

Barber, Dan. *The Third Plate: Field Notes on the Future of Food*. New York: Penguin Press, 2014.

Davidson, Alan, ed. *The Oxford Companion to Food*. Oxford: Oxford University Press, 2014.

Earnhardt, Tom. *Crossroads of the Natural World: Exploring North Carolina with Tom Earnhardt*. Chapel Hill: University of North Carolina Press, 2013.

Edge, John T., ed. *Foodways*. Vol. 7 of *The New Encyclopedia of Southern Culture*. Chapel Hill: University of North Carolina Press, 2007.

Ferris, Marcie Cohen. *The Edible South: The Power of Food and the Making of an American Region*. Chapel Hill: University of North Carolina Press, 2014.

Jacobsen, Rowan. *American Terroir: Savoring the Flavors of Our Woods, Waters, and Fields*. New York: Bloomsbury, 2010.

Jordan, Jennifer A. *Edible Memory: The Lure of Heirloom Tomatoes and Other Forgotten Foods*. Chicago: University of Chicago Press, 2015.

Kingsolver, Barbara. *Animal, Vegetable, Miracle: A Year of Food Life*. New York: Harper Collins, 2007.

Lundy, Ronni, ed. *Cornbread Nation 3: Foods of the Modern South*. Chapel Hill: University of North Carolina Press, 2005.

Remnick, David, ed. *Secret Ingredients: The New Yorker Book of Food and Drink*. New York: Modern Library, 2008.

Trillin, Calvin. *The Tummy Trilogy*. New York: Farrar, Straus and Giroux, 1994.

PREFACE

Ackerman, Diane. *A Natural History of the Senses*. New York: Vintage, 1991.

Hoffman, Peter. "Net Loss: Shad Swim against the Tide of Time." *Edible Manhattan*, 10 March 2009. https://www.ediblemanhattan.com/magazine/net_loss/.

CHAPTER 1: SNOW

Anderson, L. V. "Go Ahead, Lick That Spoon." *Slate*, 5 March 2014. http://www.slate.com/articles/health_and_science/medical_examiner/2014/03/salmonella_and_raw_eggs_how_i_ve_eaten_tons_of_cookie_dough_and_never_gotten.html.

Aneja, Viney P. Email communication, 25 January 2016.

Baird, Sarah. "We All Scream for Snow Cream." *Modern Farmer*, 22 January 2015. http://modernfarmer.com/2015/01/scream-snow-cream/.

Bramley, Anne. "Snow Is Delicious. But Is It Dangerous To Eat?" *The Salt: What's On Your Plate*, 5 March 2015. https://www.npr.org/sections/thesalt/2015/03/05/390228979 /snow-is-delicious-but-is-it-dangerous-to-eat.

Burchell, Michael. Email communication, 25 January 2016.

Diuguid, Lewis W. "Commentary: The Changing Dangers of Nuclear Radiation." *McClatchyDC*, 16 April 2011. http://www.mcclatchydc.com/opinion/article2462 2738.html.

Edwards, Joseph F., A.M., M.D., ed. *The Annals of Hygiene*. Vol. 7. Philadelphia: University of Pennsylvania Press, 1892, 428.

Grant, Marshall, and Chris Zar. *I Was There When It Happened: My Life with Johnny Cash*. Nashville: Cumberland House Publishing, 2006, 226–27.

Harker, Maxine Carey. "The Snow Eaters." *The State*, 49, no. 7 (December 1981): 14.

Kaplan, Sarah. "Snow Is Beautiful. Please Don't Eat It." *Washington Post*, 22 January 2016. https://www.washingtonpost.com/news/morning-mix/wp/2016/ 01/22/snow-is -beautiful-please-dont-eat-it/?utm_term=.f942f9fa6ca2.

Kenan, Randall. Email communication, 21 January 2016.

Lebovitz, David. "How to Buy Vanilla and Vanilla FAQs." *David Lebovitz: Living the Sweet Life in Paris* (blog), 14 November 2005. http://www.davidlebovitz.com/2005 /11/vanilla/.

McCorkle, Jill. Email communication, 3 February 2016.

McGill, Debbie. Email communication, 4 December 2015.

Morando, Lil. "Journal: Fallout Shelter Makes Architectural Note." *Hammond Daily Star*, 2 June 2001. http://www.hammondstar.com/journal-fallout-shelter-makes -architectural-note/article_e7010b78-d816-5950-b4ae-eb5992299004.html.

Nazarenko, Yevgen, Uday Krien, Oleg Nepotchatykh, Rodrigo V. Rangel-Alvarado and Parisa A. Ariya. "Role of Snow and Cold Environment in the Fate and Effects of Nanoparticles and Select Organic Pollutants from Gasoline Engine Exhaust." *Environmental Science: Processes and Impacts*, Issue 2, 2016.

"Our History." Eagle Brand. http://www.eaglebrand.com/history.

Parris, John. *Mountain Bred*. Asheville, N.C.: Citizen Times Publishing Company, 1967, 1–2.

Pearce, T. H. "More about Snow Cream." *The State*, 49, no. 9 (February 1982): 10, 28.

Quinzio, Jeri. *Of Sugar and Snow: A History of Ice Cream Making*. Oakland: University of California Press, 2010, ix.

Rosen, Diana L. *Ice Cream Lover's Companion: The Ultimate Connoisseur's Guide to Buying, Making and Enjoying Ice Cream and Frozen Yogurt*. New York: Kensington, 2000, 23–24.

Ruth, Dorothy Hall. "Real Snowcream." *The State*, 50, no. 8 (January 1983): 3.

Sauceman, Fred W. *The Place Setting: Timeless Tastes of the Mountain South, from Bright Hope to Frog Level*. Macon, Ga.: Mercer University Press, 2001, 174.

Shamp, Dawn. Email communication, 3 February 2016.

"SNOWatHOME." Snowmaking Products (website), http://www.snowathome.com /our_products.php.

State Climate Office of North Carolina. "Overview." http://climate.ncsu.edu/climate /ncclimate.html.

CHAPTER 2: GOAT'S MILK

Childs, Laura. *The Joy of Keeping Goats*. New York: Skyhorse Publishing, 2011, 191–96.

Hart, Susan. "Carl Sandburg Home National Historic Site Cultural Landscape Report." National Park Service Cultural Resources Planning Division, December 1993.

Jernigan, Adam. Interview, 4 February 2016, Black Mountain, N.C.

Liepelt, Kourtney. "Sheep and Goat Farming." Associated Press, *Los Angeles Daily News*, 21 February 2015.

Madigan, Carleen, ed. *The Backyard Homestead*. North Adams, Mass.: Storey Publishing, 2009, 258–64.

Miller, Elena Diana, ed. *Cooking at Connemara: Carl Sandburg Family Recipes*. Fletcher, N.C.: Cookbook Publishers, 1991.

Mitgang, Herbert, ed. *The Letters of Carl Sandburg*. New York: Harcourt, Brace & World, 1968, 494.

Niven, Penelope. *Carl Sandburg: A Biography*. New York: Charles Scribner's Sons, 1991, 498–99, 559–80, 624.

Plaster, Liza. Interview, 23 April 2016, Lenoir, N.C.

———. "Life at Ripshin Dairy: A Love Story." *The Dairy Goat Gazette*, The Piedmont Dairy Goat Association Newsletter, November/December 2009.

Polega, Paula Steichen. Phone interviews, 25 January 2016 and 4 January 2017.

Steichen, Paula. *My Connemara*. New York: Harcourt, Brace & World, 1969, 41–42.

Weaver, Sue. *The Backyard Goat*. North Adams, Mass.: Storey Publishing, 2011, 3–12.

CHAPTER 3: SHAD

Ashley, Keith, and Kevin Dockendorf. "American Shad *Alosa sapidissima*." North Carolina Wildlife Resources Commission website, http://ncpedia.org/wildlife/american-shad (2007).

Faulkner, William. *Light in August*. New York: Vintage International/Random House, 1990, 119.

Holt, Craig. "River-Run Shad Are Harbingers of Great North Carolina Spring Fishing." *Carolina Sportsman*, 28 February 2006. http://www.northcarolinasportsman.com /details.php?fb_comment_id=946585382074847_947004568699595#f3d58d4c5915bfc.

Lewis, Edna. *The Taste of Country Cooking*. New York: Alfred A. Knopf, 2015, 19.

"Living Waters—Trent River." Official website of Jones County, 2011. http://www.jones countync.gov/index.asp?SEC=C643CD5A-62EF-4DA3-BB21-8D9144460BC7& Type=B_BASIC

McIver, Stuart. "The Tragic Mistress of Whitehall." *Sun-Sentinel*, 2 July 1989. http:// articles.sun-sentinel.com/1989-07-02/features/8902190293_1_robert-worth -bingham-coffin-henry-morrison-flagler/2.

McPhee. John. *Founding Fish*. New York: Farrar, Straus and Giroux, 2003, 158, 177.

Mitchell, Joseph, and David Remnick, eds. "The Rivermen." *Up in the Old Hotel*. New York: Vintage Books, 1993, 610.

Raabe, Joshua K., and Joseph E. Hightower. "American Shad Migratory Behavior, Weight Loss, Survival, and Abundance in a North Carolina River Following Dam Removals." *Transactions of the American Fisheries Society*, 29 April 2014. http://afs.tandfonline.com /doi/full/10.1080/00028487.2014.882410.

Washington, George. "[April 1791]." *Founders Online*, National Archives, last modified 6 December 2016. http://founders.archives.gov/documents/Washington/01-06-02 -0002-0003-0016. Original source: *The Diaries of George Washington*, vol. 6, *1 January 1790–13 December 1799*, edited by Donald Jackson and Dorothy Twohig, 107–25. Charlottesville: University Press of Virginia, 1979.

CHAPTER 4: RAMPS

Cozzo, David. Interview, 6 April 2016, Cherokee, N.C.

Davis, Jeanine, and Jackie Greenfield. "Cultivation of Ramps (*Allium tricoccum* and *A. burdickii*)." NC State and A&T State Cooperative Extension, 30 June 2001. https:// content.ces.ncsu.edu/cultivation-of-ramps-allium-tricoccum-and-a-burdickii.

Davis-Hollander, Lawrence. "Ramps (Wild Leeks): When Is Local Not Kosher?" *Grit: Rural American Know How*, 1 April 2011. http://www.grit.com/food/ramps-wild-leeks.

Fiegl, Amanda. "Stinging Nettle Soup." *Smithsonian*, 5 May 2010. http://www.smithsonian mag.com/arts-culture/stinging-nettle-soup-87199507/.

Harrison, Jean, and Christopher Rogers. Interview, 19 September 2016, Barnardsville, N.C.

Jackson, Sara. Phone interview, 18 September 2016.

Junaluska, Marie. Interviews, 25 May 2016, Raleigh, N.C., and 6 September 2016, Cherokee, N.C.

McClellan-Welch, Sarah. "Grow Your Own Ramp Patch." *Cherokee One Feather*, 31 January 2014. https://theonefeather.com/2014/01/grow-your-own-ramp-patch/.

Merwin, Hugh. "How Ramps Became Spring's Most Popular, and Divisive, Ingredient." *Grub Street*, 23 April 2013. http://www.grubstreet.com/2013/04/the-history-of-ramps -popularity.html.

Orr, Eric. "Foraging, Storing and Eating Ramps." *Wild Edible* (blog), 2016. http://www .wildedible.com/blog/foraging-ramps.

Ozersky, Josh. "For Foodies, Ramps Are the New Arugula." *Time*, 13 April 2010. http:// content.time.com/time/nation/article/0,8599,1981446,00.html.

Reusing, Andrea. *Cooking in the Moment: A Year of Seasonal Recipes*. New York: Clarkson Potter, 2011.

Ross, Kirk. "Shad Fry Tradition Honored." *Carolina Mercury*, 7 March 2013. http://www .carolinamercury.com/2013/03/shad-fry-tradition-honored.

Wade, Yona. Interview, 25 May 2016, Raleigh, N.C.

Werner, Tommy. "Everything You Need to Know about Ramps." *Epicurious*, 30 March 2015. http://www.epicurious.com/ingredients/ramp-season-recipes-history-article.

CHAPTER 5: SOFT-SHELL CRABS

Biennial Report of the North Carolina Department of Conservation & Development. Issue 7, 1937, 28.

Bridges, Murray. Interviews, 15 April 2016 and 12 May 2016, Colington, N.C.

Dore, Ian. *The New Fresh Seafood Buyer's Guide: A Manual for Distributors, Restaurants and Retailers*. New York: Springer Science+Business Media, 1991, 38–39.

Hawthorne, Rosie. "When It Comes to Soft Shells, Timing Is Everything." *The Outer Banks Voice*, 30 June 2011. http://outerbanksvoice.com/2011/06/30/the-art-of -cleaning-and-cooking-softshell-crabs/.

Lubasch, Arnold H. "Mafia Runs Fulton Fish Market, U.S. Says in Suit to Take Control." *New York Times*, 16 October 1987. http://www.nytimes.com/1987/10/16/nyregion /mafia-runs-fulton-fish-market-us-says-in-suit-to-take-control.html.

Perry, Harriet M., and Ronald F. Malone. "Proceedings of the National Symposium on the Soft-Shelled Blue Crab Fishery." Louisiana Sea Grant College Program, 1985, 91.

Phillips, Feather. Email communications, April–May 2016.

Phillips, Willy. Interview, 15 April 2016, Colington, N.C.

———. Phone interview, 6 July 2016.

Rhodes, Keith. Interview, 13 May 2016, Wilmington, N.C.

Simpson, Bland. *Inner Islands: A Carolinian's Sound Country Chronicle.* Chapel Hill: University of North Carolina Press, 2010, 17.

CHAPTER 6: SERVICEBERRIES

Dixon, Amy. "Dixon: Invasive Nature of Bradford Pears." *Winston-Salem Journal*, 6 May 2016. http://www.journalnow.com/home_food/columnists/amy_dixon/dixon -invasive-nature-of-bradford-pears/article_d9517cf6-3516-516d-8926-32c49548 9974.html.

Elliott, Doug. Phone interview, 17 July 2016.

Gage, Sarah. "Plant Profile: Serviceberry (*Amelanchier alnifolia*)." *Botanical Rambles*, Washington Native Plant Society blog, 29 May 2013. https://www.wnps.org/blog /?s=Plant+Profile+Serviceberry.

Gilman, Edward F., and Dennis G. Watson. *Amelancier x grandiflora 'Autumn Brilliance' 'Autumn Brilliance' Apple Serviceberry.* University of Florida Horticulture Fact Sheet ST-78, November 1993. http://hort.ufl.edu/database/documents/pdf/tree_fact _sheets/amegrab.pdf.

Halsey, Evalynn. Interview, 14 September 2016, West Jefferson, N.C.

Hamby, Zetta Barker. *Memoirs of Grassy Creek: Growing Up in the Mountains on the Virginia–North Carolina Line.* Jefferson, N.C.: McFarland, 1998, 189.

J. C. Raulston Arboretum at N.C. State University. "*Amelanchier.*" https://jcra.ncsu.edu /horticulture/plant-profiles/details.php?ID=35.

Logan, William Bryant. *Oak: The Frame of Civilization.* New York: W. W. Norton, 2005, 18.

Mazza, G. "Chemical Composition of Saskatoon Berries (*Amelanchier alnifolia* Nutt.)." *Journal of Food Science*, http://onlinelibrary.wiley.com/doi/10.1111/j.1365-2621.1982 .tb05022.x/abstract.

Mills, David G. "Serviceberry Group." 2016. Wild Foods Home and Garden. http://wild foodshomegarden.com/Serviceberry.html.

Missouri Botanical Garden. "*Amelanchier* x *grandiflora* 'Princess Diana.'" http://www .missouribotanicalgarden.org/PlantFinder/PlantFinderDetails.aspx?taxonid=242791 &isprofile=1&.

North Carolina State University. "Invasive, Exotic Plants of the Southeast, Callery 'Bradford Pear.'" Growing Native: Urban Landscaping with Native Plants. https:// www.ncsu.edu/goingnative/howto/mapping/invexse/bradfor.html.

Parris, John. *Mountain Bred.* Asheville, N.C.: Citizen Times Publishing Company, 1967, 214.

Peattie, Donald Culcross. *A Natural History of Trees of Eastern and Central North America.* Boston: Houghton Mifflin, 1991, 336–37.

Saskatoon Berry Institute of North America website, http://saskatoonberryinstitute.org.

Siverson, Caroline. Phone interview, 10 September 2016.

Walls, Rhonda. Phone interview, 22 November 2016.

Wild, Hollis. Interview, 19 October 2016, Ashe County, N.C.

Winston, Gayle. Phone interview, 13 October 2016.

CHAPTER 7: CANTALOUPES

Barr, Katie. "Waldorf Astoria New York—2009 Fact Sheet." https://docuri.com/down
load/hotel-fact-sheet_59c1e3ecf581710b286af72c_pdf.

Bumbalough, Barbara Sinn. *Come with Me to Germantown: Ridgeway, North Carolina
Revisited.* Warrenton, N.C.: Record Print. Co., 1998, 11, 73–79.

Carver, Ven. "Cantaloupe Capital Falls on Hard Times." *Anniston Star,* Anniston, Ala.,
21 August, 1983, 49.

Evans, Jasper, Spencer Evans, and Edward Earl Leary. Interviews, 23 July and 1 August
2016, Rocky Hock, N.C.

George Matjelan Foundation. The World's Healthiest Foods website. http://www
.whfoods.com.

Holtzmann, Richard. Interviews, 1 July and 23 July 2016, Ridgeway, N.C.

Jacobs, Sarah. "New York City's Most Iconic Hotel Is Closing Indefinitely—Take a Look
Back at Its Star-Studded Past." *Business Insider,* 4 January 2017. http://www.business
insider.com/the-waldorf-astoria-is-closing-2017-1.

Morrison, William Alan. *Waldorf Astoria.* Charleston, S.C.: Arcadia, 2014, 121.

CHAPTER 8: FIGS

Ballance, Alton. *Ocracokers.* Chapel Hill: University of North Carolina Press, 1989, 4.

Burk, C. John. "A Botanical Reconnaissance of Portsmouth Island, North Carolina."
Journal of the Elisha Mitchell Scientific Society, May 1961, 72–74.

Cumo, Christopher, ed. *Encyclopedia of Cultivated Plants: From Acacia to Zinnia.* 3 vols.
Santa Barbara: ABC-CLIO, 2013, 416–19.

Fabricant, Florence. "Food Stuff; Heady Scent from the Grill: The Wood of the Fig." *New
York Times,* 23 May 2001. http://www.nytimes.com/2001/05/23/dining/food-stuff
-heady-scent-from-the-grill-the-wood-of-the-fig.html.

Glen, Charlotte. "Figs—the Forgotten Fruit." NC State Cooperative Extension, 27 July
2011. https://pender.ces.ncsu.edu/2012/07/figs-the-forgotten-fruit/.

Harb, Jim. Email communications, 9 August–11 September 2016.

Hatch, Peter J. "Figs: 'Vulgar' Fruit or 'Wholesome' Delicacy?" *Twinleaf Journal Online,*
January 1996. https://www.monticello.org/site/house-and-gardens/figs-vulgar-fruit
-or-wholesome-delicacy.

Hopper, Kim. Interview, 11 August 2016, Beaufort, N.C.

Joyce, Christopher. "Ancient Figs May Be First Cultivated Crops." Transcript from *All
Things Considered,* National Public Radio, 2 June 2006. http://www.npr.org/templates
/story/story.php?storyId=5446137.

Lawrence, D. H. *Birds, Beasts and Flowers: Poems.* London: Martin Secker, 1923, 18–21.

Leinbach, Connie. "A 'Fig-for-All' in Community Square; Celebration Continues Today."
Ocracoke Observer, 13 August 2016, 1.

Lynn, Chester. Interview, 12 August 2016, Ocracoke Island, N.C.

————. Phone interview, 22 December 2016.

Polomski, Bob. "Fig." School of Agricultural, Forestry, and Environmental Science, Clemson University, October 2012. http://www.clemson.edu/extension/hgic/plants /vegetables/tree_fruits_nuts/hgic1353.html.

Sutton, David C. *Figs: A Global History*. London: Reaktion Books, 2014, 7–8, 11–15, 52, 100.

CHAPTER 9: SCUPPERNONGS

Bishop, Jack. Interview, 23 September 2016, Columbia, N.C.

————. Phone interview, 13 December 2016.

Bledsoe, Jerry. *North Carolina Curiosities*. 3rd ed., revised by Sara Pitzer. Old Saybrook, Conn.: Globe Pequot Press, 1999, 38.

Brickhouse, Clara. Interview, 24 September 2016, Travis, N.C.

Chesnutt, Charles W. *The Goophered Grapevine and Other Stories*. Gloucester, U.K.: Dodo Press, n.d.

Hariot, Thomas. *A Brief and True Report of the New Found Land of Virginia*. 1588. Electronic ed., Academic Affairs Library, University of North Carolina at Chapel Hill, 2003. http://docsouth.unc.edu/nc/hariot/hariot.html.

Helsey, Alexia Jones. *A History of North Carolina Wine: From Scuppernong to Syrah*. Mt. Pleasant, S.C.: History Press, 2010, 18, 26–27, 36.

"History of Duplin Winery." Duplin Winery website, https://www.duplinwinery.com /story/.

Houston, Lebame, and Wynne Dough. "Indian Food and Cooking in Eastern North Carolina." Expanded from David Stick's "Indian Food and Cooking in Eastern North Carolina 400 Years Ago." Harpers Ferry, W.Va.: National Park Service, 2016. https:// www.nps.gov/fora/learn/education/indian-food-and-cooking-in-eastern-north -carolina.htm.

Lawrence, Elizabeth. *Through the Garden Gate*. Chapel Hill: University of North Carolina Press, 1995, 193.

McKimmon, Jane S. *Canning and Preserving with 4-H Recipes*. North Carolina Agricultural Extension Service Circular No. 11 (rev.). Raleigh: Edwards & Broughton Printing, 1917, 37.

National Institutes of Health. "Unique Grape Skin Extract Inhibits Prostate Cancer Cell Growth in the Laboratory." Press release, 31 August 2007. https://www.nih.gov/news -events/news-releases/unique-grape-skin-extract-inhibits-prostate-cancer-cell -growth-laboratory.

Simpson, Bland. "The History of the Scuppernong." *Our State*, 29 September 2014. https://www.ourstate.com/scuppernong-nc/.

Steelman, Ben. "North Carolina Has Complex History with Liquor." *Star News Online*, Wilmington, N.C., 6 March 2016. http.://www.starnewsonline.com/news/20100306 /north-carolina-has-complex-history-with-liquor.

CHAPTER 10: APPLES

Behr, Edward. *The Artful Eater*. New York: Atlantic Monthly Press, 1992, 159–60, 166.

Brown, Tom. "Junaluska Apple Discovery." Apple Search website, © 2008–2016, http:// www.applesearch.org/Junaluska_Apple_Discovery.html.

————. "Man Keeps History Alive with Junaluska Apple Find." *Times-News Online,* Hendersonville, N.C., 17 January 2011. http://www.blueridgenow.com/news/20110117 /man-keeps-history-alive-with-junaluska-apple-find.

Calhoun, Creighton Lee, Jr. *Old Southern Apples: A Comprehensive History and Description of Varieties for Collectors, Growers, and Fruit Enthusiasts.* White River Junction, Vt.: Chelsea Green Publishing, 2010, 40, 106, 108, 168.

Carson, Bill. Interview, 23 October 2016, Altapass, N.C.

————. *Stories of Altapass.* Spruce Pine, N.C.: The Orchard at Altapass, 2002.

Downing, A. J. *The Fruits and Fruit Trees of America.* New York: John Wiley, 1854.

Joyner, Ron, and Suzanne Joyner. Big Horse Creek Farm: Antique Heirloom Apple Trees website, http://bighorsecreekfarm.com/.

————. Interviews, 17 September and 18 October 2016, West Jefferson, N.C.

Medford, Houck. Interview, 22 October 2016, near Blowing Rock, N.C.

North Carolina Department of Agriculture. "Goodness Grows in North Carolina: Apple Outline." http://www.ncagr.gov/agscool/teacher/commodities/apple.htm.

Ragan, W. H. *Nomenclature of the Apple: A Catalogue of the Known Varieties Referred to in American Publications from 1804–1904.* Bulletin No. 56. Washington, D.C.: United States Department of Agriculture, 1905.

CHAPTER 11: PERSIMMONS

Breyer, Melissa. "10 Things You Didn't Know about Opossums." Mother Nature Network, 14 November 2012. http://www.mnn.com/earth-matters/animals/stories/10-things -you-didnt-know-about-opossums.

Briand, C. H. "The Common Persimmon (*Diospyros virginiana* L.): The History of an Underutilized Fruit Tree (16th–19th Centuries)." *HUNTIA,* 12, no. 1 (2005): 71–89.

Bunker, Melissa. Interview, 24 November 2015, Star, N.C.

Council, Mildred. *Mama Dip's Kitchen.* Chapel Hill: University of North Carolina Press, 1999, 209.

Fletcher, W. F. "The Native Persimmon." *United States Department of Agriculture Farmers' Bulletin* #685, 12 October 1915, 1–2. https://naldc.nal.usda.gov/download/47502/PDF.

Greenlee-Donnell, Cynthia. "Native Persimmons Are Overabundant and Underappreciated Backyard Delights." *Indy Week,* 14 January 2009. http://www. indyweek.com/indyweek/native-persimmons-are-overabundant-and-under appreciated/Content?oid=1213280.

Hariot, Thomas. *A Brief and True Report of the New Found Land of Virginia.* 1588. Electronic ed., Academic Affairs Library, University of North Carolina at Chapel Hill, 2003. http://docsouth.unc.edu/nc/hariot/hariot.html.

Hensley, Jan G. "Persimmons." Unpublished essay, 21 December 2016.

Holland, Charles, and Peyton Holland. Interview, 24 November 2015, New Hill, N.C.

Kephart, Horace. *Camp Cookery.* New Orleans, La.: Cornerstone Book Publishers, 2013.

Krause, William J., and Winifred A. Kraus. *The Opossum: Its Amazing Story.* Columbia, Mo.: Department of Pathology and Anatomical Sciences, School of Medicine, University of Missouri Columbia, 2006, 6.

Lawson, John. *A New Voyage to Carolina.* Chapel Hill: University of North Carolina Press, 1967, 180.

Lembke, Janet. *Shake Them 'Simmons Down.* New York: Lyons and Burford, 1993, 49.

Bibliography

Lucky 32 Southern Kitchen. "Shaking Down Persimmon Recipes: Pie, Glaze, and Southern Comfort Hard Sauce." *Lucky 32 Southern Kitchen* (blog), November 2012. https://lucky32southernkitchen.com/2012/11/01/shaking-down-persimmon-recipes -pie-glaze-and-southern-comfort-hard-sauce/.

May, Robert. *The Accomplisht Cook; or, The Art and Mystery of Cookery.* London: Printed for Obadiah Blagrave at the Bear and Star in St. Pauls Church-Yard, 1685.

McDermott, Nancie. *Southern Pies: A Gracious Plenty of Pie Recipes, from Lemon Chess to Chocolate Pecan.* San Francisco: Chronicle Books, 2010, 94–95.

McPhee, John. "A Forager." In *Secret Ingredients: The New Yorker Book of Food and Drink,* edited by David Remnick, 208. New York: Modern Library, 2009.

Michael, Jeff. Phone interview, 11 December 2015.

Nagy, Seth. "Persimmon Tree." North Carolina Cooperative Extension (Caldwell County Center), 6 December 2012. https://caldwell.ces.ncsu.edu/2012/12/persimmon -tree/.

Reich, Lee. "Ugly, but Tasty Old Fruit." *Lee's Garden Now* (blog), 26 December 2013. http://www.leereich.com/2013/12/ugly-but-tasty-old-fruit.html.

Smith, Captain John. *Works, 1608–1631.* Vol. 1, edited by Edward Arber. Westminster: Archibald Constable and Co., 1895.

Stafford, Gene. Interview, 24 November 2015, Colfax, N.C.

Tartan, Beth. *North Carolina and Old Salem Cookery.* Chapel Hill: University of North Carolina Press, 2000, 218–19.

"What Does the Persimmon Lady Say about Winter 2015?" *Farmer's Almanac,* 26 September 2014. http://farmersalmanac.com/blog/2014/09/26/persimmon-lady -winter-2015/.

CHAPTER 12: OYSTERS

Bevans Oyster Company. "Bevans IQF Half-Shell Oysters." Kinsale, Va. http://www .bevansoyster.com/products/iqfhalf.htm.

Blackburn, Brady. Interview, 7 February 2016, Carrboro, N.C.

Blackburn, Brady, Emma Louise Boyd, Anna Brodmerkel, Walter Coker Holmes, Claire Johnson, Christy Korzen, Cinnamon Moore, Nicholas Reschly, Holly Roberts, and Caitlin Seyfriend. *Investigation on the Half Shell: The Social Ecological Role of Oyster Aquaculture in North Carolina.* UNC Institute for the Environment Outer Banks Field Site 2015 Capstone Report, 7 December 2015, 50.

Bowers, George M. *Report of the Commissioner for the Year Ending June 30, 1903.* U.S. Commission of Fish and Fisheries, Part 29. Washington, D.C.: Government Printing Office, 1905, 276.

Butler, Stephanie. "Oyster Stew on Christmas Eve: An American Tradition," History.com, 24 December 2013. http://www.history.com/news/hungry-history/oyster-stew-on -christmas-eve-an-american-tradition.

Candelario, Michael. "Recycling the Coast." *Carolina Shore,* September 2015, 56, 62.

Cecelski, David. *A Historian's Coast: Adventures into the Tidewater Past.* Chapel Hill: University of North Carolina Press, 2000, 87.

———. "The Oyster Shucker's Song." *Cornbread Nation 3,* edited by Ronni Lundy, 180– 87. Chapel Hill: University of North Carolina Press, 2005.

Daniels, Joey, and Emma Daniels. Interviews, 13 March and 3 November 2016, Wanchese, N.C.

Dean, Cornelia. "A North Carolina Lifeline Built on Shifting Sands." *New York Times*, 6 March 2012. http://www.nytimes.com/2012/03/06/science/highway-12-outer -banks-lifeline-is-under-siege-by-nature.html.

Gallant, André. "Why Are Coon Oysters Called Coon Oysters?" *André Gallant* (blog), 2 February 2015. http://www.andre-gallant.com/blog/2015/2/2/why-are-coon -oysters-called-coon-oysters.

Hardy, Craig. "The Oyster Resource in North Carolina." PowerPoint presentation, North Carolina Division of Marine Fisheries, November 2010.

Herring, David. "Hurricane Floyd's Lasting Legacy: Assessing the Storm's Impact on the Carolina Coast." *Earth Observatory*, 20 March 2000. http://earthobservatory.nasa.gov /Features/FloydFear/.

Jacobsen, Rowan. "Crab Slough Oysters from NC." *The Oyster Guide* (blog), 31 December 2013. http://www.oysterguide.com/new-discoveries/crab-slough-oysters -from-nc/oysterguide.com.

————. *The Essential Oyster*. New York: Bloomsbury USA, 2016.

————. *A Geography of Oysters: The Connoisseur's Guide to Oyster Eating in North America*. New York: Bloomsbury USA, 2008, 39.

Keeler, Andrew. Interview, 7 March 2016, Carrboro, N.C.

Lee, E-Ching. "Home in an Oyster Shell." *Coastwatch*, Winter 2014, 14–19.

Miller, Todd. Email communication, 10 January 2016.

————. Interview, 4 December 2015, Newport, N.C.

Millis, Randy. Interview, 5 December 2015, Snead's Ferry, N.C.

Moore, Cinnamon. Interview, 7 February 2016, Carrboro, N.C.

North Carolina Coastal Federation. "The Napa Valley of Oysters." *Our Coast*, 2015 ed., 16–17.

————. North Carolina Oyster Blueprint: An Action Plan for Restoration and Protection (website). 2016. ncoysters.org.

————. "Oysters: Restore and Sustainably Manage Oysters." North Carolina Coastal Federation. http://www.nccoast.org/protect-the-coast/oysters/.

North Carolina Department of Environment and Natural Resources. "New License Requirement in Effect for Mechanical Harvest of Shellfish." Marine Fisheries nr-54-13 Mechanical Oyster Harvest, 1 November 2013.

Pamlico County Chamber of Commerce. *About Pamlico County*. Grantsboro, N.C.: Pamlico County Chamber of Commerce, 2012. http://www.pamlicochamber.com /about-pamlico-county-1.html.

Phillips, Willy. Phone interview, 5 July 2016.

Prioli, Carmine, and Martin, Edwin. *Hope for a Good Season: The Ca'e Bankers of Harkers Island*. Winston-Salem, N.C.: John F. Blair, 1998.

State of New Jersey. *Report of the Bureau of Shell Fisheries*. Trenton, N.J.: MacCrellish and Quigley, State Printers, 1905, 70.

Trillin, Calvin. "Newspaper Columnists Are Infallible." *St. Louis Post-Dispatch*, 16 December 1993. https://www.questia.com:newspaper:1P2–32844876:newspaper -columnists-are-infallible.

Index

Page numbers in *italics* indicate illustrations.